NEWTON RIGG COLLEGE PENRITH

This book is due for return on or before the last date shown below

To renew please telephone (01768) 893503 with your library card number.

Part of Askham Bryan College

Geotourism

Front cover images:

- Iguazu Falls, Argentina, Brazil, Paraguay Border. *Source*: Ross Dowling
- Bourke's Luck Potholes, Mpumalunga Province, northern South Africa. *Source*: Ross Dowling
- Paradise Bay, Antarctic Peninsula, Antarctica. This place is definitely a geotourist's paradise. *Source*: Ross Dowling
- Kandovan village, Sahand Mountain, Iran. *Source*: Alireza Amrikazemi
- Tourists on mule back viewing the Grand Canyon, beneath the rim, Arizona, USA. *Source*: Ross Dowling
- Uluru (Ayers Rock), Northern Territory, Australia.
- Geo-interpretation, Network Partner Tuebingen, Germany. *Source*: Andreas Megerle
- Our Dynamic Earth, Edinburgh, Scotland. *Source*: Our Dynamic Earth

Back cover images:

- Knockan Crag, Northwest Highlands, Scotland. *Source*: Lorne Gill, Scottish Natural Heritage
- Chimney Rocks, Mahneshan Region, Iran. *Source*: Alireza Amrikazemi
- Table Mountain, Cape Peninsula, South Africa. *Source*: South African Tourism
- Mapungubwe World Heritage Site, Limpopo Province, South Africa. *Source*: M. J. Viljoen
- The Grand Canyon, Arizona, USA, one of the most spectacular examples of geotourism on the planet. *Source*: Ross Dowling
- Spectacular confined gorge, Yuntaishan Mountain Geopark, Henan, China. *Source*: Jiang Jianjun
- Katalehkhor Cave, Iran. *Source*: Alireza Amrikazemi
- Giant Geode of Pulpí, Almería, Spain. *Source*: José M. Calaforra.

Geotourism

Edited by
Ross K. Dowling and David Newsome

ELSEVIER
BUTTERWORTH
HEINEMANN

AMSTERDAM   BOSTON   HEIDELBERG   LONDON   NEW YORK   OXFORD
PARIS   SAN DIEGO   SAN FRANCISCO   SINGAPORE   SYDNEY   TOKYO

Elsevier Butterworth-Heinemann
Linacre House, Jordan Hill, Oxford OX2 8DP
30 Corporate Drive, Burlington, MA 01803

First published 2006

British Library Cataloguing in Publication Data
A catalogue record for this book is available from the British Library

Library of Congress Cataloguing in Publication Data
Control Number: 2005927528

ISBN   0 7506 6215 8

For information on all Elsevier Butterworth-Heinemann
publications visit our website at www.elsevier.com

Typeset by Charon Tec Pvt. Ltd, Chennai, India
www.charontec.com
Printed and bound in Great Britain by MPG Books Ltd, Bodmin, Cornwall

To our wives and families

*Wendy Dowling, Jayne, Trevor, Shenee and Paige Belstead,
Simon Maclennan and Lynette McGrath, Mark and Kelly
Dowling, Tobias Dowling, Aurora and Helena Dowling and
Francis Dowling*

and

Jane, Benjamin and Rachel Newsome

Contents

List of figures

List of tables

List of case studies

Contributors

Authors

Alireza Amrikazemi, Planning & Program Management, Geological Survey of Iran, Ministry of Industries and Mines, Tehran, Iran
Alireza Amrikazemi is Manager of the Geotourism Project in the Geological Survey of Iran. He is a geologist and has great experience of specialized photography and documentary-making in Geosciences. His research focuses on the geological phenomena, and their introduction and documentation in pursuit of conservation and protection goals.

Georg Büchel, Institute for Applied Geology, Jena, Germany
Professor Georg Büchel has been Professor of Applied Geology at the Institute of Geosciences, Friedrich-Schiller-Universität Jena, since 1995. His main research focuses on geo–biointeraction, groundwater prospection and exploration, acid mine drainage in the former uranium mining site in Eastern Thuringia, and the formation of groundwater (maar) volcanoes in Alaska, Java and the Eifel area. He holds degrees in Applied Geology, Hydrogeology, and Volcanology, and has particular expertise in transferring geo-issues, especially volcanology, to the broad public as well as safeguarding geo-resources for geoscientific research by innovative approaches.

José M. Calaforra, Department of Hydrogeology, University of Almería, Almería, Spain
Professor José M. Calaforra is Titular Professor of Geodynamics at the University of Almería. He has been President of the Spanish Speleological and Karst Science Society (SEDECK) since 1998. He works in the Water Resources and Environmental Geology Research Group on special topics such as karst hydrogeology and geomorphology, and also teaches courses on geology, hydrogeology and cave environmental protection in the Faculty of Environmental Science.

Ian F. Clark, School of Natural & Built Environments, University of South Australia, Mawson Lakes, Australia
Dr Ian Clark is a Senior Lecturer in Geoscience and Park Management at the School of Natural & Built Environments at the University of South Australia. He holds degrees in Geology and Science Education. He is the President of the International Geoscience Education Organisation, and his research focuses on geoscience education and its contribution to studies of the Earth as a system.

Ángel Fernández-Cortés, Department of Hydrogeology, University of Almería, Almería, Spain
Dr Ángel Fernández-Cortés graduated in 1999 from the University of Almería with a degree in Environmental Science, and joined the Water Resources and Environmental Geology Research Group. His PhD is concerned with the environmental monitoring of show caves. His current research interest covers time series analysis and the use of geostatistical tools, both applied to cave management and protection.

Marie-Luise Frey, Welterbe Grube Messel GmbH, Messel, Germany
Dr Marie-Luise Frey has been Manager of the World Heritage Site Messel Pit GmbH (Ltd) in Messel, Hesse, Germany, since 2003. She holds degrees in Geology and Applied Geology, and has particular expertise in promoting geosciences and transferring geoscientific issues to the public. During her work in the Gerolstein Geopark in the Vulkaneifel region from 1992 to 2003 she was the project officer responsible for the foundation of the European Geoparks Network, created in 2000.

Alexander E. Gates, Department of Earth and Environmental Sciences, Rutgers University, Newark, New Jersey, USA
Professor Alexander Gates is Chair of the Graduate Program of the Department of Earth and Environmental Sciences, Rutgers University, Newark. His research career began in regional and plate tectonics and structural geology, and later branched into environmental geology. He also conducts projects in formal and public geoscience education, and geotourism on geologic provinces.

Thomas Hose, Principal Lecturer in Tourism, Buckingham Chilterns University College, High Wycombe, UK
Dr Thomas Hose is Principal Lecturer in Heritage and Tourism Management at Buckingham Chilterns University, UK. He has a BSc in Geology and an MA in Museum Administration. His PhD examines the development of the geotourism concept. He is a consultant on geotourism and geology-focused interpretive provision and is a council member of the British Institute of Geological Conservation.

Jane A. James, School of Humanities, Flinders University, Adelaide, Australia
Associate Professor Jane James is Head of Cultural Tourism, and also the Department of Cultural Studies, in the School of Humanities at Flinders University in Adelaide. Her research interests include effective and sustainable management of natural and cultural heritage sites, the delivery of authentic interpretation, the evaluation of visitor experiences, and festival and event management. She has two

degrees in geology, began her professional life as consultant geologist, and has had several reincarnations since – including environmental and adult education, land management and tourism education. She is good at managing change.

Patrick James, School of Natural & Built Environments, University of South Australia, Mawson Lakes, Australia
Professor Patrick James is Foundation Professor and Head of the School of Natural and Built Environments at the University of South Australia in Adelaide. He has research interests in tectonics and mapping, environmental geoscience, remote sensing, regional geology, geoscience education and the application of learning technology to tertiary studies. He has taught on these topics in university, externally, and in industry short course modes.

Jiang Jianjun, Department of Geological Environment, Ministry of Land and Resources, Beijing, People's Republic of China
Dr Jiang Jianjun is the Director General of the Department of the Geological Environment, Ministry of Land and Resources of People's Republic of China. He holds a doctorate in Palaeontology, and his work focuses on management of geological environment in China. He is a member of the Leading Group of National Geoparks of China.

Jonathan Larwood, Environmental Impacts Team, English Nature, Peterborough, UK
Dr Jonathan Larwood is Senior Geologist and Palaeontologist with English Nature. He has fifteen years' experience in geological conservation. In recent years he has been involved in the development of the Dorset and East Devon Coast World Heritage Site and a number of high profile geotourism initiatives throughout England.

Patrick J. Mc Keever, Geological Survey of Northern Ireland, Colby House, Stranmillis Court, Belfast, County Antrim, Ireland
Dr Patrick Mc Keever is a geologist with the Geological Survey of Northern Ireland, managing that organization's Landscape Heritage section. He holds degrees in Geology and works on public outreach and developing the geological heritage of Northern Ireland as a sustainable economic resource through the development of geotourism. He is currently Vice Coordinator of the European Geoparks Network, and an advisor to UNESCO on Global Geoparks.

Alan McKirdy, Scottish Natural Heritage, Battleby, Redgorton, Perth, Scotland, UK
Alan McKirdy is Head of Scottish Natural Heritage's Natural Heritage Data Unit. He has a BSc (Hons) from Aberdeen University, has written or edited over twenty popular books on the geology of Scotland, and has helped to promote the study of environmental geology.

Abbas Mehrpooya, Geological Survey of Iran, Tehran, Iran
Professor Abbas Mehrpooya is Freelance Translator and Professor of English in the Geological Survey of Iran, and Head of English Translation Group and Editor-in-Chief for the Iran Industrial Estates Organization. He holds degrees in

English literature and English teaching (TOEFL). His research focuses on the translation of geosciences, geotourism, economics and literary texts, including poetry and prose, and he has also particular expertise in the translation and narration of scientific and literary texts in documentaries.

Andreas Megerle, Institute of Regional Science, University of Karlsruhe (TH), Karlsruhe, Germany
Dr Andreas Megerle is Lecturer in Regional Science at the University of Karlsruhe, and also a consultant for tourism and nature conservation planning. His main research interests are the development of competencies within cooperation networks and sustainable tourism, with a special focus on geotourism and geoparks.

Margarete Patzak, Division of Earth Sciences, UNESCO, Paris, France
Dr Margarete Patzak is Assistant Professional for the Geoparks Activities and the International Geoscience Programme at UNESCO. She holds degrees in mineralogy and geology. The main focus of her work is on international project management related to matters in applied and theoretical geosciences and geological and cultural heritage.

Christof Pforr, School of Management, Curtin Business School, Curtin University of Technology, Perth, Australia
Dr Christof Pforr is Lecturer in Tourism Management at the School of Management, Curtin University of Technology. His main research interests include tourism policy and planning, sustainable tourism, ecotourism, and policy analysis with a focus on policy processes and policy networks.

Wolf Uwe Reimold, Impact Cratering Research Group, School of Geosciences, University of the Witwatersrand, Johannesburg, South Africa
Professor Uwe Reimold is Professor of Mineralogy and Head of the Impact Cratering Research Group at the University of the Witwatersrand in Johannesburg. He has MSc and PhD degrees in Mineralogy from the Westfalian Wilhelms University in Münster, Germany. Uwe has carried out numerous multidisciplinary, geoscientific studies of meteorite impact craters and associated impact-generated rocks, in particular in the world's largest and oldest impact structure, the Vredefort Structure in South Africa. He is a past President of the Geological Society of South Africa, and for a number of years chaired the Geoconservation and Geotourism Committee of this Society.

Klaus Schäfer, Verw.-Betriebsw., Eifel Tourism GmbH, Kalvarienberg, Prüm/ Eifel, Germany
Klaus Schäfer has been Directing Manager of the Eifel Tourism GmbH (Ltd) Prüm, for the Eifel region covering Rhenania-Palatinate and North Rhein-Westfalia in Germany, since its foundation in 2000. He has been Manager of the Eifel Touristic Agency North Rhine-Westfalia e.V. and of the EVIV–European Economy Interest Association since 2003. He holds a degree in administrative economics, and has particular expertise in marketing, tourism, public relations and geotourism. He collaborates with scientists in the field of geology as well as volcanology, cultural geography, agriculture and sustainable regional development.

Felix Tongkul, School of Science and Technology, Universiti Malaysia Sabah, Kota Kinabalu, Sabah, Malaysia
Associate Professor Felix Tongkul is an Associate Professor and Deputy Dean of the School of Science and Technology, Universiti Malaysia Sabah, East Malaysia. He holds BSc and PhD degrees in geology. His research interest is the sedimentology, tectonics and geotourism of NW Borneo.

Thomas Wallmach, Ferret Mining and Environmental Services (PTY) Ltd, Lynnwood Ridge, South Africa
Dr Thomas Wallmach is a Senior Environmental Scientist at Ferret Mining and Environmental Services (Pty) Ltd. He has an MSc degree in Mineralogy from Johannes-Gutenberg University, Mainz, Germany, and a DSc from the University of Pretoria. From 1988 to 1997 he lectured in geology and mineralogy at the University of the Witwatersrand in Johannesburg and the University of Pretoria. He then was employed as a geologist at the Miningtek Division of the Council for Scientific and Industrial Research (CSIR) in Johannesburg. In May 1999 he left the CSIR to develop and promote geotourism and educational tourism in South Africa.

Glen Gavin Whitfield, Explorers for Africa, Pinegowrie, South Africa
Gavin Whitfield is a Geological Consultant and Specialist Tourist Guide based in Johannesburg, South Africa, from where he operates a variety of geologically-oriented tours. He holds an MSc in geology from Rhodes University, Grahamstown, and for many years worked in mineral exploration in southern Africa. Gavin is a Fellow of the Geological Society of South Africa and a member of that Society's Council, where he is currently the Convener of the Conservation Committee, and the Geotourism Interest Group.

Chen Youfang, Department of International Cooperation, Science and Technology, Ministry of Land and Resources, Beijing, People's Republic of China
Chen Youfang is Divisional Director in the Department of International Cooperation, Sciences and Technology, Beijing.

Zhao Xun, Chinese Academy of Geological Sciences, Beijing, People's Republic of China
Zhao Xun is a member of the International Advisory Group for Geoparks and is Vice President of the Chinese Academy of Geological Sciences.

Editors

Ross K. Dowling, School of Marketing, Tourism & Leisure, Faculty of Business & Law, Edith Cowan University, Joondalup, Western Australia, Australia
Professor Ross Dowling is Foundation Professor of Tourism, and Head of the Tourism Program, School of Marketing, Tourism & Leisure, Faculty of Business & Law, Edith Cowan University. He is an Executive Board Member of the Indian Ocean Tourism Organisation (IOTO) and a Board Member of Ecotourism Australia. In Western Australia he is Chairperson of The Forum Advocating Cultural and Ecotourism (FACET), and a Council Member of both the National Trust, the Royal Automobile Club and the Royal Agricultural Society.

He is an international speaker, author, researcher and consultant on tourism, with over 200 publications. His research focuses on the intersection between tourism and the environment, and he has a particular passion for geotourism, ecotourism, wildlife tourism and cruise ship tourism.

In 2002 he was Western Australia's sole Ambassador for the International Year of Ecotourism, and he co-authored two books on the subject – *Ecotourism* and *Natural Area Tourism: Ecology, Impacts & Management*. In 2003 he co-edited the books *Ecotourism Policy and Planning* and *Tourism in Destination Communities*. In 2005 he co-authored the book *Wildlife Tourism*, and he is currently preparing the edited book *Cruise Ship Tourism* for publication in early 2006. Many of these books have been written or edited in collaboration with David Newsome.

Dr Dowling holds a BSc in Geology, an MSc (Hons) in Geography and a PhD in Environmental Science, as well as Diplomas in Educational Administration, Sport & Recreation, and Teaching. His Master's thesis was on karst geomorphology and hydrology in an International Hydrological Decade Basin at the top of the South Island, New Zealand, and his doctoral dissertation was on an environmentally based approach to tourism planning, carried out in the Gascoyne Region of Western Australia. His model has since been applied in Australia, Canada, Indonesia, Malaysia and the USA.

He has 30 years' experience working in the field of the environment and has been a tour guide in wilderness areas and national parks in many parts of the world, including Asia, the Pacific and the Antarctic. For his contributions to the environment he has been awarded a New Zealand Conservation Foundation Citation.

David Newsome, School of Environmental Science, Murdoch University, Perth, Western Australia, Australia
Dr Newsome is Senior Lecturer in Environmental Science at Murdoch University, Perth, Western Australia. His principal research interests are geotourism, human–wildlife interactions, and the biophysical impacts of recreation and tourism. He has twelve years' experience in natural resource management as a lecturer and researcher in Environmental Science at Murdoch University. David's research and teaching, and the activities of his research group, focus on the sustainable use of landscapes and the assessment and management of recreational activity in natural areas.

Dr Newsome holds a BSc (Hons) in Botany and Geography, an MSc in Geography and a PhD in Geomorphology, as well as a Diploma in Environmental Impact Assessment. His Master's thesis was on soil formation on the Yorkshire Wolds in eastern England, and his doctoral dissertation was on the origin of sandplains in Western Australia.

David has expanded his interests in natural area tourism by virtue of travel in various parts of the world. Countries visited include Norway, Costa Rica, Argentina, Chile, South Africa, Botswana, Zimbabwe, Cameroon, India, Nepal, Sri Lanka, Malaysia and Indonesia. This has fostered a strong interest in the management and protection of nature reserves and national parks from a tourism perspective.

The publication of this book follows from the success of two other books (*Natural Area Tourism* and *Wildlife Tourism*) where he led the authorship. David has a strong interest in setting up geotourism as an applied science and using it to expand the scope of natural area tourism.

Preface

Planet Earth is dynamic, and the one constant about it is that it is in a state of continual change. The major geological features that we see on the landscape are the landforms which have been formed by a variety of processes. The word *geology* comes from the Greek words *geo*, meaning earth, and *logia*, meaning study or science. Geologists study the Earth, and how it evolved and developed. They investigate it from the rocks and minerals, at a micro-scale, to the movement of the earth's crust through the study of plate tectonics, at the macro-scale. Somewhere between lies geomorphology, the study of landforms – or the part of the geological landscape which is visible and obvious.

While many books have been written about geology and a host of others have been penned on the subject of tourism, few (if any) have brought the two subjects together. However, a recent offering moves towards this integration of disciplines, especially with regard to geology and its conservation value. Murray Gray's *Geodiversity: Valuing and Conserving Abiotic Nature* (published by John Wiley & Sons Ltd, 2004) presents the subject from the perspective of maintaining geodiversity. The author approaches the link between geology and tourism as being an area of 'important economic activity but one that can lead to damage to biodiversity and geodiversity' (p. 159). Whilst totally agreeing with the author that landform features should be conserved, and in some cases, preserved, this book explores the positive links between geology and tourism.

We are passionate about the subject. Both of the editors have trained as geologists and now work in tourism education. We hold geology dear to our hearts and wish to share that with like-minded people. We believe that through geotourism a better understanding of the Earth can be achieved so that its geological attributes can be acknowledged alongside the more commonly held view that such attributes are only useful when exploited as resources.

The Earth's geological wonders have always fascinated people, and many form the basis for the establishment of protected areas and World Heritage Sites. From Uluru (Ayers Rock) in Australia to the Grand Canyon in the United States of America, examples abound of outstanding geological features which have attracted visitors from time immemorial. It is not just spectacular landforms but also the processes which have shaped the Earth that attract interest, so tourists visit sites where glaciers are in action, volcanoes are active and rivers are causing erosion. It is the understanding of this 'form–process' link that is important in geology and, by extension, geotourism. Through geotourism the relationship is explored and the consequences of geological landforms and activities on our lives is more fully understood.

This book uses the term *geotourism* essentially to mean geological tourism rather than geographical tourism. Thus it focuses upon the 'geo' niche and bounds the subject accordingly. It pertains to tourists looking at natural landscapes, including the landforms within, as well as the processes that shaped them.

In this book we have tried to present a snapshot of what is happening in the world of geotourism at this time, in the mid-2000s. It is not meant to provide a comprehensive overview as the subject is still in its infancy, with the term being only derived within the last decade. Thus the contributions represent a varied approach to the subject with a range of shades of meaning ascribed to the subject and differing levels of understanding about it. Some of the chapters are well detailed and illustrated, others are more elementary. All are included because they represent the views of people who are passionate about the subject and come from a number of countries around the world. Whereas some chapters are little more than resource inventories, others illustrate geotourism in practice. Issues such as environmental impact and geoconservation are explored, together with those of access and interpretation. Case studies provide real-world examples of geotourism in action and the rise of the geopark movement. Through it all our hope is that we have generated further interest in this rapidly emerging subject, which we are sure will be the subject of considerably more books and papers in future years.

The book is organised into three sections. The first provides a descriptive overview of the resources for geotourism in a number of countries. The second addresses the rise of the geopark movement and provides case studies of geoparks in Europe and China. The third section presents case studies of geotourism in practice at a range of levels in differing settings. The final chapter is a brief summary of the findings, with the editors highlighting some of the themes that weave throughout the pages.

We wish the reader to note that this book is neither a definitive text nor an encyclopaedic overview of the subject. It has been compiled simply as an 'entrée' to the subject, served with passion by both the contributors and editors in order to communicate our love of the subject so that more will be done for it. We know that more detailed, scholarly research volumes will follow, and we present the book as a marker to stimulate further interest and research in the subject. Having said this, however, we wish to point out that this text marks the introduction of geotourism as an applied science and sets the foundations for teaching and research in geotourism. If this occurs, then we will have achieved our goal.

Finally, the book has been compiled for a broad audience, including natural area tourism professionals, planners and managers; government and business decision-makers; and students from a wide range of disciplines seeking general information on geotourism development in one volume. We hope that you enjoy it.

Ross Dowling and David Newsome

June 2005

Acknowledgements

The editors would like to thank a number of people who have contributed to this book, including the authors and publishing staff. The authors are to be thanked for their willing participation in this project. They come from around the world and are acknowledged experts in their fields. While most are academics, a number are from government organizations and private businesses, and through the course of the book many have become valuable resources of information and firm friends.

We particularly wish to thank the Butterworth-Heinemann Team at Elsevier, Oxford, England. On numerous visits to them to discuss and further the book they have always been extremely professional, encouraging and helpful. We wish especially to thank Sally North (Senior Commissioning Editor, Hospitality, Tourism & Leisure), Tim Goodfellow (Senior Production Editor) and Francesca Ford (Editorial Assistant). We also wish to thank Alan Rossow, Chief Technician (Geomatics), School of Environmental Science, Murdoch University, Western Australia, for taking some of the rudimentary diagrams hand-drawn by the editors and converting them into excellent end-product illustrations for the book.

In addition we wish to acknowledge our earlier discussions with Jonathan Tourtellot, Geotourism Editor, National Geographic Society, USA. Through earnest discussions with him in Australia in February 2004 we recognised that the character of geotourism commonly ascribed to a widely quoted 2002 US Tourism Industry Association and National Geographic Report on the subject is very broad and is more aligned to the 'geo' in 'geographic' tourism than 'geologic' tourism. Whilst appreciating the former view, we firmly espouse the latter.

Individually as editors we wish to thank some people.

Ross Dowling:
I would like to thank my co-editor David Newsome. We have worked well together over the years authoring and editing a number of books. As always, the experience in co-editing this book has been extremely productive and very enjoyable.

My love of geology began through the interest of a friend, Donald Lumsdon, from Nelson, New Zealand. He started my lifetime fascination with the subject. It was professionally encouraged and enhanced by the comprehensive knowledge of an early lecturer and mentor, Professor Paul Williams, Professor of Geography and globally recognised Karst Geomorphologist, whilst I studied under his direction at the University of Auckland, New Zealand. In recent years I acknowledge that my renewed interest comes from working with my co-editor David Newsome, a passionate advocate of exploring and understanding the world through landforms.

As with all previous books, I wish to acknowledge the support of my employer, Edith Cowan University, one of Australia's leading new-generation universities that is committed to excellence in teaching and research. It is a truly great university. I particularly wish to thank my mentor there, Professor John Wood, Deputy Vice-Chancellor (Students, Advancement & International), for his ongoing support and encouragement. This is very much appreciated.

Finally I wish to thank my wife Wendy for her unfailing love and support through this my sixth book in the last four years. I could not have achieved this without her. I also wish to acknowledge my children Aurora, Francis, Jayne, Mark, Simon and Tobias, as well as my three grand-daughters Helena, Paige and Shenee. This book is partly for you all.

David Newsome:
I would like to thank my wife Jane for her support whilst working on my third book in as many years. I am particularly grateful to Tom Hose and his family for assistance and transport in the field, for helpful discussion and insights into the interpretation of geological sites, and for doing much for the promotion of geotourism in England.

I would also like to thank Noella Ross for assistance with word processing, and Ross Lantzke and Colin Ferguson for providing technical expertise in the use of various computer software packages. All are important members of the team in the School of Environmental Science, Murdoch University.

Most importantly of all, I would like to show my appreciation to my father and mother, Ken and Mary Newsome, who, when I was a child, took the family on holiday to exciting places like Cornwall and Northumberland in England. It was during these summer and autumn days that as a boy I could explore cliffs and rocky coastlines, wade through braided rivers and marvel at the wonder of nature. It was during these times, and especially in Cornwall, that a sense of wonder and appreciation of natural landscape developed in me. I thank them both for these times, and this book is for them.

Part One: The Resources for Tourism

1

The scope and nature of geotourism

David Newsome and Ross Dowling

Geotourism: the appreciation of geology and landforms

Geotourism sits within a spectrum of definitions (Figure 1.1). For example, Stueve *et al.* (2002) provide a very broad definition of geotourism – one that encompasses wider geographical, socio-economic and cultural contexts which sit under the umbrella of geographic tourism. Such reasoning probably relates to geology being the basis for the physical environment and therefore ecological systems, with extension into the cultural, spiritual and economic interface. Frey *et al.* (see Chapter 6) embrace geotourism at the level of social and community development according to the concept of the geopark. However, in our definition of geotourism the 'geo' part pertains to geology and geomorphology and the natural resources of landscape, landforms, fossil beds, rocks and minerals, with an emphasis on appreciating the processes that are creating and created such features.

At the same time the tourism component of geotourism (Figure 1.2) involves visitation to geosites for the purposes of passive recreation, engaging a

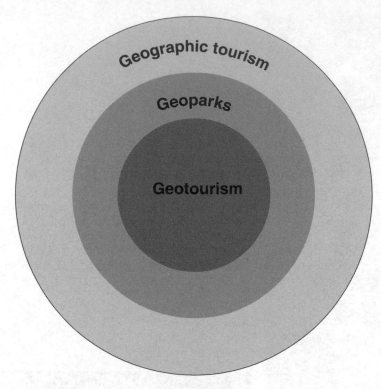

Figure 1.1 The existing spectrum of tourism.

sense of wonder, appreciation and learning. In association with this visitation there may be regular tours, specific activities and even the development of accommodation facilities. In addition to this there may be various forms of geosite planning and management in place. We thus posit that geotourism is a distinct subsector of natural area tourism, and not a form of tourism that also includes wider cultural and heritage components or tourism that focuses on wildlife, all of which can be considered as distinct and separate aspects of tourism in their own right.

Geotourism can therefore be mostly conceptualized according to Figure 1.2. Form represents the existing landscape and its features and materials. Landscapes of geotourism interest include mountain ranges, rift valleys, great escarpments, volcanoes, karst landscapes and arid environments. Within these landscapes there may be characteristic landforms or an array of landforms. For example, within a particular mountain range there may be glacial and fluvial geomorphic features. Moreover, a hierarchy of features of geotourism interest may be identified within a landscape; these may range from individual landforms through to geological materials such as rocks, sediments and fossils (Figure 1.3).

The concept of process (Figure 1.2) can be conceptualized in relation to the dynamic Earth. Process involves geological and geomorphological activity, including volcanic eruptions, the action of running water, and sediments being

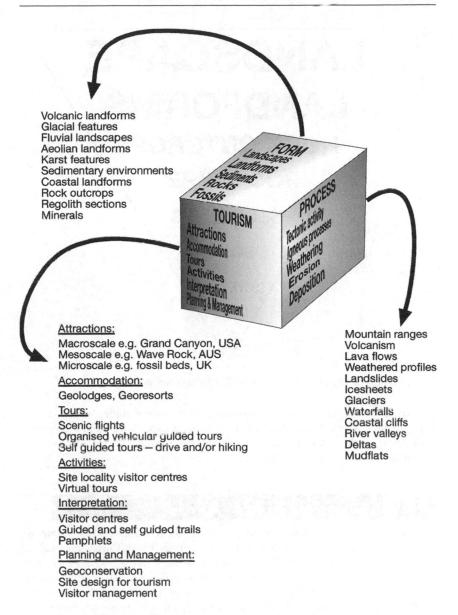

Volcanic landforms
Glacial features
Fluvial landscapes
Aeolian landforms
Karst features
Sedimentary environments
Coastal landforms
Rock outcrops
Regolith sections
Minerals

Attractions:
Macroscale e.g. Grand Canyon, USA
Mesoscale e.g. Wave Rock, AUS
Microscale e.g. fossil beds, UK

Accommodation:
Geolodges, Georesorts

Tours:
Scenic flights
Organised vehicular guided tours
Self guided tours – drive and/or hiking

Activities:
Site locality visitor centres
Virtual tours

Interpretation:
Visitor centres
Guided and self guided trails
Pamphlets

Planning and Management:
Geoconservation
Site design for tourism
Visitor management

Mountain ranges
Volcanism
Lava flows
Weathered profiles
Landslides
Icesheets
Glaciers
Waterfalls
Coastal cliffs
River valleys
Deltas
Mudflats

Figure 1.2 Conceptualization of the nature and scope of geotourism.

weathered, liberated and moved from one site (eroded and transported) to another (deposited). This can readily be appreciated when volcanic activity is observed or where people can see rivers in flood and recent landslide events.

Superimposed on this is the human dimension as reflected in tourism activity. Visitation to geosites may take the form of bus tours, boat trips, scenic flights, self-guided driving, hiking trails, and patronage of viewpoints. Sites selected and

Figure 1.3 Hierarchy of features of potential geotourism interest.

developed for geotourism may contain accommodation facilities and attendant infrastructure. Services designed to enhance visitor experience include purpose-built access roads, visitor centres, interpretive geotours and virtual tours, such as can be conducted by an IMAX cinema.

The relationship of geotourism to other types of tourism

It is our view that the bulk of geotourism takes place in the natural environment. Geotourism may thus be considered to be a part of natural area tourism and ecotourism (see Newsome *et al.*, 2002 for definitions), but is a specialized form of tourism in that the focus of attention is the geosite. A geosite can be a landscape, a group of landforms, a single landform, a rock outcrop, a fossil bed or a fossil. This approach provides a clear distinction from other forms of tourism that take place in the natural environment, such as visiting natural areas to view wild flowers or animals, or simply for recreating a natural area. In relation to this latter point, many people visit sites for a combination of natural values some of which are geological in character. These values include appreciation of scenery, hiking, and bird watching.

In the geotourism described here the attention is primarily on geological phenomena, where the objective of the trip is to visit and view a geological attraction. Where fossils are involved, an extension into early evolutionary processes and the evolution of humans (anthropology) and other vertebrates can also fall

Figure 1.4 Glacier trek, Nigardsbreen Glacier, Jostadelen Region, Norway (photograph courtesy of David Newsome).

under the umbrella of geotourism. Furthermore, landscapes and some geosites provide for aesthetic values and cultural, historical and adventure tourism. 'Geological' tourism can focus on cultural and historical aspects, such as buildings constructed from local rocks and stones and various forms of mining activity. Of particular relevance are mine sites where the impact of geology on people can be readily appreciated (for example, see Pretes, 2002). Old mine sites, such as former gold mines, can provide tourism interest relating to the issues surrounding the importance of geology in people's lives and also to aspects of environmental degradation.

There is a crossover into adventure tourism, as many sites of geological interest are also destinations for thrill-seekers. Cheddar Gorge in England is promoted as a natural attraction. It comprises an area of carboniferous limestone in which a deep gorge (the largest in Britain) has been cut by meltwaters during glacial periods. The gorge and its caves are sites for climbing, abseiling and caving activities. Here the gorge, like so many areas of geological interest, provides the site and backdrop for adventurous activities. Of interest, however, are those situations where the adventure is directly linked to the geology, with the visitor gaining satisfaction from visiting a risky and hazardous site. In these cases the geological attraction frequently forms the centrepiece rather than the backdrop to the activity. Examples of this include trekking on glaciers (Figure 1.4), visiting active volcanoes (Figure 1.5) and undertaking boat trips to the base of powerful waterfalls as at the Iguacu Falls in northern Argentina.

Themes and subject matter in geotourism

The global diversity of landscapes and geological materials in association with the body of knowledge relating to Earth history and geological processes provides for immense scope within the context of geotourism. Many parts of the world show evidence of current tectonic processes, while in others the past legacy of tectonics is evident in rocks and landscapes. Accounts of landscape evolution are written for virtually every part of the world, and an impressive diversity of rocks and minerals have been comprehensively described. Geotourism can be

Figure 1.5 Eruption of Anak Krakatau, Indonesia (photograph courtesy of David Newsome).

developed at the landscape scale – for example, as in the Grand Canyon, Big Bend and Guadalupe Mountains in the USA. Various landforms provide sites of scientific, photographic and cultural interest and a sense of wonder. Geotourism can also comprise visits to road sections, cuttings and quarries in order to view exposed rocks that may show folds, faults, phenocrysts and distinctive assemblages of minerals. Activities can take place in all environments, including coastlines, river valleys and tropical rainforests. Geosites are also not necessarily confined to natural areas such as national parks and other protected areas; they can also be found in agricultural settings and even in urban environments – as in the case of Arthur's Seat in Edinburgh. Road cuttings may sometimes offer views of impressive rock structures, but such sites may fail to provide for the additional components that add to visitor experience, such as interpretation, visitor centres, walk trails and a sense of naturalness and wildness.

Geotourism is thus an option for all countries and parts of the world. Western Australia provides a useful example of some geosites that are present in the Australian regional context. The sites indicated in Table 1.1 range from landscape-level attractions through to geosites that demonstrate specific landforms. These sites are visited by car and hiking trails and, depending on the situation, various facilities are available, such as visitor centres and interpretive trails. Some sites, such as the Bungle Bungle Range (Figure 1.6), can be viewed as part of a scenic flight and/or via walk trails of varying length. Much larger areas that have a diversity of features of geological interest can be viewed as part of a self-guided car tour, as in the case of the 'Rocks and Roads' excursion guides available in Western Australia which cater for car-based journeying (Baxter, 2000a, 2000b).

For example, the 'Rocks and Roads' excursion guide developed by Baxter (2000a) is a travel map indicating the location of various sites of geological interest. The guide briefly interprets and identifies the location of the Leeuwin Block (coastal exposures of igneous and metamorphic rocks), the Darling Fault, the Bunbury Basalt, karst and thrombolites at Lake Clifton. In addition, coastal

Table 1.1   Examples of regional geosite diversity in Australia: the case of Western Australia

Site	Feature	Geological characteristics
Bungle Bungle Range	Sandstone towers and gorges	Devonian Sandstone Ancient current ripples Banding Large-scale cross bedding
Wolfe Creek Crater	Meteorite impact crater	Second largest meteorite crater in the world – measures 900 m across and 60 m deep
Windjana Gorge	Inland gorge	Former barrier reef; cross-sections can be seen in walls of Windjana Gorge
Nambung National Park	Limestone pillars and rhizoliths	Aeolian bedforms preserved in many of the pillars Egg-shaped features preserved in the limestone are fossilized pupal cases of a weevil
Wave Rock	Granite outcrop	Flared slope landform with vertical streaking caused by algal growth
Lake Clifton	Thrombolites	Microbes precipitate calcium carbonate into rock-like structures called thrombolite
Margaret River and Leeuwin-Naturaliste National Park	Cave systems	Speleothems formed from re-deposition of calcium carbonate; forms include stalactites, stalagmites, helictites, pillars, flowstones, shawls and straws
Broome	Dinosaur footprints	Footprints of *Megalosauropus broomensis* visible at low tide at Gantheaume Point
Fitzgerald River National Park	Spongelite Cliffs	Pallinup Siltstone made up of marine sponge silica spicules; other fossilized remains include nautiloids, bivalves, gastropods and echinoids

Derived from Hoatson *et al.* (1997), Tyler (2000), Copp (2001).

geomorphological features are identified and the role of jointing in creating blowholes, natural bridges and coastal gaps is explained.

In Kalbarri National Park in Western Australia (Figure 1.6), geotourism takes the form of car-based visits to coastal gorges. Here the Tumblagooda Sandstone outcrops at the coastline, where marine erosional processes have carved natural arches and sea stacks. The sandstone is overlain by a highly weathered and friable limestone, and solutional weathering processes have produced calcretes, where calcium carbonate has been re-deposited at depth. The limestone also displays many examples of fossil root channels and, because of its friability, is subject to collapse and provides examples of mass wasting events. An interpretive walk trail has been developed at one of the gorges, where examples of bedding planes and weathering features are explained for the Tumblagooda Sandstone. Inland the Murchison River provides an example of incised meanders (Figure 1.7) and the

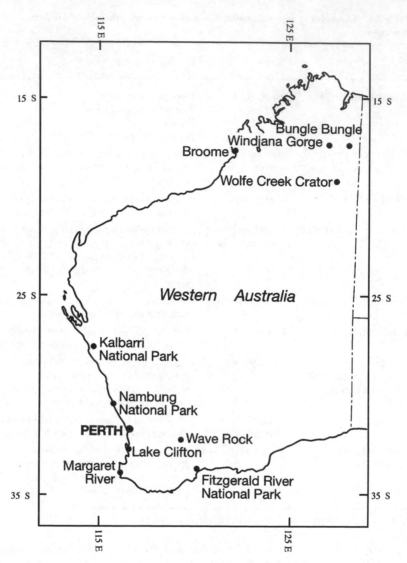

Figure 1.6 Location of selected geotourism sites in Western Australia.

down-cutting has created spectacular gorges where viewing points have been developed. Visitors can also complete walk trails of varying length.

In some parts of the world geotourism is centred on a particular theme. One such example is the Lake District of Iowa in the USA (Table 1.2). This area provides for appreciation of the geological significance of the Pleistocene glaciations. Here the role of glacial processes in creating landscape can be explored. A diversity of related landforms can be seen which reflect the geomorphology resulting from the advance and retreat of ice. Active contemporary glacial processes can be observed at other sites, such as at the Nigardsbreen Glacier in Norway and the

Figure 1.7 Incised meanders, Murchison River Gorge, Kalbarri National Park, Australia (photograph courtesy of David Newsome).

Table 1.2 Site/theme geosite diversity in a previously glaciated landscape: Lake District of Iowa, USA

Feature	Geological characteristics
End moraine	Rock and regolith left by stagnating glacial advances
Erratics	Large stones and boulders that have been transported by glaciers; in many cases their geology reflects being transported a considerable distance from their origin
Glacial lakes	When glaciers advanced over the landscape they scoured basins into their valleys, and these basins have filled with water arising from the melting of stagnant ice over a long period of time
Kettleholes	Formed as a result of a residual block of ice gradually melting and forming a wet depression
Kames	Sediment-laden streams flow from beneath glaciers, and kames develop where the debris accumulates in a cavity in the ice. A hill is left following glacial retreat and after the ice has melted
Eskers	Meltwater stream channels flow in tunnels beneath the ice. Eskers are long, winding ridges that are left in the landscape following retreat of the ice

Franz Joseph and Fox Glaciers in New Zealand. Other sites that focus on just one theme include volcanic sites such as the Hawaii volcanoes (Table 1.3). The Kilauea Visitor Centre has displays on the formation of volcanoes and geological processes, and film of previous eruptions. Roads provide for access to a number of sites (see Table 1.3); in addition, visitors may camp, cycle and utilize hiking trails.

Fossils are often the focus of attention, as in the case of the Karoo Fossil Trail in South Africa. Here the attention is on fossils *in situ*, but visitors may also

Table 1.3 Volcanic features that can be seen on a visit to the Mauna Loa and Kilauea Volcanoes, Hawaii

Feature	Aspects of geological interest
Recent and active volcanism	Shield volcanoes Basaltic lava flows Kilauea is one of the world's most active volcanoes
Calderas (Mauna Loa and Kilauea have summit calderas)	Large basin-shaped depressions – Kilauea caldera measures 4.5 × 3 km across
Pit craters (e.g. Kilauea)	Smaller craters on the edge or inside the main caldera, formed as a result of local sinking and collapse giving rise to a crater shape
Cinder cones (e.g. Puu Puai, Kilauea)	Small hills formed by cinders arising from an eruptive event
Spatter Cones (e.g. Kilauea)	Low, steep-sided cones composed of deposited lava
Littoral cones (e.g. Kilauea)	Cones that develop where lava has flowed into the sea. The cone develops as a result of water exploding into steam as lava enters the water
Lava tubes (e.g. Nahuku lava tube)	A tube-like space that has developed beneath the surface of a lava flow. The space is created when hot lava flows out from beneath the solidified surficial crust
Steam vents (e.g. Kilauea)	Hot groundwater and steam produced as a result of geothermal heating
Sulphur banks (e.g. Kilauea)	Volcanic gases have seeped out with the groundwater, precipitating sulphur at the surface
Black sand beaches (Hawaii)	Derived from the erosion of volcanic rocks/lavas and dominated by minerals such as the pyroxenes and iron oxides

appreciate other geological and geomorphological features of the area. The fossils are contained in the Karoo Supergroup, which is an accumulation of clayey and sandy sediments. The sedimentary rocks show impressions of leaves, preserved tracks and burrows, shells, and the skeletons of reptiles. Visitors are presented with exciting interpretive questions on the age, appearance and ecology of the fossils.

The vital role of interpretation: the case of Wave Rock, Western Australia

For many people, rocks do not command the same attention as a living forest or elicit the interest that animals do by virtue of movement, colour, sound and interaction. This makes the issue of bringing rocks 'alive' to the visitor a critical aspect of geotourism. Although many landforms are visually impressive, what really matters are accounts of palaeo landscape and formation. This requires knowledge and therefore trained interpreters who can deliver the information and inspire the geotourist. As in other forms of natural area tourism, the visitor needs to be

Case study 1.1: Geotourism Development Project, Indonesia (after Amin, 1999)

In Indonesia, a Geotourism Development Project (GDP) has been formed to supply geological information for the national tourism industry. It defines geotourism as tourism activities in which geological concepts are used to explain the formation of landforms and natural phenomena. The GDP's tourism project is based on geological conservation that is characterized as the identification and protection of areas possessing highly aesthetic natural phenomena due to their geological uniqueness and/or rarity. It aims to assist the tourism sector to create selected nature-based tourism objects and identify areas as diverse, unique and valuable geotourism attractions which can provide a natural alternative to existing attractions.

By 1999, the Project had produced a number of informative and educational geotourism products including six guidebooks, three maps, six videos and three graphic animated CD-ROMs. The GDP views the benefit of geotourism products as:

1. The diversification and enrichment of geotourism objects
2. The production of geotourism guide books for the tourist guides to explain the natural phenomena using accurate geological information
3. An appreciation of nature through geotourism, and the appreciation of nature through the application of geoconservation principles.

left with a sense of wonder and challenged as to where we sit as a species within the timescale of planet Earth.

Materials that can be used to assist in interpreting geosites include: books, displays, videos, slide shows, interactive touch panels, models, specimens, computer animations and activities. Although these are extremely useful (see Case study 1.1), and in many cases an essential part of presenting geotourism to the visitor, there is no substitute for being in the field. On-site interpretation is very dependent on face-to-face communication, but selected materials can also be used in the field in order to enhance the interpretive process.

Wave Rock in Western Australia (see Figure 1.6) provides an example of the importance of interpretation at an established geotourism destination. Wave Rock is a 12-metre overhanging natural wall of granite which extends for a length of about 100 m. The granite underwent weathering when most of it was covered by regolith. The process, occurring over a long period of time, involved rainwaters running off exposed parts and ponding around the base of the outcrop. Here the rock was slowly dissolved, and when the overlying regolith was removed due to erosion a concave and smooth slope was revealed (Figure 1.8). Grey vertical streaks and lines that are evident on the rock face are the result of algal growth (Copp, 2001). The formation is unique and spectacular, and over the years a tourism industry has developed based on a long-distance day-trip coach tour to view the rock formation. An accommodation facility has been developed in the nearby town of Hyden, designed to service more independent travellers and those that wish to stay overnight.

Figure 1.8 Wave Rock, Western Australia (photograph courtesy of David Newsome).

One of the issues associated with Wave Rock is that it sits in a remote location and entails a four-hour journey by road from Perth. Interviews with recent visitors indicate disappointment and dissatisfaction associated with the length of the journey 'just to see Wave Rock'. In addition, visitors have complained that there is no decent walk trail and that interpretation is lacking. What is needed here is an expansion of the Wave Rock experience according to a number of stops that break up the journey, providing an interpretive story that concludes at Wave Rock. This way several layers of geological content can be incorporated, thus reducing the focus on a single site (Figure 1.9). The journey could start at a quarry close to Perth, where the regolith that overlies most of the rocks in south-western Australia can be examined and explained. Face-to-face interpretation could address questions like 'What is this stuff made of?' and 'How did it form?' Visitors could handle the materials and become more attuned to the nature of the ground beneath their feet.

The journey to Wave Rock takes place across an essentially flat landscape which reflects the geological stability of the Yilgarn Craton. This stable landmass, which forms much of the basement geology of south-west Australia, can be easily overlooked because of the flat terrain, few rock outcrops and an extensive covering of regolith. This is where interpretation is vital and opportunities arise for drawing attention to less obvious aspects of the landscape.

The sight of an almost flat landscape, therefore, particularly requires interpretation of what is being seen and explanation of what it means. Because rocks and landscapes are not alive in the sense that plants and animals are, geotourism is particularly reliant on explanation of origin and meaning. With appropriate interpretation, any landscape, rock outcrop or landform can be made as exciting as spectacular displays of wildflowers or concentrations of wild animals. To be able to understand a geosite makes the experience much more rewarding. Visitors could be asked how the landscape came to look like this, or to take their minds back to the Pre-Cambrian age and imagine a mountain range and the forces that

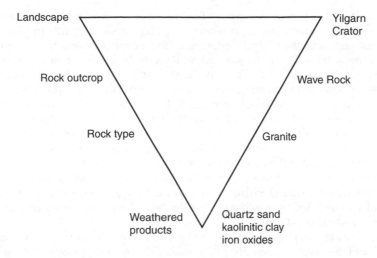

Figure 1.9 Linkages in relation to the interpretation of Wave Rock.

created it. Such a story could also be further developed with the aid of models and diagrams. Visitors could be led through the environmental changes of the Tertiary period and 'provoked' into considering the origin of lateritic regolith. Clients might be asked to reflect on how we know about geological materials and consider how the evidence is gathered. Grains of sand could be examined under a binocular microscope and visitors allowed to discover shape and colour for themselves and, more importantly, consider the 'why?'. Such self-discovery based insight activities could then be supported with the viewing of enlarged electron-micrographs of the surfaces of sand grains, thus allowing the geotourist to appreciate fully the story that unfolds from viewing a grain of sand. A suitable rock outcrop could be examined before finally arriving at Wave Rock, with interpretation here focusing on whether the rocks seen earlier are the same or different from Wave Rock and why.

The main focus of interpretation, however, will be at the main site itself. The ultimate objective is to increase understanding and enhance the enjoyment of Wave Rock. By instilling interest via interpretation, appropriate visitor behaviour at the site can be achieved. The final desirable outcome should be to encourage appropriate minimal-impact behaviour, increase the visitor's awareness of impacts, foster conservation of the site and promote an interest in geoconservation.

The impacts of geotourism

All tourism causes impacts, which can be both beneficial (good) and adverse (bad). The type of disturbance brought about by recreation and tourism is multifaceted and reliant on a number of factors and, depending on the nature, can be permanent. Negative human disturbance caused by direct visitation or recreation in the geological environment commonly results in graffiti, erosion of friable rocks, spoiling of sensitive features such as speleothems, and damage as a result of hammering, digging and collecting fossils. The role of planning and management therefore is to increase the beneficial impacts and reduce the adverse ones. In Mathieson and Wall's (1982) famous treatise, *Tourism: Economic, Physical and Social Impacts*, the authors stated that 'information on the effects of tourism on geology are scarce' (p. 112). They noted that rock formations and caves had been impacted by both amateur collectors of minerals, rocks and fossils and professional souvenir hunters. To this was added vandalism at popular cave sites by visitors carving their names or initials into the rock formations. They also pointed to the damage caused by climbers cutting footholds in popular climbing routes – although this was not caused by tourists, but rather by recreationalists. The authors noted that the impacts on geology were restricted to special environments and were largely confined to the vandalism of unique features, concluding that this would not be a major problem in most tourist areas in future.

Two decades later, natural areas are viewed as being visited to 'get away from it all', and this involves many recreational activities that take place within natural eco- and geo-systems (Newsome *et al.*, 2002). With a rapidly increasing number of people visiting natural areas there is much scope for negative impacts to occur, and the nature and degree of impact can be complex and variably significant depending on the situation. Impact significance can depend on the type and source of impact, the environmental sensitivity, other cumulative pressures, and the effectiveness of any management that is in place. Moreover, what is a well-recognized and significant impact in one country or environment may not be a problem elsewhere.

Sources of impact

There are various ways of categorizing the potential environmental impacts of tourism. Buckley and Pannell (1990) divide these into transport and travel, accommodation and shelter, and recreation and tourism activities in the natural environment. In terms of tourism and recreational activities, common sources of impact include boating, off-road vehicles, hiking, camping, mountain-bike riding, horse riding and caving. In some cases all three impact categories may occur together, leading to a cumulative impact situation. The degree of physical impact, however, will depend on the location, diversity, intensity and duration of the activities themselves. Environmental response varies according to individual geosystem resistance and resilience.

Impacts on the natural environment can be divided into a number of categories according to whether they are 'direct' or 'indirect'. Direct impacts on geosites can be caused by broadscale tourism development, such as the clearance of vegetation leading to increased erosion or the levelling of terrain for tourist development. Specific localized impacts are caused by trampling on paths, fossicking for minerals or fossils, or the use of trail bikes and other off-road vehicles causing erosion and scarring. Whilst some environmental impacts are deliberate acts of vandalism, others are more benign; however, their cumulative impact can cause problems.

Geotourism sites are often perceived to be at low levels of risk of physical damage where there are only few trails, limited access and few visitors. This situation often fits in with the concept of wilderness tourism. A number of studies of recreational impacts, nevertheless, show that significant impacts can occur at campsites after only short periods of time and low levels of use (Hammitt and Cole, 1998). A high and continuous impact potential may exist where there are many trails, roads and facilities, and a large infrastructure. Concentrations of use mean that although intense and severe impacts may occur at a popular tourist site or along a well-used trail, only small parts of large natural areas are impacted.

There are several examples of adverse environmental impacts caused by geotourism. Some include litter and pollution of geological environments, the removal of specimens, the effects of tourists on enclosed environments such as caves, and the damage created by off-road vehicles.

Nepal contains some of the most spectacular areas in the world in a remarkable physical setting. The altitude ranges from 100 metres above sea level in the south to the top of Mount Everest (8848 m) in the north (Wells and Sharma, 1998). Whilst climbing and trekking are the mainstay of the tourism industry, the majority of international tourists travel to the country to view its spectacular landscape, its culture and its biological diversity. Overshadowing the country's physical attributes are the high Himalayan Mountains, and underpinning the international visitation is the geotourism experience. Problems exist as the rising number of tourists has exacerbated the demand for fuel-wood, causing deforestation. In addition, they have created litter and pollution problems along the major trekking routes and trails. However, a new zoning approach is being introduced to advance a sustainable future for the country. In Sagarmatha (Mount Everest) National Park, a World Heritage Region, two-thirds of the families living in the park have direct income from tourism, working as guides or porters, or selling food, lodgings, clothing, equipment and handicrafts. The main tourism centre in the park is a thriving village with many new tourist lodges. This growing geotourism industry is still in its infancy, with an emphasis by the tourists still more on adventure than on geological appreciation. However, as guides become more educated and tourists more genuinely interested in their hosts, then the focus of Nepal's future tourism industry will embrace geotourism as a 'softer', more informed tourism niche than its mountaineering-based counterpart.

Petrified wood can be found all over the world, and one of the world's most extensive concentrations of petrified wood is at the Petrified Forest National Park (PFNP) in north-eastern Arizona. The trees are 225 million years old, and represent an extraordinarily visible record of Earth's past. The barren hills are tinted with delicate bands of reds, oranges, greys and whites, and have been eroded to reveal the remains of life, preserved in stone. A 46-kilometre scenic drive loops throughout the park, winding past overlooks and short walking trails. The PFNP has a visitor centre, a museum (Rainbow Forest) and a number of walk trails. Visitors are allowed to touch the logs, but it is illegal to take even the smallest piece of petrified wood from the park. Unfortunately visitors cannot resist the temptation to remove specimens, and, when multiplied by hundreds of thousands of visitors every year, these small thefts add up to a loss of approximately 1 tonne of petrified wood each month (Seely, 2002).

The environmental impact of tourist pressure on caves has been investigated in Spain (Calaforra *et al.*, 2003). Cave temperature monitoring was carried out in the Cueva del Agua de Iznalloz, Granada, Spain – a cave that has great tourist potential and has been maintained under natural conditions for over 30 years. The Cueva del Agua is located in the Sierra Arana Mountain, Granada, Spain, at an altitude of 1700 metres (see Chapter 11, Figure 11.2). It includes 3000 metres of passages, extending to a depth of 165 metres. The particular lithological and structural features of the cave have led to the development of unique speleothems. The study was carried out because there has been a marked increase in the development of tourist caves, yet the sustainability of this has not really been investigated. Cave lighting and the presence of visitors alter the conditions inside a cave, leading to a number of changes in relative humidity, air temperature, carbon dioxide concentration, algal proliferation and altered fauna habitat. These processes produce a progressive deterioration in ambient quality, and increase the degradation of speleothems, cave art and troglobite biodiversity.

The experiments were designed to determine the possible effect of visitors on the cave. There was a large response from the city of Granada, with 3068 people participating in open days on 22 and 29 April 1995. Controlled experiments investigated the effect of two large-scale visits (980–2088 visitors per day). The effect of both mass visits on the air temperature in the interior of the cave was very rapid (2.5 minutes). The maximum perturbation of air temperature within the cave during the two experiments was after 30 and 70 minutes. The results indicate that in order to maintain a sustainable cave temperature, visitors to the cave would need to comprise groups of fewer than approximately 50 people, with the cave open for a maximum of 4 hours daily. To avoid a cumulative thermal impact the period between closure of the cave and a subsequent visit would need to be 4–5 hours in order to allow complete recovery.

In the small town of Horse Cave, Kentucky, USA, tourist caves give rise to significant economic activity. In 1941 the US federal government opened the Mammoth Cave National Park, and today it attracts 1.5 m visitors a year, with people required to book visits in advance. The cave experience has subsequently evolved into an 'environmental edutainment' experience (Anonymous, 2000). The caves are marketed as places where visitors can learn about geology and conservation. The promotional literature states that: 'It's not some cold fact in a science book, things here come alive'. Mammoth Cave attracts nearly two million visitors annually, and it is a designated World Heritage Site and International Biosphere Reserve. In addition to touring the cave, visitors hike, canoe and fish throughout the park's extensive hardwood forest. With a rich history of conservation and tourism, the US National Park Service and caver lobby groups are now questioning the environmental soundness of a proposed industrial park, shipping complex and airport being proposed for development about 8 kilometres southwest of the cave complex. The project could pose serious risks to the world's longest cave system. Environmentalists believe that the project is not compatible with the region's unique karst geology (Daerr, 2001). Moreover, this environmental view is supported by the economic benefits generated by the cave. A 1994 survey by the Kentucky Department of Travel estimated that the Cave filters more than $115 million into the state's economy annually.

Mountain areas are also subject to ever-increasing access by all-terrain vehicles, resulting in accelerated hillside and rock erosion caused by track cutting and use (Worboys *et al.*, 2001). Recreational off-road vehicles (ORVs) include four- and six-wheel drive cars and coaches, all-terrain vehicles (ATVs), trail and dirt bikes, and snowmobiles (Buckley and King, 2003). These can all have adverse environmental impacts on soils and rock formations. It is suggested that the geological impacts of ORVs are created through the compaction of soils, break-up of surface crusts, wear of rock surfaces and tyre scars on rocks.

Off-trail biking is creating a number of adverse impacts on geological features. One area that is causing particular concern is the canyon country of southern Utah, USA (Egan, 2001). The area is characterized by eroded rock maze scenery near the southeast town of Moab, with Arches and Canyonlands National Parks nearby. Remains of one of the three major Indian cultures in the prehistoric Southwest region are also in evidence (Walker, 1993). In the early stages of the tourist boom tourists visited the area primarily for its archaeological attributes, or to roam and search for solitude. However, about fifteen years ago the canyon country was rediscovered, and an influx of visitors have come to explore the region by both pedal- and motor-powered all-terrain vehicles.

The town of Moab, with its 6000 inhabitants, now has almost 2000 hotel rooms. Visitors to Arches National Park have more than tripled in 20 years, from 270 000 in 1979 to 870 000 in 1999, and have grown six-fold in Canyonlands National Parks over the same period, to 447 000. Near Moab, the Slickrock Trail now attracts over 100 000 mountain-bike cyclists each year. All-terrain vehicles have disturbed much of the fragile crust of the open land and eroded many of the back roads. Park rangers state that 'hyper-recreating tourists' are having the same adverse impacts on the land that mining and over-grazing once did. Federal land managers have tried to keep the region's campgrounds from becoming outdoor waste dumps, and now they educate visitors on the fragility of the land (Egan, 2001).

Park rangers know that the undulating topography of the canyon country is not a simple desert with a large river running through it. The ground is held together by a cryptobiotic crust – a thin tangle of lichens, bacteria, mosses and other components – and bike and jeep bike trails lead to its destruction. Park management is now concerned that naturally weathered arches could be chipped or marred by visitors, or that the innumerable Anasazi archaeological sites in the south could be vandalized. Increasingly, the rangers have had to referee conflicts between the different groups scrambling for their piece of the canyon country – hikers versus bikers, horseback riders versus four-wheelers, target shooters versus birdwatchers – as new forms of recreation expand into the area (Egan, 2001). The latest craze around Moab is base-jumping, in which people with parachutes jump from the tops of tall spires and cliffs. The development of adventure-based geotourism is having spiralling effects on the small town of Moab. Like a number of other settings in the west, it may now be expanding into second-home developments. Plans are under way to develop 150 condominiums, a 225-room lodge and 110 houses on 2-acre sites. Overall, the face of the region is changing as adventure recreationalists and other tourists are visiting in ever-increasing numbers.

The examples described here serve to point out the multifaceted nature of tourism impacts in geo-locations. The Arches and Canyonlands National Parks

19

situation demonstrates the complex interface between the benefits and problems caused by tourism and recreation. It is evident that certain stakeholders and service providers are benefiting from increased visitation, but the increased human pressures – and especially conflicting recreational activities – are also potentially damaging the geotourism experience and natural values.

Planning and management in geotourism

This section will provide some examples of management issues and approaches (see Case studies 1.2 and 1.3). As with other forms of natural area tourism, geotourism's impacts are neither all good nor bad, but the key task is to ensure that any negative impacts are minimized whilst at the same time maximizing any positive impacts. This poses a challenge for planners and managers, but it is not an insurmountable one and lessons presented in the various case studies in this book can assist in the development of a sustainable form of geotourism which is environmentally appropriate, community endorsed and economically viable.

The importance of ranger presence

A brief example from the USA provides an insight into the importance of management having face-to-face contact with the public. Yellowstone National Park, located in the states of Wyoming, Idaho and Montana, USA, is the world's first national park. It comprises 2.2 million acres of geological attractions with 10 000 thermal displays and an extensive array of wildlife, scenery and recreation opportunities. Lava flows are visible, and the landscape is punctuated with geysers and hot springs. Mammoth Hot Springs and Old Faithful are two of the park's major attractions. Here, interpretation is a significant tool in enhancing visitor experience and reducing negative impacts (Williams, 2002). The geyser basin can be viewed from the many boardwalks and understood through guiding and information given by the park rangers. Ranger-led hikes in the park are scheduled most days of the week in many different areas throughout the park. The length and difficulty of the hikes vary, ranging from two hours to a half-day. The rangers are more teachers than tour guides, and they stop frequently along the trail to show how geology and biology interact and inform visitors about minimizing their impact on the environment.

Management issues at waterfalls in Australia

For a largely arid country with generally low relief, Australia has a remarkably large number of waterfalls. Found mainly near the coast, close to where most of the population lives and to the major tourist resort areas, Australia's waterfalls have long been popular scenic attractions and places for recreation (Hudson, 2004). They play an important role in the country's tourism, even in seaside resort

Case study 1.2: Managing geotourism: the case of Waitomo Caves, New Zealand (after Doorne, 2000)

New Zealand contains mountain ranges, glacial features, dormant and active volcanoes, impressive river systems, and many examples of coastal processes and landforms. The country's largest attraction is the Waitomo Caves, in the King Country region of the North Island. Here, the karst landscape comprises numerous caves and underground river systems. The local village has a resident population of approximately 500 people and a tourist population of around 450 000 international, predominantly Asian, visitors per annum. The visitors come to the area principally to undertake one experience – that is, to visit the Glow-worm Cave. Tourists undertake a guided tour of the cave system, visit the 'cathedral' or main chamber, then go on a boat ride through the Glow-worm Grotto. A large calcite crystal column dominates the Cathedral Room, where stalactites and stalagmites can be viewed. Both are hollow, straw-like 'spears', and where they grow together columns form. The floor and walls are covered with flowstone, forming 'curtains', 'draperies' and 'shawls' where the water has flowed in sheets down the cave walls. The cave is widely regarded as a geological attraction of considerable aesthetic and ecological significance.

From a planning and management perspective, the cave is designated as a 'sacrificial cave', concentrating tourist activity in one spot so as to protect more environmentally significant sites. A major issue for the operation of the cave is its amount of carbon dioxide at any one time. A limit of 2400 ppm has been placed on ambient levels, which amounts to around 300 people per hour, because beyond this level the speleothems (limestone formations) begin to corrode.

Tourist numbers are an issue, and investigations have been made into crowding and social impact. A survey of 2000 visitors indicated a high level of satisfaction with the overall product. However, they were less satisfied with the number of groups in the cave, waiting for other groups during the tour, and access to some of the tourist facilities. Domestic tourists registered high perceptions of crowding, whereas some of the Asian tourists (notably the Koreans) were dissatisfied with having to wait for other groups during their tour. All visitors regarded crowding as a problem during the high visitation periods around midday during the summer months.

These findings are significant for the future of the cave, which is a major national tourism icon and forms the hub of tourism in the surrounding region. On the one hand the cave is viewed as public property to which access is guaranteed, but on the other commercial expediency suggests that overseas tourists with their higher level of tolerance for crowds is economically more viable. However, the case of the Glow-worm Cave is more complex than its money-making or 'cash cow' element. It suggests that the issue of domestic visitor displacement needs to be addressed at the political level in order to maintain a stable sustainable future for the cave for the benefit of both the visitors and the community (local, regional and national).

areas where the main attractions are sandy beaches and surf. Before European settlement and the development of the tourism industry Aboriginals visited waterfalls, as recorded in drawings and paintings by nineteenth century European explorers and artists. With European settlement, waterfalls became among the main forms of landscape features visited by tourists.

Today the enjoyment at waterfalls can take many different forms. While it is the aesthetic appeal of waterfalls that attracts many visitors, for some they are not just beautiful landscape features to look at and photograph but also places for rest and recreation. To facilitate access and allow visitors good views in comfort and safety, footpaths, lookouts, viewing platforms, handrails, fences, direction signs and warning notices have been provided at many waterfall sites. Many sites also have nearby car parks.

In addition to more passive recreation, waterfalls also attract more adventurous visitors seeking activities such as diving or jumping into the plunge pools, canyoning and bungee jumping. Where the rock faces are suitable, waterfalls provide opportunities for rock climbing and abseiling. Canoeing, white-water canoeing and kayaking, tubing and rafting are popular. Some waterfalls are accessible by boat and are popular cruise destinations; however, most visitors arrive by road and gain access via walk trails. Easy access and tourist development can thus pose a great threat to the conservation of waterfall sites. Perhaps the most serious dangers are soil erosion and damage to vegetation, particularly where visitors leave the footpath to take shortcuts or obtain different views (Hudson, 2004). Vandalism, including littering and the removal of plants, in order to acquire better views and access is quite common, and graffiti are often seen on rocks and trees along footpaths and at the falls.

Careful planning and management are therefore needed to ensure that waterfalls retain their aesthetic appeal, while providing means of access that allow people to visit them in relative comfort and safety. In view of the large number of different stakeholders, including tourism developers, operators, and promoters, environmental conservationists and bushwalkers, and tourists of all kinds, the appropriate level of development at waterfall sites is likely to remain a contentious issue. Probably the best solution lies in providing a diversity of waterfall experiences, with some remote or inaccessible falls being kept as far as possible in their pristine state while others are developed for access and, in some cases, provided with appropriate amenities. The challenge for tourism planners and developers responsible for areas endowed with attractive waterfalls is to provide appropriate amenities at carefully selected sites, while at the same time preserving the experience of nature that the visitors seek.

Planning and management are essential components of geotourism development. It can be seen from this brief introductory account that geotourism can provide substantial economic benefits, but also needs to be subject to the same planning and management controls as other forms of natural area tourism. With any geotourism attraction that is developed there will be a number of issues that will need to be addressed. These include wider landscape threats to the site, over-development of tourism facilities, analysis of how the sites will be/ are viewed, overcrowding, visitor conflict, visitor displacement, degradation of trails and other facilities in the vicinity of the site, and degradation of the geosite itself.

Case study 1.3: The issue of aircraft noise at the Grand Canyon, USA (after Schwer et al., 2000)

The Grand Canyon is a World Heritage Site of global significance that attracts well in excess of 1 million visitors each year. As an aside, it is interesting to note that more visitors each year see the IMAX theatre presentations on the Canyon at the town of Williams, just outside the southern boundary of the park, than actually visit the Park (Grand Canyon National Park Ranger, 2003, personal communication).

In 1997 over 100 000 tourists visited the park by air to see the Canyon's outstanding landform features, of whom 60 per cent used the nearby city of Las Vegas as their point of departure. The tourists are mainly from Asia, and visit the Canyon in a single air trip one-day visit. However, proposed regulations to tighten up over-flight rules in the Canyon in the late 1990s fuelled concern for the future of this lucrative industry. The major aim of the proposed regulations was to ensure continued provision for the safety of the flights as well as to restore the natural quiet of the park. This situation has been defined by the US National Park Service as meaning that 50 per cent or more of the park must be free from aircraft noise for 75 to 100 per cent of the day. Special US Federal Aviation Regulations resulted in the establishment of four flight-free zones over the Canyon, covering 45 per cent of the park. The regulations also established minimum flight altitudes and provided special routes for air-tour operations. Already this 1997 regulation has been superseded by proposals to tighten up the regulations even further, by maintaining flight-free periods (or curfews) as well as restricting noisy aircraft.

Using a regional impact model, Schwer et al. (2000) estimated that the annual Grand Canyon air-tourism industry directly contributed US$ 444 million to the southern Nevada economy, with a further $316 million in indirect expenditure. After full accounting for expenditures, it was estimated that this activity contributed as much as $504 million to the economy. Further, it was suggested that if the tours were eliminated, the region could suffer a loss of around $250 million through the sum of the lost revenues of operators and the lost expenditures of tourists who would no longer visit the region without the option of a Canyon air tour. This account therefore serves to illustrate the balance that has to be struck between economic development and the maintenance of a quality experience for all visitors, while at the same time catering for a diversity of different human needs.

Scope and contents of this book

The generalist perspective of Stueve et al. (2002) is so broad that it is not a meaningful definition of geotourism. Our definition of geotourism puts geology and geomorphology as centrepiece components and the main focus of tourism interest. The contents of this book reflect this, and we have included a number of chapters that provide a perspective on current practice from around the world. In this book we have brought together a number of writers who are involved with developing and practising geotourism. This book therefore constitutes a first in attempting to set up geotourism as an applied science. We have deliberately included a range of views, first by presenting a global perspective, and secondly by presenting the ideas of writers with different approaches and views on the subject.

The book is arranged in three parts. Part One examines the resources for geotourism and contains chapters on the geotourism resources of Malaysia, South Africa, Australia and Iran. Part Two explores the concept of the geopark according to the international movement embraced by UNESCO, which is based on georesources. In addition to this, accounts of geoparks are supplied in the form of case studies from Germany and China. Part Three considers geotourism in action. The book is not a comprehensive overview, but instead sets the scene for the ongoing and proposed practice of geotourism. Case studies of existing geotourism activities are provided from the USA, Ireland, Great Britain and Spain. Some of the issues surrounding the interpretative component of geotourism are contained in Chapter 12, which focuses on interpretive geotourism in England and Scotland.

Finally we conclude by noting that the accounts of geotourism presented in this book illustrate the immense scope for tourism based purely on geology and geomorphology. Here we also flag the idea that there are many sites that remain to be identified and developed properly. It is very likely that, in many parts of the world, hundreds and even thousands of geosites await discovery and to be developed as natural area tourism products. In combination with other forms of tourism, geotourism adds another dimension and diversity to the natural area tourism product. Most important of all, we recognize that natural landscapes, landforms, rocks, fossils, and even soils and sediments need to be preserved before they are lost. We can only achieve this by recognizing and valuing these resources, planning for tourism and setting in place the appropriate management actions. The exploration of geotourism as an applied science is one way of doing this.

References

Anonymous (2000). United States: open for business. *The Economist*, 356(8189), 37.

Baxter, J. (2000a). *Perth to Albany Geology*. Rocks and Roads of Western Australia. Hermitage Holdings.

Baxter, J. (2000b). *Perth to Augusta Geology*. Rocks and Roads of Western Australia, Hermitage Holdings.

Buckley, R. C. and King, N. (2003). Visitor-impact data in a land-management context. In: R. C. Buckley, C. Pickering and D. B. Weaver (eds), *Nature-Based Tourism, Environment and Land Management*, CAB International, pp. 89–99.

Buckley, R. and Pannell, J. (1990). Environmental impacts of tourism and recreation in national parks and conservation reserves. *Journal of Tourism Studies*, 1(1), 24–32.

Calaforra, J. M., Fernandez-Cortes, A., Sanchez-Martos, F. *et al.* (2003). Environmental control for determining human impact and permanent visitor capacity in a potential show cave before tourist use. *Environmental Conservation*, 30(2), 160–167.

Copp, I. (2001). *Geology and Landforms of the South-West*. Department of Conservation and Land Management, Perth, Western Australia.

Daerr, E. G. (2001). Mammoth Cave waters at risk. *NPCA Park News*, Nov/Dec, 10–11.

Doorne, S. (2000). Caves, cultures and crowds: carrying capacity meets consumer sovereignty. *Journal of Sustainable Tourism*, 8(2), 116–130.

Egan, T. (2001). A landscape in peril. *The New York Times Magazine*, 18 Nov, 18.

Hammitt, W. E. and Cole, D. N. (1998). *Wildland Recreation: Ecology and Management*. John Wiley & Sons.

Hoatson, D., Blake, D., Mory, A. *et al.* (1997). *Bungle Bungle Range*. Australian Geological Survey Organisation, Canberra.

Hudson, B. J. (2004). Australian waterfalls as tourism attractions. *Tourism Review International*, 7, 81–94.

Mathieson, A. and Wall, G. (1982). *Tourism: Economic, Physical and Social Impacts*. Longman.

Newsome, D., Moore, S. and Dowling, R. (2002). *Natural Area Tourism: Ecology, Impacts and Management*. Channel View Publications.

Pretes, M. (2002). Touring mines and mining tourists. *Annals of Tourism Research*, 29, 439–456.

Schwer, R. K., Gazel, R. and Daneshvary, R. (2000). Air-tour impacts: the Grand Canyon case. *Annals of Tourism Research*, 27(3), 611–623.

Seely, K. B. (2002). Stone forests. *Scientific American Explorations*, 5(1), 11.

Stueve, A. M., Cook, S. D. and Drew, D. (2002). *The Geotourism Study: Phase 1 Executive Summary*. National Geographic Traveller, Travel Industry Association of America.

Tyler, I. (2000). *Geology and Landforms of the Kimberley*. Department of Conservation and Land Management, Perth, Western Australia.

Walker, S. L. (1993). *The Southwest: A Pictorial History of the Land and its People*. Camelback/Canyonlands Venture, Arizona.

Wells, M. P. and Sharma, U. S. (1998). Socio-economic and political aspects of bio-diversity conservation in Nepal. *International Journal of Social Economics*, 25(2–4), 226–243.

Williams, C. (2002). Rangers' knowledge adds much to hikes. *The Atlanta Journal Constitution*, 13 Jan, K9.

Worboys, G., Lockwood, M. and De Lacy, T. (2001). *Protected Area Management: Principles and Practice*. Oxford University Press.

2

Geotourism in Malaysian Borneo

Felix Tongkul

Introduction

The term *geotourism* used in this chapter refers to the utilization of geological heritage resources for education-based tourism. The geological heritage resource is based on the intrinsic values of geological and geomorphological features. These intrinsic values may include scientific, aesthetic, recreational and cultural values. The *scientific* value refers to important geological records or history of the earth (e.g. fossils, rock types and unconformity). It may also be understood in terms of the diversity of minerals, rocks, fossils, structures and landforms. The *aesthetic* value refers to breathtaking and unusual landscapes (e.g. mountains, valleys, lakes, rivers, waterfalls and beaches). The *recreational* value refers to landscapes that are suitable for various nature recreation (e.g. mountain hiking, rock climbing, white-water rafting and swimming etc.). The *cultural* value is associated with traditional use, local beliefs, and historic and archaeological records.

As in many other countries in the world, Malaysian Borneo (which includes the East Malaysian states of Sabah and Sarawak) inherited many geological features through its long (more than 200 million years) and complex geological history. Some of them are rarely found in other parts of the world, and are already declared as World Heritage. Examples include the intrusive rocks of Mount Kinabalu in Sabah and the lime-stone complex of Mulu in Sarawak. While this geological heritage has long been popular with tourists, its main attractions have been mostly limited to aesthetic and recreational values. Scientific values are often ignored or not included at all as part of the attraction. One of the reasons for this is the lack of scientific informa-tion related to a particular site that can be easily understood by the public. The concept of geotourism as understood here is therefore relatively new in Malaysia. The concept only started to evolve systematically in 1996 with the establishment of a Malaysian Geological Heritage Group comprising geologists from local uni-versities, government agencies (e.g. the Department of Mineral and Geosciences) and oil companies (e.g. PETRONAS and Sarawak Shell). This was formed in order to address the lack of scientific knowledge and its dissemination in the development of existing and potential tourism sites. In 1999 this informal group was formalized to facilitate research into, and the conservation and development of, geological sites that have heritage value for geotourism. Furthermore, system-atic efforts to identify, map, characterize and evaluate geological features nation-wide are an ongoing activity of this group. This group also advises the government regarding appropriate conservation strategies to be implemented. Discussion with other interested parties to introduce a strategy to conserve geological resources is ongoing at the national and international levels (Komoo *et al.*, 2003).

Geotourism and conservation

Conventional geological resources (e.g. minerals, rocks, hydrocarbons, water, soils, sands, gravels, clays and salt etc.) have played an important and increasing role in the industrial development of Malaysia and throughout the world. Unfortunately the path to wealth creation has been environmentally destructive, as extraction through mining and quarrying leaves behind considerable unwanted waste that ends up polluting the surrounding areas. Extraction also leaves scars on natural landscapes and alters ecosystem structure and function. In Malaysia, several unique tropical karst morphologies have been destroyed through quarrying for rock aggregates, cement and dimension stones (Komoo and Desa, 1997). As geotourism is focused on the appreciation of the intrinsic values of geological resources, it also falls under the concept of utilization without destruction. This concept is similar to the practice in the evaluation of work of arts and antiquities. The promotion of geotourism is therefore integral to the conservation and systematic development of geological features and landscapes.

The presence of outstanding geological features and landscapes generally con-tributes to the conservation of a particular area in Malaysian Borneo (Figure 2.1). In Sabah, several important geological attractions are located within protected areas. The remnants of the Mount Kinabalu granitic intrusion (Figure 2.2) in Ranau District and the Mount Maria volcanic cone in Tawau District contributed to the establishment of the Kinabalu Park in 1964 and Tawau Hills Park in 1979, respectively (see Figure 2.1). The presence of an active mud volcano in the island of Pulau Tiga in the district of Kuala Penyu has become a key

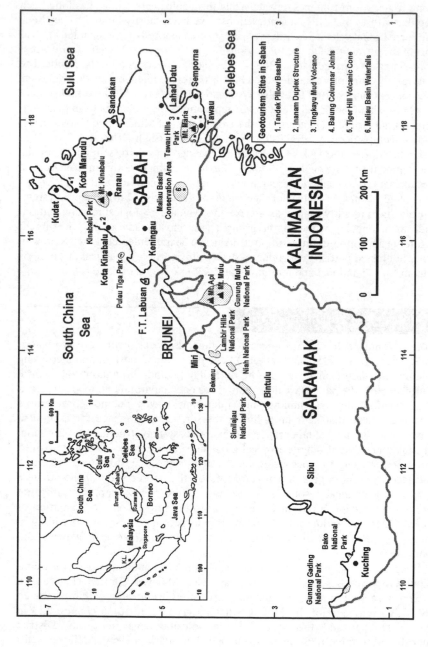

Figure 2.1 Geotourism sites in Sabah and Sarawak.

Figure 2.2 Mount Kinabalu, the highest peak in Southeast Asia, overlooks the Crocker Range Mountains of Sabah.

attraction to visitors, prompting the government to gazette the whole island as a national park in 1978. The occurrence of a circular sedimentary basin in central Sabah prompted the State government to gazette Maliau Basin Conservation Area as a Protection (Class 1) Forest Reserve in 1997.

In Sarawak, the presence of limestone caves, limestone pinnacles, waterfalls, coastlines and beaches have contributed to the establishment of several national parks (Figure 2.1). Bako National Park, Sarawak's oldest park, established in 1957, as well as Semilijau National Park, opened in 1995, are both well known for their picturesque coastlines, where constant erosion caused by waves at the base of cliffs has carved and created many sea arches and sea stacks. Niah National Park and Gunung Mulu National Park are well known for their karst topography, a distinct landscape where vast limestone terrain is carved out by river and ground water. Gigantic caves and cave systems, some of the largest in the world, are found in both parks. Waterfalls and pools constitute some of the key attractions at Lambir National Park and Gunung Gading National Park.

Development of geological features for geotourism

In Sabah and Sarawak, the development of geological features for geotourism is yet to be fully realized. Two approaches have been adopted by the Malaysian Geological Heritage Group in the development of geological sites for geotourism. The first takes advantage of existing ecotourism areas and uses the support system already available. In these areas, additional work is carried out to uncover and promote specific geological sites. This approach has been carried out

Table 2.1   Proposed geotourism at Kinabalu Park, Sabah (based on Dana Badang, 1999)

Geological site	Brief description of site
Mt Kinabalu plateau	The plateau, underlain by plutonic igneous rocks (mainly adamellite), has a smooth surface with a gentle to moderate slope gradient. The peaks of Mt Kinabalu, reaching up to 4095 m above sea level, are located here. At the summit there are 25 peaks and several gulleys left by glacial erosion during the Pleistocene. Cirques, U-shaped valleys, broken and plucked surfaces of the peaks and *rochee mountonees* are some of the glacial features that can be seen here.
Panar Laban plain	The small plain, where the main camping ground is located, lies at a height of between 3500 and 3700 m above sea level. The different rock types of the Mt Kinabalu pluton, comprising hornblende adamellite, porphyritic adamellite and aplite veins, can be seen here. Glacial deposits, called tilloid, also occur. The scour effects of glacial erosion (e.g. grooves, plucked surface) can be observed here.
Park HQ, Panar Laban Traverse	The 6-km traverse, following the trail to the peak of Mt Kinabalu, exhibits the different rock types found in the park. The first 3.5 km consists mostly of slightly metamorphosed sandstone and mudstones of the Trusmadi formation. This is followed by another kilometre of ultrabasic rock (serpentinite) with several stocks of microgranite. The plutonic igneous rock of Mt Kinabalu, comprising of adamellites, intruded into the Eocene Trusmadi Formation and Cretaceous ultrabasic rock which forms the cover rock of the Mt Kinbalu pluton.
Pinousuk plain	The plain of about 60 km^2 lies southeast of Mt Kinabalu near the town of Kundasang at a height of between 800 and 1700 m above sea level. The plain comprises a thick sequence of glacial deposit, referred to as the Pinousuk gravel. Blocks and cobbles of sandstone, serpentinite, granodiorite and porphyritic adamellite, loosely held by a sand and mud matrix, characterize this Quaternary deposit.
Poring hot spring	The hot spring occurs near Poring, a small village lying southeast at the edge of the park at a height of about 500 m above sea level. The hot spring can reach to a temperature up to 60°C, and is thought to be associated with the magmatic intrusion of Mount Kinabalu. Areas of relatively recent magmatic activities have a higher heat flow than the earth's average – in other words, the heat sources are nearer to the ground surface. Thus, percolating groundwater has a greater chance of being heated, and stored as hot water. Faults or fractures may have acted as conduits for the heated water to flow out to the surface at Poring.

at Kinabalu Park in Sabah, where a systematic study was carried out to map and characterize accessible geological sites within the park area (Badang, 1999). Some of the most important features recognized within Mount Kinabalu include glacial features, glacial deposits, rock unit contacts and hot springs (Table 2.1).

Figure 2.3 Columnar joints on andesitic rocks along the Balung River in Tawau District, Sabah.

Representative rock and mineral samples from the area have been collected and are exhibited at the park's mini rock museum. A geological model of Mount Kinabalu is also on display at the museum. Several park guides have undertaken short courses on basic geological mapping, rock identification and the geological history of Mount Kinabalu in order to enhance their scientific knowledge of the park.

The second approach involves the planned development of a specific site and a network of sites that have unique geological heritage value. The research and development activities focus on mapping, characterization, and the evaluation of new and established sites with the aim of educating visitors about the special intrinsic value attached to each site. Based on this approach, several examples have been established in Sabah and Sarawak. In Sabah and the Federal Territory of Labuan, 63 sites have been mapped and characterized (Tongkul, 2003). Some of the potential sites that could be developed for geotourism include columnar basalts, pillow basalts, an extinct volcanic cone, active mud volcanoes, tectonic structures (e.g. faults and folds) and waterfalls (Figure 2.3, Table 2.2).

While detailed studies have been carried out on some of these selected sites, efforts to promote the sites to the public are still in their early stages. In Sarawak, similar work has been carried out by geologists from the Department of Mineral and Geosciences, and from Sarawak Shell. One well-studied site is the karst topography of Mulu National Park (Figure 2.4, Case study 2.1). Unlike in Sabah, some efforts have been carried out in Sarawak to promote selected geological sites for geotourism, with some success. Since 1998, geologists from Sarawak Shell have been promoting geological-based tours in the Miri area (Table 2.3). Case study 2.1 illustrates how a small roadside outcrop in Sarawak has been developed for geotourism.

Table 2.2 Proposed geotourism sites in Sabah and the Federal Territory of Labuan

Geological site	Brief description of site
Tandek pillow basalts	Well-exposed pillow basalts associated with chert layers of the Cretaceous age occur along the Baliojong River in the district of Kota Marudu in North Sabah. The pillow basalts are well developed, showing radial cooling joints with thin skin. The basalts are interpreted to be remnant of an ancient oceanic crust formed around 90–120 million years ago (Tongkul, 1997). The site, which is easily accessible, is ideal for research and education in geosciences, and is visited regularly by local geology students.
Inanam duplex structure	This duplex structure located inside an abandoned sandstone quarry in the district of Kota Kinabalu shows excellent compressive deformation structure. The duplex structure is associated with thrust faults. The thrust fault resulted in the repetition of Oligocene sandstone and mudstone layers of deep-water sediments. The deformation is interpreted to be related to subduction–accretion processes in NW Borneo. The site is visited regularly by local geology students.
Tingkayu mud volcano	An active mud volcano found near the Tingkayu River in Lahad Datu District is one of the most impressive found in Sabah. The mud volcano spews out small fragments of rocks from the underlying strata. The mud volcano produces a cone structure of about 2 m in height, occupying an area of about 1500 m^2. The mud volcano is thought to be related to ongoing compressive tectonics in this region. It is located near an oil-palm plantation settlement, and has been turned into a recreation site by the plantation manager.
Balung columnar joints	Columnar joints, which occur along the Balung River in the district of Tawau, are a rare geological feature in Sabah. Columnar and horizontal joint structures are well developed on andesitic rocks. The columnar joints have produced four-, five- and six-sided blocks with a diameter about 30–40 cm. The horizontal joints have produced polygon-shaped blocks having a thickness of between 20–30 cm.
Tiger Hill volcanic cone	An ancient volcanic cone occurs on Tiger Hill in the district of Tawau. Quarrying on the hillside has exposed the impressive internal structure of the volcanic cone. The exposed cone, about 25 m high and 100 m wide, shows at least four episodes of deposition of volcanic ash and scoria bombs. The site is visited regularly for field excursions by local geology students.
Maliau Basin waterfalls	Maliau Basin, located in Tawau, forms an almost circular amphitheatre, about 25 km across and sharply defined on all sides by steep slopes or cliffs reaching over 1700 m high (Phillipps, 2002). The basin is underlain by sedimentary formation of gently inclined beds of sandstone and mudstone. The basin formed as a result of subsidence due to extension tectonics in this region (Tongkul and Chang, 2003).

Table 2.2 (*Continued*)

Geological site	Brief description of site
	Maliau Basin is well known for its many spectacular water-falls; about 30 waterfalls higher than 5 m have so far been mapped. The Basin is thought to have more waterfalls in its 390 km^2 area than any other place in Malaysia. The high density of waterfalls here can be attributed to the right combination of rock types (hard sandstone and soft mud-stone layers), geological structures (vertical fractures and gentle dipping layers) and morphology (a saucer-like sur-face). The Basin is a protected area managed by the State government. The seven-tier Maliau Fall has become one of the major attractions for visitors.
Labuan Island sedimentary facies	Labuan Island, located southwest of Sabah, is comprised of two major Neogene sedimentary rock units, the Setap Formation and the Belait Formation. Such formations occur widely offshore Sabah and Sarawak, and are rock-equivalent to those sedimentary formations producing oil and gas. The sedimentary rock units, exposed along the coast, exhibit a variety of interesting sedimentary structures, sedimentary facies, depositional processes and depositional environments. Three geotourism sites have been identified to demonstrate the diversity of sedimentary facies here (Tongkul, 2002). At Tanjong Punei, the Setap Formation is characterized by two sedimentary facies – namely disturbed sandstone-mudstone facies and bedded sandstone-mudstone facies. These sedimentary facies shows slumping processes on the conti-nental slope and turbidite depositional process in the deep-water environment, respectively. At Tanjong Layang-Layang and Tanjong Kubong, the Belait Formation is characterized by three sedimentary facies – namely mudstone facies, mud-stone-thin sandstone facies and pebbly sandstone facies. The sedimentary facies shows depositional processes on shelf, tidal delta and fluvial environments. The sites, which are easily accessible, are popular with local geology students and professional geologists.

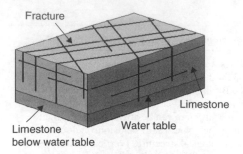

A thick limestone deposit forms a plateau. Rain and ground water seep into fractures of the brittle rock, dissolving the limestone and widening fractures into fissures and caves.

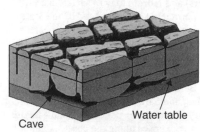

Caves develop along the line of the water table and fractures. They increase in size as further weathering takes place and as their roofs and walls collapse.

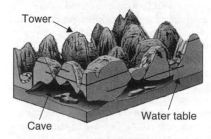

When the water table remains deep, the landscape eventually becomes rugged, consisting of limestone towers.

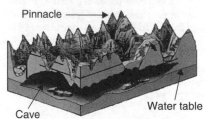

Erosion by heavy tropical rainfall results in the formation of razor-sharp Pinnacles. During cave creation, exquisite deposits of calcium carbonate form depositional features such as stalactites and stalagmites.

Figure 2.4 The development of tropical karst landscape in Sarawak.

Case study 2.1: Miri Airport Road Outcrop Museum, Sarawak

The Miri Airport Road Outcrop is the first geological site to be set up as an outdoor museum in Malaysian Borneo. This museum is a joint community project by the Miri Municipal Council and the Miri Outcrop Museum Working Group. The museum was established to preserve key geological features in and around Miri and to promote geotourism in Miri town (Lesslar and Lee, 2001). The outdoor museum is a popular site for local residents, especially school children.

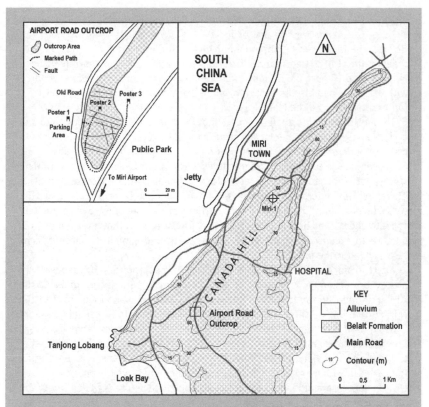

Figure 2.5 Location and general geology of the Miri Airport Road Outcrop Museum in Sarawak.

Background

Miri is a town located on the northern part of Sarawak, close to the border of Brunei. The Miri Airport Road Outcrop lies about 3 km south of the Miri town centre, located along the road to the airport (Figure 2.5). The outcrop is located towards the southwestern end of Canada Hill, a NE–SW elongated anticlinal structure about 8 km long and 1 km wide. The outcrop lies across the road from a recently completed public park.

Miri was the first oil town in Malaysia. Its first commercial oil well, Miri-1, was located on Canada Hill. The oil well, dubbed the Grand Old Lady, produced oil for 62 years until it was retired in 1972. The growth of the oil industry has helped to transform Miri from a small fishing village at the turn of the century into a modern and prosperous town of 170 000 residents, comprising various ethnic backgrounds.

The geological attraction

The key importance of the Miri Airport Road Outcrop lies in its scientific value in that a well-preserved faulted sedimentary rock sequence provides a record of the geological and tectonic history of the area dating back fifteen million years.

The faults and associated deformation features can be observed in three dimensions, thus making the site one of the best outcrops of its kind in Malaysian Borneo. The faults can be observed in high resolution from millimetre to metre scales. A total of 30 normal faults with a throw of 10 cm or more have been mapped here (Figure 2.6). Many interesting deformation structures associated with the faults can also be observed, including fault gouge, fault bed, fault lens, fault end and drag of bedding.

The interesting thing about a fault is that it compartmentalizes rocks into discrete blocks. Petroleum geologists need to map the fault through fault blocks in order to understand the distribution of oil and gas deposits. In the subsurface, faults can act as seals, trapping the fluids within fault blocks. The Miri Oilfield consists of a large number of fault blocks, similar to the ones exposed here. Therefore, this outcrop provides an excellent analogue to help understand the subsurface geology of the Miri Hill. Structural geologists study the fault in order to understand how and why the rocks fracture. With that information, it is possible to reconstruct the history of the earth and explain the mechanisms responsible for the formation of mountains.

Apart from the faults, sedimentary structures produced by depositional process are also quite common and well preserved. The rocks that make up the Airport Road Outcrop consist of interbedded sandstones and mudstones of the Miri Formation (Liechti *et al.*, 1960) deposited about ten to fifteen million years ago in a shallow marine to deltaic environment. The sandstones range from very fine-grained, laminated tidal deposits to medium-grained, cross-bedded or bioturbated shoreface and offshore bar deposits. Trace fossils, such as the distinctive pellet-lined burrows of shrimps (*Ophiomorpha*) that lived in shallow marine environment, are abundant, and rare star-shaped trace fossils (*Asterosoma*) can also be found here.

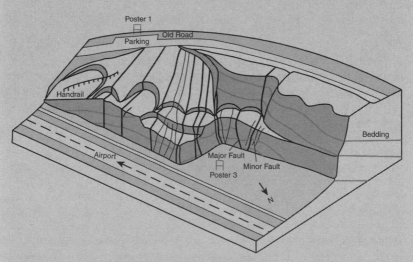

Figure 2.6 A three-dimensional sketch of the Miri Airport Road Outcrop showing the fault lines (based on Lesslar and Wannier, 2001).

Development of the site

The Outcrop Museum project was conceptualized in 1998 by a group of volunteers from Sarawak Shell. This project was part of a larger project, proposed earlier by the group, which includes two more sites – the Tanjong Lobang Sea Cliff and Canada Hill. The early idea of the group was to develop interesting outcrops, and particularly those that are accessible along the roadside, in order to create and develop interest among the people of Miri. However, the volunteers were faced with a number of challenges. First, local awareness and interest in geology is not that high among the people of Miri. Secondly, there was no example of a similar project available locally to learn from. Thirdly, the volunteers were not sure if there would be any support for such a project by the public. Fourthly, funding was unavailable to start the project, and finally, a small group, working voluntarily to provide ongoing management of the site, was not available.

After completing the geological documentation of the three proposed outcrops in early 1999, posters were prepared to highlight the geological attraction of each outcrop. These attractions were presented to the Deputy Chief Minister and local ministers of Sarawak, and later to the Miri Municipal Council, in order to seek their support in protecting the area. The response from the relevant authorities was very positive. Because the concept of preserving outcrops is new and in order to learn progressively from experience, the volunteers, together with the Miri Municipal Council, decided to proceed first with one outcrop. The Airport Road site, which was the one chosen, is the most interesting geologically as well as the most accessible. In 2000, with financial and construction support from the Miri Municipal Council, the first posters were installed on site at three strategic locations. Apart from information on the site, the posters also included contact information should visitors to the site wish to pursue the topics further. A brief geological guide in the form of flyers was also produced to introduce the site. Following this, the first group tour was organized in October 2000. Later, paths and guide-rails were constructed to facilitate easier movement and increase safety around the site.

To promote the newly established geological outcrop, letters from the museum were sent to all secondary schools in the area. A website (www.ecomedia-software.com/museum/museum) was set up and a multimedia CD of the Airport Road Outcrop was produced for sale. The website and CD have information on the background of the project, as well as details of progress and activities carried out. A working group comprising dedicated volunteers, both geologists and non-geologists, maintains the website and the overall development of the physical site. To create awareness among a broader audience, the project was presented at the Geological Society of Malaysia Petroleum Conference in Kuala Lumpur in 2000 and at the Second National Heritage Geology Conference on Langkawi Island in 2001. On both occasions the project received substantial interest and encouraging feedback.

To date, the visitors to the outcrop museum have comprised mostly secondary school students and teachers from Miri (Figure 2.7). People attend for free two-hour guided excursions or onsite geological exercises conducted by a group of volunteers from Sarawak Shell. These are normally carried out during the weekends and public holidays. In June 2002, petroleum technology students

Figure 2.7 Students looking at one of the major faults at the Miri Airport Road Outcrop in Sarawak (photograph reproduced courtesy of Phillip Lesslar).

visited from Norway to view the outcrop. The site is now being used by Shell and other oil companies for their in-house geological studies.

Management and sustainability

The Miri Airport Road Outcrop Museum is managed by a Working Group comprising of volunteers from Sarawak Shell and Miri Municipal Council. The team of geologists from Sarawak Shell provides the scientific knowledge, while the Miri Municipal Council looks after the physical aspects of the site. Potential problems faced by the Working Group include vandalism and site degradation due to intense tropical weathering. Tropical weathering associated with high temperature and heavy rainfall results in rapid chemical and physical breakdown of the exposed surface of solid rocks into soft and friable soil materials. During this process sedimentary features (e.g. lamination, cross-bedding, trace fossils) and tectonic features (e.g. faults and fractures) associated with the rock are destroyed. The newly formed soil materials become colonized with vegetation, which will eventually cover the whole area within the relatively short period of a decade. To ensure the sustainability of the museum, the rock outcrops will therefore have to be protected from weathering. In order to slow down the weathering process, water will have to be prevented from interacting with the rock – especially the rock surface. One of the possible ways of doing this is by constructing a roof above some of the most important geological features.

Table 2.3   Geological tourism in Miri, Sarawak (based on Lesslar and Wannier, 1998)

Geological tour area	Brief description of tour
Mulu	The main attraction is the limestone karst landscape of the Gunung Mulu National Park. Within the park's perimeter are the world's largest chamber, the largest cave passage known to man, Southeast Asia's longest cave system, and the highest pinnacle in the world (see Case study 2.1).
Niah	The main attraction is the Niah cave complex, which is easily accessible. Inside the cave there are historical wall paintings and archaeological sites. Another attraction is the rock outcrop of the Subis limestone complex, which is well-exposed along the Subis quarry face. The limestone complex shows many sedimentary features, and contains diverse microfossils. Along the Miri–Bintulu road, the sedimentary facies of the predominantly mudstone beds of the Setap shale formation is well-exposed. The mudstone shows interesting sedimentary structures and contains microfossils.
Bekenu	There are three main attractions in this area. The first is an active mud volcano at Ngebol. The mud volcano, located within an oil-palm plantation, consists of a mud mountain with crater-like formations produced by erupting gases. The mud volcano is thought to be related to over-pressured mud underlying the area. The mud volcano acts as a tiny pressure valve. The second attraction is a sedimentary sequence of the Lambir Formation located at Auban and Tanjong Batu coastal cliffs. The Lambir formation, which consists of sandstone and mudstones, shows interesting sedimentary structures and contains a rich assemblage of fossils such as gastropods, bivalves and crabs. The third attraction is a sedimentary sequence of the Setap shale formation exposed along the Miri–Bintulu Road. The outcrop shows interesting sedimentary structures, such as channels and slump structures.
Lambir	The Lambir National Park, underlain by a Miocene sedimentary sequence of the Lambir formation, is one of the main attractions here. Within the park area several medium-sized waterfalls occur, frequently visited by tourists. The other attractions are sedimentary sequences of the Lambir and Sibuti formation outcropping along the Miri–Bintulu Road. Near Entulang and Liam, marine shelf mudstone of the Sibuti formation, which contains a rich micro-fauna and micro-flora, is overlain by shore-face sandstones of the Lambir formation.
Miri	Four outcrops have been identified to illustrate the tectonic and sedimentary structures of the Miri formation along the Canada Hill area. The first outcrop, the Airport Road Outcrop, is a spectacular outcrop along the main road showing large scale block faulting (see Case study 2.1). The second outcrop, located near the Hospital Road, extends along a 20-m high cliff which follows the Canada Hill transpressional thrust zone. The upthrusted fault block which causes the Canada Hill relief is characterized by subhorizontal layering, while the downthrown block is characterized by near vertical strata. Oil-impregnated

(Continued)

Table 2.3 (*Continued*)

Geological tour area	Brief description of tour
	sandstones can be observed at various places along the outcrop. The third outcrop, at Jalan Lopeng, is characterized by aggrading shallow marine clastics. At various levels in the outcrop, shell lags associated with rip-up clasts are present at the base of sandstones. The fourth outcrop, at Pujut, is characterized by two major lithostratigraphic units of the Miri formation, a lower and an upper sandy sequence, separated by a flooding episode.

Prospects for geotourism in Malaysia

The paradigm shift in the geological community in Malaysia towards the conservation of geological heritage resources provides an impetus to more intensive collaborative research in this field between institutes of higher learning and government agencies. The increased emphasis placed by the Malaysian Government on the role played by the tourism industry in generating income and employment means that more financial resources are becoming available for the research and development of geological heritage resources in Sabah and Sarawak. The support given by state and local government to the Miri Working Group in the establishment of the Miri Airport Road Outcrop Museum points to a bright future for geotourism development in Malaysia.

Conclusion

The intrinsic value of geological features is often invisible to the untrained eye and can only be fully revealed and appreciated if systematic research and development are carried out by professionals. The volunteers from Sarawak Shell combined their expertise in different fields (e.g. structural geology, sedimentology, palaeontology, regional geology and software development) in the preparation of the posters, flyers and a multimedia CD for the Miri Airport Road Outcrop Museum.

The sustainability of conserved geological heritage requires some form of social and economic returns to be derived from them. The volunteers in the Miri Airport Road Outcrop Museum recognize that concentrating on geological aspects alone is insufficient. Their initial ideas were further developed to integrate geological goals into the aspirations of the community in terms of ecotourism and education. The Miri Working Group hopes to work closely with tour operators to help create a demand for better-trained and knowledgeable tour guides, which will in turn benefit the state tourism industry in the longer term.

To be successful, conservation of geological heritage requires the concerted involvement of all stakeholders, both geologists and non-geologists (e.g. politicians, planners, landowners, developers and the public/local communities). The volunteers in the Miri Airport Road Outcrop Museum project realized from the beginning that a project like this could not be sustained simply by a group of volunteers but would need ongoing maintenance effort that could only come from local authorities. Hence, it was a very clear requirement to involve relevant authorities as early as possible.

References

Badang, D. (1999). *Geologi pelancongan Taman Kinabalu, Sabah* [*Geotourism at Mt Kinabalu, Sabah*]. Unpublished MSc thesis, Universiti Kebangsaan Malaysia.

Komoo, I. and Desa, K. Md (1997). Conservation geology: a case for the tourism industry. In: I. Komoo, S. Leman, K. Md Desa and I. Abdullah (eds), *Warisan Geologi Malaysia* [*Geological Heritage of Malaysia*]. LESTARI, Universiti Kebangsaan Malaysia, pp. 85–95.

Komoo, I., Othman, M. and Aziz, S. (eds) (2003). Earth heritage conservation strategy. In: I. Komoo, M. Othman and S. Aziz (eds) (2003) *Proceedings of the International Dialogue on Earth Heritage Conservation, Kota Kinabalu, 8 July 2002*. LESTARI, Universiti Kebangsaan Malaysia, pp. 1–85.

Leichti, P., Roe, F. W., Haile, N. S. and Kirk, H. J. C. (1960). The geology of Sarawak, Brunei and the western part of North Borneo. *British Borneo Geological Survey Bulletin*, 3, 1–360.

Lesslar, P. and Lee, C. (2001). Preserving our key geological exposures – exploring the realm of geotourism. In: I. Komoo, H. D. Tjia and S. Leman (eds), *Warisan Geologi Malaysia – 4* [*Geological Heritage of Malaysia – 4*]. LESTARI, Universiti Kebangsaan Malaysia, pp. 417–425.

Lesslar, P. and Wannier, M. (1998). *Destination Miri – A Geological Tour of Northern Sarawak's National Parks and Giant Caves*. Multimedia CD, EcoMedia Software, Miri, Sarawak.

Lesslar, P. and Wannier, M. (2001). *Geology of the Miri Airport Road Outcrop*. Multimedia CD, EcoMedia Software, Miri, Sarawak.

Phillipps, A. (2002). *Secrets of the Lost World: Sabah's Maliau Basin*. Yayasan Sabah/Innoprise Corporation Sdn Bhd.

Tongkul, F. (1997). An ancient oceanic crust in Tandek, Sabah – a unique geological heritage. *Sabah Society Journal*, 14, 1–10.

Tongkul, F. (2002). Geotapak Pulau Labuan. In: I. Komoo and S. Leman (eds), *Warisan Geologi Malaysia – 5* [*Geological Heritage of Malaysia – 5*]. LESTARI, Universiti Kebangsaan Malaysia, pp. 196–218.

Tongkul, F. (2003). *Pencirian, penilaian dan pembangunan fitur geologi untuk geopelancongan di Sabah dan Labuan* [*Characterization, evaluation and development of geological features for geotourism in Sabah and Federal Territory of Labuan*]. Unpublished Research Report (UMS17/99), Universiti Malaysia Sabah.

Tongkul, F. and Chang, F. K. (2003). Structural geology of the Neogene Maliau Basin, Sabah. *Bulletin of the Geological Society, Malaysia*, 47, 51–61.

3

Geotourism potential of southern Africa

Wolf Uwe Reimold, Gavin Whitfield
and Thomas Wallmach

Introduction

The South African government regards tourism as
one of its main economic development strategies.
In 2002, South Africa was rated the fastest-growing
tourism destination worldwide, with a 12 per cent
increase in the third quarter of 2002 alone. In 2003 a
4.2 per cent increase in overseas visits was recorded,
against a global drop of this figure by 1.2 per cent.
From a mere 640 000 arrivals in 1994, this figure had
exploded to 6.5 million in 2003 (*Sawubona*, 2004a).
It has been estimated that by 2010 the South African
tourism industry will employ no less than 1.2 million
people, either directly or indirectly. Apparently, for
each eight new tourists, one permanent job can be
created (*Sawubona*, 2003a). South Africa's tourism
market does not only cater for international tourists;
in 2002, 67 per cent of the total South African tourism
market comprised domestic tourists. Some 15 million
South African tourists undertook 34 million domestic
trips and boosted the economy of the country by
nearly 10 billion Rand (*Sawubona*, 2003b; exchange
rate approximately R7/1US$).

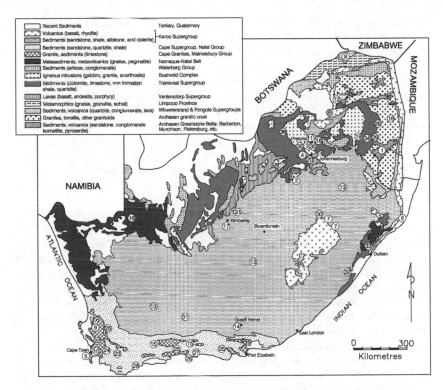

Figure 3.1 Simplified geological map of South Africa (after Viljoen and Reimold, 1999). This figure indicates the locations of important sites and areas referred to in the text. (1) Barberton Mountain Land; (2) Vredefort impact structure; (3) Freedom Park/Pretoria; (4) Cradle of Humankind; (5) Robben Island World Heritage Site; (6) Greater St. Lucia Wetland Park World Heritage Site; (7) uKhahlamba-Drakensberg World Heritage Site; (8) Mapungubwe World Heritage Site; (9) Cederberg Wilderness Area; (10) Table Mountain World Heritage Site/Cape Peninsula; (11) Tswaing mete-orite crater; (12) Makapans Valley; (13) Karoo Basin; (14) Valley of Desolation; (15) Klein Karoo; (16) Richtersveld National Park/Aughrabies Fall; (17) Kimberley; (18) Kruger National Park; (19) Dwars River National Natural Monument; (20) Gold Discovery Site at Langlaagte/Johannesburg; (21) Nooitgedacht glacial pavement and petroglyphs; (22) Paarl Mountain; (23) Kogmann's Kloof; (24) Brandvlei hot springs; (25) Cape Fold Belt; (26) Tsitsikamma Coastal National Park; (27) Robberg Nature Reserve; (28) Blombos Cave; (29) Great Escarpment in Mpumalanga; (30) Golden Gate National Park; (31) Karoo National Park; (32) Oribi Gorge; (33) Valley of the Thousand Hills; (34) Pilgrim's Rest; (35) Magaliesberg; (36) Pilanesberg Volcanic Complex and National Park.

Geotourism can make a major contribution to the alleviation of poverty in rural parts of southern Africa, as in many other parts of the developing world. It has the potential to open up new regions to tourist influx – for example, the mountain terrain around Barberton in eastern Mpumalanga Province, an area of ancient geology and gold mining history dating back to the nineteenth century (Figure 3.1 (1)). Another example is the Vredefort Dome near Johannesburg (Figure 3.1 (2)), the central part of the world's largest and oldest meteorite impact structure, which is

43

crossed by the Vaal River in scenic mountain terrain, and abounds with geological, archaeological and historical heritage. It is a little known fact that this area represents a window through which can be observed three billion years of geological evolution of the Kaapvaal craton.

On the outskirts of Pretoria, the new 35-hectare Freedom Park (3) is currently being developed as a national heritage precinct. It will depict South Africa as the 'Cradle of the Earth', illustrating the earliest life forms of about 3.5 billion years of age, and telling the story of the early hominids of millions of years ago and of more modern man as early as 150 000 years ago. South Africa also hosts one of the world's most important palaeo-anthropological sites, the Cradle of Humankind World Heritage Site (4) (Hilton-Barber and Berger, 2002), centred on the Sterkfontein Caves northwest of Johannesburg, which is heavily marketed as a tourist destination.

In recent years, much emphasis has been placed on the growing number of World Heritage Sites declared in South Africa. Currently six such sites have been approved by UNESCO: Robben Island off Cape Town (5) in Western Cape Province, the Greater St Lucia Wetland Park (6) and the uKhahlamba-Drakensberg Park (7) in KwaZulu-Natal, the Cradle of Humankind in Gauteng (3), and, the most recent additions, the Mapungubwe (8) iron age archaeological site in the far northwest of Limpopo Province and the Cape Floral Region. This latter site collectively refers to eight mountainous terrains in the Western Cape, including, for example, the awesome sandstone formations of the Cederberg Wilderness Area (9). Soon, Table Mountain (10) is expected to be declared a World Heritage Site, and a number of other sites have been listed tentatively or already proposed to UNESCO. These include the Tswaing Meteorite Crater (11) in Gauteng (Reimold *et al.*, 1999), one of the best-preserved and most accessible meteorite craters in the world; the fossil-rich Makapans Valley (12) in Limpopo Province; and parts of the Vredefort meteorite impact structure (2) that encompasses the entire Witwatersrand Basin region of north-central South Africa. More than half of these current and proposed World Heritage Sites represent entirely natural geological heritage and illustrate geological processes. They include mountain ranges, cave formations, fossil sites, meteorite impact sites and coastal formations. The remainder represent cultural or socio-political heritage. However, it is interesting to note that when South Africa's heritage is discussed, generally only cultural and historical aspects are referred to.

Southern Africa's geological heritage

Southern Africa includes a number of countries, such as South Africa, Namibia, Zambia and Zimbabwe. The region reveals a great diversity of geological resources; in fact it can be characterized as a virtual geological wonderland. With the exception of active glaciers and volcanoes (though both these environments can be studied in the stratigraphic record of the Karoo Basin (Figure 3.1 (13))), every geological process can be observed, covering a time span of 3600 million years (Table 3.1). This includes the evolution of the Earth, since the formation of the 3500 million year nucleus of an Archaean continent, with microfossils of some of the earliest lifeforms on this planet, to the presently active beach processes and desert development. The coastline of South Africa and its scenic coastal mountain

Table 3.1   South Africa: some 3600 million years of Earth's history in one country

Millions of years ago	*Events*	*Area(s) in South Africa*
3600–3100	Formation of granite-greenstone terrance and amalgamation into proto-Kaapvaal craton (early microfossils)	Barberton Mountain Land, Vredefort Dome, Johannesburg Dome
3080	Rifting and massive volcanic event (Dominion Group volcanics)	Vredefort Dome, environs of the Witwatersrand region
3080–2700	First major sedimentary basin: Witwatersrand Supergroup sedimentation	Witwatersrand Basin, Vredefort Dome, central Johannesburg
ca. 2700	Rifting and Ventersdorp flood volcanism	South of Johannesburg, North West Province
ca. 2600–2150	Transvaal Basin (giant stromatolites)	Mpumalanga Province, Pretoria–Johannesburg region, Northwest Province and Northern Cape
2060	Bushveld and Phalaborwa complex emplacement	Bushveld region of Limpopo and Mpumalanga provinces (world-class igneous ore deposits)
2020	Vredefort impact	Vredefort Dome and surrounding Witwatersrand Basin
ca. 1800	Waterberg Basin	Waterberg/Soutpansberg region of Limpopo Province
ca. 1300	Pilanesberg Volcano	Pilanesberg National Park (Northwest Province)
	Kimberlite intrusions	Cullinan: Premier Diamond Mine
ca. 1100–1000	Natal–Namaqualand orogeny	KwaZulu-Natal and Namaqualand/Bushmanland of Northern Cape
ca. 550–350	Sedimentation in the Western Cape region followed by mountain building (280–230)	Cape Fold Belt, Cederberg mountains
300–180	Karoo Basin development	Karoo of central South Africa (mountain ranges of Eastern and Western Cape interior, Drakensberg range)
60–120	Kimberlite volcanism	Kimberley (Northern Cape), Premier Mine near Pretoria
2.5	Early Hominid development	Cradle of Humankind near Johannesburg, Makapansgat; sites along south and west coast
0.25	Meteorite impact	Tswaing meteorite crater near Pretoria, Kalkkop meteorite crater south of Graaff-Reinet
Current	Beach processes, wetlands, erosion, desertification	Entire coastline; Lake St Lucia World Heritage site; many sites in the Karoo; Richtersveld and Trans-Kalahari national parks

ranges provide fine examples of processes related to continental drift, the collision and splitting apart of crustal plates, and the formation of continents over hundreds of millions of years.

Other countries of the Southern African Development Community (SADC) also have much geological heritage and beauty to offer. Namibia (Grünert, 2003; Schneider, 2004), for example, is a country that has a vibrant tourism industry which is nearly entirely based on the promotion of natural assets. These include various mountain ranges, coastal beauty, cultural heritage in the form of petroglyphs on the Brandberg mountains, desert geomorphology and dune formations (such as those at Sossusvlei), the deep and extensive Fish River Canyon, and fantastic rock structures in the Kuiseb-Naukluft National Park. The phenomenal diamond riches that have been extracted along the coast of the Namib Desert and from the lower reaches of the Orange River provide further tourism interest. Since the well-known 'Finger of God', which had been a geological icon of Namibia, collapsed owing to natural causes in the early 1990s, much effort has been made to protect and responsibly utilize this country's natural heritage (Figure 3.2). Nevertheless, proposals have been made to allow mass tourism access to the superb Roter Kamm meteorite crater in the southern Namib Desert by daily helicopter safari! The Geological Society of Namibia and the Geological Survey of Namibia are actively campaigning for sustainable development of the country's natural resources, both with regard to geotourism as well as to responsible mining development. At this stage, the Roter Kamm fragile desert has been declared a Conservancy and now cannot be disturbed by 4WD vehicles.

By the 1970s Zambia had already identified a number of national natural monuments, and a booklet, now long out of print, was produced providing much geological and natural historical information. Some of the national monuments and prominent natural heritage sites that are worth noting include: the Kundalila Falls near Kanona on the Great North Road; the 221-metre high Kalambo Falls in the far north near Lake Tanganyika; the Kapishya hot springs at Shiwa Ng'andu near the North Luangwa National Park and the skull of the Broken Hill (alias Rhodesian) Man (*Homo rhodesiensis*) from present-day Kabwe, reportedly unearthed during mining operations 80 metres underground at the Broken Hill zinc–lead mine in 1921; the petrified fossil forest of Karoo-age near Chirundu in the south, a national monument; and the well-revealed, fault-controlled Zambezi rift valley. The mineral riches and mining heritage of the Katangan Copperbelt could also be made accessible to the public. Some of these places are well signposted and listed on maps, and tourist guides are posted at a number of these sites. Still today a guide is present at the Kundalila Falls, with interesting information, although the geological information is questionable. At other sites only relics of the original facilities remain, as at the Nsalu cave that reportedly has good examples of San rock paintings. Unfortunately, visitors to this country are often left to their own devices to explore the beautiful sites of geological or archaeological interest. However, one notable exception is the Victoria Falls on the Zambezi River near Livingstone and the impressive Batoka Gorge downstream, where a fully-fledged tourism infrastructure exists.

Zimbabwe, which until the recent decline of its economy and breakdown in the rule of law was a booming tourism destination, also has some remarkable geotouristic sites to offer. Foremost is Victoria Falls, a natural wonder in itself and another World Heritage Site, but one that is largely marketed for its general tourist

Figure 3.2 The famous, now destroyed by natural weathering, Finger of God sandstone erosion feature, formerly of southern Namibia (photograph reproduced courtesy of Wolf Uwe Reimold).

appeal. For those visitors who are prepared to search a bit, some background information about the progressive geological development of the Falls and gorge can, however, be found locally. The craggy Chimanimani Mountain Range, a 2400-metre high volcanic range along the eastern border with Mozambique, provides numerous outstanding vistas and hiking trails, but the underlying geology is not explained anywhere. Near Bulawayo, the spectacular Matopos Hills, granite whalebacks polished by ancient glaciers and crowned by enormous tors of granite

47

boulders, are widely known for being the gravesite of Cecil John Rhodes, but not for their interesting geological history. These are just a few of the many outstanding geosites scattered throughout Zimbabwe, highlighting the geological heritage in this country. Zimbabwe is also widely known for its excellent 'soapstone' (talc schist and serpentinite) sculpture. This thriving cottage industry provides an ideal opportunity to educate tourists about the country's geology and possibly to promote tourism to more remote parts.

Geotourism development in the southern African region

Overall, none of the SADC countries have even come close to recognizing the potential value that their natural geological heritage provides, despite the fact that it is the foundation upon which their cultural and historical heritage has developed. The countries have not realized that their geological resources present an additional facet that could, if properly developed and marketed, form another attractive approach to tourism, complementing the many existing tourist destinations. The African continent seems to have remained largely indifferent to the increasingly strong trend of educational tourism, which should take its rightful place besides traditional safari and adventure tourism. This is in contrast to what has occurred in many developed countries, such as Europe, and developing countries like China, where, for example, geopark documentation and declaration (both national and cross-border) and promotion of these as tourism attractions is well advanced.

The geopark concept is an attractive idea for southern Africa. As an example, the semi-desert plain of the Great Karoo (Figure 3.1 (13)) of central South Africa is not a region that tourists normally flock to, unless they take the accidental land route from Johannesburg to Cape Town. However, the often very scenic Mesozoic (*ca.* 300–180 million years ago) geological formations of the Karoo Supergroup contain numerous palaeontological sites of note. This stratigraphic interval also spans the major mass extinction at the Permian/Triassic boundary (250 million years ago) and a second, minor one at the Triassic/Jurassic boundary (205 million years ago). The geology of this region reveals diverse stages of palaeoclimate and geological environment, including exposures of the Permian Dwyka glaciation (21) and the Jurassic Drakensberg (7) continental flood volcanism. The Karoo is also well known for the spectacular rock formations of the Valley of Desolation (14) outside of Graaff-Reinet and, in the south, for the Cape Fold Mountain ranges of the Klein Karoo (15) in Western Cape Province. Another potential geopark development could be considered for the desert region of the Richtersveld (16) geological terrain in Northern Cape Province, straddling the border of South Africa and southern Namibia. This region contains the Richtersveld National Park, the Fish River Canyon, and the Ai-Ais hot springs within a planned trans-frontier conservation area.

Geotourism development in South Africa

In South Africa, geotourism has not yet been officially recognized. The promotion of this important national resource has been driven almost solely by the independent Geological Society of South Africa (GSSA), as well as by staff of the Council for Geoscience (CGS), both aiming at increasing public awareness of the existing geological resources and their protection and sustainable use. The GSSA has a formal Conservation and Environment Committee/Geotourism Interest Group dedicated to these issues. Recently, this group began discussions with government tourism organizations. The Geological Society has published *An Introduction to South Africa's Geological and Mining Heritage* (Viljoen and Reimold, 1999), 5000 copies of which were made freely available to all secondary schools in the country as the Geological Society's and the Council of Mineral Technology's contribution to the country's 'Year of Science and Technology 1998'. Some 7000 copies have been sold to the public, which is indicative of the great interest in South Africa's geological heritage – so much so that a second edition is in preparation. The two organizations have published other materials, such as posters, brochures and booklets, promoting South Africa's natural heritage, explaining the geological processes that have led to the development of geosites, landscapes and mineral deposits, and educating society to manage its resources responsibly (e.g. Laubscher and Reimold, 2003). A popular book on the natural and historical heritage of the Vredefort Dome has recently been published (Reimold and Gibson, 2005).

A number of relevant museums exist, including the iZiko Museum (formerly the South African Museum) in Cape Town, the National Museum in Bloemfontein, the Geoscience Museum housed within the Transvaal Museum in Pretoria, and the Geological Museum contained in Museum Africa in Johannesburg. The Geology Departments of the Universities of KwaZulu-Natal in Durban and of the Witwatersrand in Johannesburg, as well as a number of smaller and more focused museums, such as the Gold Mine Museum at Gold Reef City in Johannesburg, the Gold of Africa Museum in Cape Town, or the Kimberley Mine Museum at the Big Hole in Kimberley (17), present geoheritage to the public and raise awareness of its responsible use. Hands-on geological and mining education will also be part of a new Science Centre developed in the Newtown District of Johannesburg.

South Africa is a country with a large number of national, provincial and private game reserves and parks (www.parks-sa.co.za). As expected, wildlife and ecology dominate in these protected areas, and the geological background is often missing. The South African National Parks organization has produced booklets on the Kruger National Park (18), where an introduction to the geology and the concept of geologically related ecozones is presented. A recent popular article by travel journalist Bridget Hilton-Barber (2003) illustrated the interaction between geology and the distribution of game in the Kruger National Park. Other exceptions include a comprehensive handbook on the Tswaing Crater (Reimold *et al.*, 1996) and a booklet available on the geology of the Pilanesberg (36) Game Reserve (Cawthorn, 1988). Overall, personnel of the South African National Parks Board and in private reserves are not trained in geology and related disciplines. Nevertheless, mention should be made of efforts, generally through the personal dedication of often-retired members of the Geological Society, aimed at documentation of important geological sites within game reserves (e.g. Schutte, 2003, 2004).

The Council for Geoscience (CGS) has also embraced conservation and promotion of geotourism, through its mandate to educate the public about South Africa's geological heritage. It has undertaken to develop a detailed geosite database, which in effect will form a national register of geological sites – a long overdue measure. The CGS, with its several regional offices, is ideally positioned to compile such a national inventory with all relevant data, including the importance of sites, threats to these sites, and any opportunities presented by them. As a start, it would be desirable to document geosites in already existing game parks and reserves (such as the Kruger National Park) as not only are these areas already dedicated as conservation areas but also they are widely known and extensively promoted as tourism destinations. It should be noted that the incorporation of important geoheritage into officially protected areas does not provide sufficient protection from geo-vandalism, as was recently noted upon a visit to the famous Komati River Gorge of the Mpumalanga Province's Singimvelo game reserve in the southern part of the Barberton Mountain Land (Figure 3.1 (1)). The gorge provides a transect through 3200- to 3400-million-year-old metasedimentary and metavolcanic strata, but had unfortunately been drill-sampled for geoscientific analysis in such a way that all major exposures have now been permanently defaced.

Numerous geological sites throughout rural South Africa and the other southern African countries have enormous potential to be developed as tourist attractions, thereby creating jobs as part of poverty alleviation programmes. However, these sites are generally located in economically deprived regions, where provincial and local governments do not have the expertise or experience required to make use of these resources. Clearly this is an opportunity for authorities to follow up, perhaps through a tourism development strategy. At the same time, it is important to entrench conservation and geoheritage issues into local communities so that they can begin to realize the potential benefits of taking such an initiative themselves. There is a need for trained geologists to become involved in conservation, education and geotourism activities. A number of geologically trained, partially retired colleagues are involved in geotouristic endeavours, though mostly through arranging geotours for international groups.

The government's role in conservation and geotourism

The National Heritage Resources Act of 1999 provides the legislative basis for the protection of South Africa's natural and cultural heritage. South Africa's heritage resources of geological interest (now defined at national, provincial and municipal levels) include:

> Rare geological materials (meteorites and fossils), unique sites of scientific, cultural and historic value, typical sites (including characteristic landforms such as desert, mountain ranges, natural lakes), historically important sites [for example, Johannesburg's Main Reef Gold Discovery site at Langlaagte, or the Big Hole in Kimberley], and culturally important sites.

The South African Heritage Resource Agency (SAHRA; www.sahra.org.za) took over from the erstwhile National Monuments Council in 1999. The main function of this central body is general supervision, while protective and conservation activities, with the exception of a small number of sites that are considered to be of national importance, have been devolved to provincial and municipal structures. While national and provincial registers are being reorganized, however, quite a few of the unattended former National Monument sites in South Africa have been vandalized or fallen into disrepair. Examples include explanatory plaques stolen at the famous Dwars River (19) geological site in the Bushveld Complex; the partial destruction of exhibits at the Main Reef Gold Discovery site in Johannesburg (20), and the defacement by graffiti of the Nooitgedacht petroglyph and glacial pavement site (21) near Kimberley. Local and provincial SAHRA offices are understaffed, and lack specific expertise and experience. While these staff makes efforts to look after sites under their charge, their generally cultural and historical focus and lack of geological training make it impossible for them to protect and care for South Africa's geological heritage to the degree that this important resource deserves.

The government institution directly tasked with marketing South Africa's natural and cultural assets to the international tourism market, South African Tourism, has to date not recognized the extraordinary natural geological resources available to them, except in their broadest, general tourism context. The national government is still mostly focused on the development of cultural and some historical heritage. This was amply documented in media presentations relating to heritage and the future as part of the South African Millennium celebrations, and the reporting by the national media about the World Summit for Sustainable Development held in 2002 in Johannesburg (Reimold, 2002; see also *Sawubona*, 2004b). Overcoming this limited focus by authorities is one of the main challenges of geoconservation and geotourism in South Africa.

Geotourism's educational focus

The general education system in South Africa faces considerable challenges. The government's resources are stretched to the limit, in the face of huge needs of housing, health, education and training. Teaching resources are generally scarce, but especially so in many rural areas. The economies of the provincial government are stretched even further than the national budget. However, geological sites do provide unique and multidisciplinary outdoor classrooms, where not only physical science and geography but also natural, social and environmental science can be taught. One case in point is the Tswaing Meteorite Crater in Gauteng Province, where such subjects are being taught, though not as yet to the large numbers of learners that could be accommodated. However, with the completion of a visitors' centre and museum anticipated for 2005, this site should develop rapidly into a major educational and geotouristic location. An even better potential outdoor classroom exists in the central part of the Vredefort impact structure, located only 90 minutes by car from Johannesburg. This is viewed as an outstanding example of an outdoor geological laboratory.

Official training courses for both tourist guides and field guides should contain a geological curriculum component, but training staff, with the exception of a few locally employed retired geologists, lack this expertise themselves. At some tertiary education institutions efforts have been made to educate teachers in geology, especially regarding regional geology of southern Africa, but these programmes have been short-lived due to a lack of funding.

Informal education on geoheritage is also required. Local communities throughout the country need to be educated about geological heritage, and how they

51

could benefit from the development of geosites through the establishment of tourism facilities, the production and sales of arts and crafts, and, by becoming tourist guides, presenting local culture to tourists. At the same time, this would contribute to the education of other South Africans about the geological heritage of their country (see, for example, Reimold, 1999, 2001, 2002; Schlueter, 1999; Schlueter and Kibundjia, 1999). The responsibility and challenge throughout the SADC region is considerable: to take stock of the geological assets, tackle the underlying ignorance about the various countries' geological heritage resources, and train all involved – particularly teachers, heritage officials, tour operators and tourist guides – in basic geoscience.

South Africa's geotourism resources

South Africa is a country of great geological diversity, which is expressed in a variety of spectacular landscapes and in fascinating geological and associated ecotourism attractions. It is a land of geological superlatives, reflecting the creation of many life forms dating back to 3600 million years ago, and is a treasure house of important minerals and major mines. No other country has so much to offer to the geotourist, all facilitated by a generally well-developed tourism infrastructure. South Africa is indeed a 'world in one country'. The following sections examine a variety of South Africa's geological attractions, and their development into tourism destinations.

Table Mountain and the Cape Peninsula (10)

Table Mountain, an imposing 1050-metre high plateau flanked by the Lion's Head and the Devil's Peak, is located at the northern end of the spectacular 50-km long Cape Peninsula mountain range, where it forms an amphitheatre-like backdrop to Table Bay and Cape Town. Soon to be declared a World Heritage Site, iconic Table Mountain is South Africa's best-known geological attraction. For early visitors arriving at the Cape, Table Mountain was the first landfall after weeks at sea. Today, Cape Town is visited by millions of tourists each year.

Table Mountain and its attendant range form an excellent example of a residual mountain. Four major rock formations are involved; the earliest are the steeply-dipping deformed slates of the Malmesbury Group that formed between 750 and 650 million years ago and which underlie much of Cape Town city centre. Coarse-grained Cape granite intruded these around 540 million years ago during a period of mountain building, as seen at the well-known Sea Point contact on the Atlantic seafront, which so inspired Charles Darwin when he visited the site. The overlying Table Mountain Group, deposited between 460 and 280 million years ago, consists first of about 50 metres of flat-lying, reddish, sandstone, siltstone and shale, followed by a 500-metre thick sequence of light grey, cliff-forming sandstone. The major erosional contact with the older granite is visible along scenic Chapman's Peak Drive. These sandstones make up the higher mountains and major cliff faces of Table Mountain, and extend as far south as Cape Point. The much younger sandy formations of the Cape Flats and other low-lying areas were formed from about 25 million years ago when the Cape Peninsula was an island, isolated from the mainland.

The Western Cape Branch of the Geological Society has produced a series of self-guiding tourist brochures on the geological attractions of the region, including Table Mountain, the Sea Point contact and Chapman's Peak Drive. They have also included other nearby important geological features, such as the granite domes of Paarl Mountain (22), impressive folding of Table Mountain quartzite as seen at Kogmann's Kloof (23) near Montagu, and the Brandvlei (24) hot springs near Worcester.

Cape Fold Belt mountain ranges (25)

The Cape Fold Belt mountain ranges stretch for some 600 kilometres along the southern coast of South Africa. Starting 460 million years ago, an 8000-m thick pile of sediments accumulated, forming the Cape Supergroup. This comprises the quartzite-rich Table Mountain Group at the base, the shale-rich Bokkeveld Group in the middle, and the quartzitic Witteberg Group at the top. The present mountains are the topographic end-product of a major mountain-building episode that started some 280 million years ago and culminated in a Himalaya-like range by about 220 million years ago. The present reduced elevation of the ranges is the end result of multicycled episodes of erosion, and isostatic adjustment of the Earth's crust. Precipitous mountain passes, enhanced by contrasting erosion of hard and soft formations, show the evidence of intensive folding and faulting of rock beds. The area is ideal to appreciate the tectonic forces which occur during processes of continental drift and subduction.

The 200-kilometre stretch of coastline from Mossel Bay to Storms River in Western Cape Province, with its necklace of bays, beaches and cliffs carved out of the alternating hard and soft formations of the Cape Fold Mountains, is known as the Garden Route. Places such as the Tsitsikamma Coastal National Park (26) and the Robberg Nature Reserve (27) are ideal to study ancient evidence of continental drift together with recent beach processes. Along the coastline there are many Stone Age middens and caves testifying to the inhabitation of early man in this area, dating back tens of thousands of years. One of the most important recent archaeological findings from Blombos Cave (28; www.nsf.gov/od/lpa/news/02/pr0202.htm) shows symmetrical, hatched scratchings on ochre which could be more than 70 000 years old. This is interpreted to be the oldest evidence of early behavioural modernity in the form of decoration, and is 35 000 years older than the oldest forms of decoration found in Europe.

Great Escarpment (29) and Pilgrim's Rest (34)

The Great Escarpment (29) is another of South Africa's premier tourist destinations, and is in part promoted by tourism marketers as 'The Panorama Route'. The main tourism focus extends for about 140 kilometres, from the Valley of the Olifants in the north to Kaapsehoop in the south, and lies mainly in Mpumalanga Province. The region is deeply incised by active rivers and streams, and the underlying rock formations are well exposed. There is no better place to see the role of geology than through the development of the rugged scenery.

There are two geologically distinct terrains: the crystalline granitic gneisses in the east that form the rather flat plain of the Lowveld, which includes the Kruger National Park; and, overlying these in the west, the mainly sedimentary formations of the 2600- to 2150-million-year-old Transvaal Supergroup that form the north–south trending high ground and the spectacular scenery. The basement granitic gneisses and remnants of greenstones are the oldest rocks, ranging from 3600 to 3100 million years, and the youngest are the numerous intrusive sills related to the Bushveld Complex, around 2060 million years old. The gently westward-dipping Transvaal Supergroup, up to 12 000 metres thick, is divided into four major stratigraphic groups. From the base upwards these are the Wolkberg Group (up to 2000 m thick and consisting of sediments and volcanics); the regionally extensive but thin Black Reef Formation (made up mainly of quartzite and conglomerate); the Chuniespoort Group (including up to 1500 metres of cave-forming Malmani Dolomite); and, on top, the Pretoria Group (largely comprising quartzite and shale).

The landscape is strongly controlled by the underlying geology. The erosional forces of water and wind cut through less resistant sediments to reveal the basement granitic gneisses of the Lowveld. The Black Reef Formation forms a layer of resistant quartzite that dominates the topography throughout the region, forming part of the spectacular kilometre-long drop of the Escarpment. Steady uplift of the African basement has provided the opportunity for the natural cycle of erosion to do its work, and considerable moisture derived from the warm Indian Ocean brings abundant precipitation to the Escarpment. In a region of vast timber plantations, said to be the largest in the world, there are also panoramic views from places like Long Tom Pass near Sabie, and across the entire Lowveld from God's Window. In addition to large and intriguing cave systems, the Malmani Dolomite formation displays giant stromatolites that bear witness to the fossilized remains of vast oxygen-producing algal growth around 2500 million years ago. The landforms at Kaapsehoop, Bourke's Luck potholes, the deeply incised Blyde River Canyon (the third largest canyon in the world), the Abel Erasmus Pass and numerous stunning waterfalls provide a wealth of spectacular geological sites. The region is also famous for its pioneer gold prospecting and mining activities – South Africa's first significant alluvial gold rushes took place around Sabie and Pilgrim's Rest in 1873, and at Kaapsehoop in 1882. The old mining village of Pilgrim's Rest has been preserved as a living museum, the only town in South Africa declared as a national monument in its entirety. It is now a popular tourist attraction, but with only limited geological explanation.

uKhahlamba-Drakensberg Park (7) and Golden Gate Highlands National Park (30)

The main ramparts of the Drakensberg, reaching heights of nearly 3500 m, lie in KwaZulu-Natal Province along the border with Lesotho; there they exist as a rugged, dissected mountain plateau. These mountains are the highest in southern Africa and form the most dramatic and precipitous scenery, known to the Zulu as *uKhahlamba*, meaning 'barrier of spears'. In recognition of both their outstanding scenery and their rich natural and cultural heritage, an area of 2430 square kilometres, over a distance of nearly 200 km, was declared a World Heritage Site by UNESCO in 2000. Here are found more than 40 per cent of all San cave paintings in southern Africa, in what was the Bushman's last stronghold. Game Pass Shelter in the Kamberg Nature Reserve and Main Cave at the Giant's Castle Reserve are well known for their spectacular paintings, and can be viewed by the public.

The High Berg is formed of countless flows of Drakensberg basaltic lava reaching over 1500 m in thickness, and covering the underlying Clarens Formation sandstones of the Little Berg. This massive, continental outpouring of lava took place around 180 million years ago, and heralded the break-up of the Gondwana supercontinent. Only a remnant of this volcanic plateau remains, forming the Drakensberg and the highlands of Lesotho, and it is probably the world's best example of an erosional, dissected mountain range. It also forms the watershed between the country's major west and east draining rivers. Like the Great Escarpment, its development is due to uplift and rapid erosion. The high ground was rapidly cut back to form the ever-retreating escarpment, leaving the present-day undulating coastal plain. This escarpment has retreated over 150 kilometres from the present coastline, and the rate of erosion of the Drakensberg is said to average 1.5 m per 1000 years.

Some 50 km to the northwest, forming an extension into eastern Free State Province, is the 120-square-kilometre Golden Gate Highlands National Park (30), situated in mountainous country close to the village of Clarens. Golden Gate Park has pristine highveld and montane flora, and is well stocked with game and bird life. The defining feature of the area is the red, cream and yellow weathered sandstone of the Clarens Formation that is deeply eroded to form bluffs and cliffs. The characteristic caves and overhangs have developed by selective weathering of softer strata, and the action of freeze and thaw during cold winters. Part of the upper Karoo Supergroup, the sandstone reflects a large sandy desert environment that existed around 200 million years ago. Dinosaur fossil remains are abundant in this area. Overlying the sandstone are dark layers of the Drakensberg lavas that form the highest peaks.

Karoo National Park (31)

The Karoo National Park (31), near Beaufort West in Western Cape Province, comprises an arid landscape underlain by flat-lying mudstones and sandstones of the Beaufort Group of the Karoo, and intruded by thick dolerite sills. It offers an educational trail, along which plant and animal fossils can be studied. This provides visitors with information on ecological changes from the period 300 million years ago, when glaciers covered most of the Karoo, to 190 million years ago, when the Karoo climate was desert-like owing to the effects of continental drift. The changing climate was the driving force for the evolution of reptiles and mammal-like reptiles and, finally, the emergence of early mammals. Some of the world's oldest fossils of reptiles, mammals and dinosaurs have been found in the Karoo strata, reflecting evolutionary processes during the crucial period between the Permian and Triassic epochs. The Karoo offers an almost unbroken fossil record of these times – a feat that is not repeated anywhere else in the world. Here, a number of palaeontological sites can be visited.

Vredefort (2) and Tswaing (11) meteorite impact sites

The Vredefort Dome, forming the central part of the oldest and largest impact structure known on Earth, is located some 110 km southwest of Johannesburg around the towns of Parys and Vredefort in the Free State and Northwest provinces. This complex geological feature, now visible around 90 km across, has been established as being the remnant of a catastrophic impact by a large asteroid or comet which impacted 2020 million years ago. The vast original impact crater has long since disappeared, with only the root zone of the central uplift preserved. In addition to its planetary/geological significance, the area also hosts numerous Iron Age settlements. A section of the Vredefort Mountain Land, which includes the historic Venterskroon goldfield of the Witwatersrand, has already been declared as the Bergland Conservancy. Part of the Vredefort Dome area was proposed to UNESCO in 2002 for World Heritage Site status, on the basis of its geological, archaeological and cultural importance (Reimold and Gibson, 2005).

A much smaller impact site is the Tswaing Crater, located some 40 km north of Pretoria (Figure 3.3). It provides an excellent example of how a geological feature has been turned into a tourist destination. In 1999 the Council for Geoscience produced a comprehensive popular science book on the crater (Reimold *et al.*, 1999). Previously known as the Pretoria Saltpan, this meteorite crater lies in the midst of a concentration of semi-rural settlements populated by more than a million people. Meaning 'place of salt', the impact site is at the centre of a 2000-hectare conservation area, revealing a crater about 1000 m wide and 70 m deep. Visitors are able to see and walk through one of the best preserved, and most accessible, small, bowl-shaped impact sites on Earth. At the bottom of the crater, a small crater lake once provided trona-rich brine. Originally the crater was thought to be a volcanic neck, but in 1989 it was confirmed to be of meteorite

Figure 3.3 Aerial view of the Tswaing meteorite crater, Gauteng Province (photograph reproduced courtesy of Aki Wilhelm).

impact origin, formed only about 220 000 years ago. A number of hiking trails take the visitor through the well-preserved Bushveld ecosystems and reveal the unique impact geology. A detailed exhibition provides sound understanding of the impact process, the archaeological importance and ecology of the area, and the more recent history of trona production, as well as introducing the local fauna and flora. A visitors' centre and eco-museum are close to completion.

Tswaing is a unique conservation and education area for Earth science, archaeological, ecological and cultural resources. This geological site was developed and is managed by the National Cultural History Museum in Pretoria, with the full cooperation of the local community, which benefits in terms of employment and tourism revenue. This provides a sustainable model for other geological attractions countrywide, where local people, given proper training and motivation, can take a vested interest in a geosite and make it work for them.

Sterkfontein and the Cradle of Humankind (4)

The ongoing development of the so-called Cradle of Humankind provides another example of how a number of geological and scientific attractions are being used and promoted as world-class tourism destinations. Sterkfontein Cave was made famous in 1947 when an almost complete skull of a young adult hominid known as 'Mrs Ples' (then called *Plesianthropus transvaalensis*, now *Australopithecus africanus*) was recovered and estimated to be around 2.7 million years old. In 1998 the almost complete skeleton of an older hominid known as 'Little Foot' was found and dated at 3.3 million years. The nearby Swartkrans, Kromdraai and Drimolen cave sites are almost as famous for their fossil evidence of *Australopithecus robustus*, ape-men assumed to have lived at the same time as the more evolved *Homo habilis*, ancestor to humans. Numerous fossil animals and plant material have also been found, as well as stone tools. At Swartkrans, burnt bone fragments more than a million years old have been found and interpreted as being the first-known evidence that our ancestors were able to control fire.

In 1999 a 470-square-kilometre area underlain by ancient, cave-forming Malmani Dolomite, extending from the Witwatersrand in the south to the Magaliesberg in the north, was declared a World Heritage Site. The very accessible area is considered to be of universal value because of the outstanding richness of at least thirteen documented fossil hominid cave sites, all of which have produced a wealth of material for ongoing palaeo-anthropological research. These sites have provided important information on the very early development of the human family in Africa, and the environment in which our remote ancestors evolved. The caves of the Sterkfontein valley are a world-class geotourism destination, particularly in the context of recent genetic studies, which show that all modern humans have their genetic roots in sub-Saharan Africa (Cann, 1987; Oppenheimer, 2003).

Because of its importance as a World Heritage Site, and the potential value of mass tourism, the development of the Cradle of Humankind sites is under the prime management of the Gauteng Provincial Government. Development is currently taking place, and at nearby Mohale's Gate a major new interpretation centre will be able to cater for 3000 visitors per day. At Sterkfontein Caves the facilities will be significantly upgraded, and orientation 'information gateways' are envisaged for coming years, to stimulate tourism and improve the economy of the area. Being very accessible from both Johannesburg and Pretoria, the area is being developed as a premier domestic and international tourism destination and educational area.

Pilanesberg Complex and National Park (36)

The Pilanesberg National Park, covering 550 square kilometres, is founded on a unique geological structure. It is also one of South Africa's premier ecotourism destinations, and a compact, world-class conservation area possessing considerable ecological diversity. Approximately 120 000 visitors pass through the park annually, creating considerable sustainable local employment. It is ideally located, 50 km north of Rustenburg in Northwest Province and only 90 minutes' drive from Johannesburg. It provides an excellent case study of how a natural geological feature has been successfully developed into an integrated and world-class tourist destination through vision and hard work.

Geologically, the Pilanesberg consists of an almost perfectly circular dissected mountain massif of some 25 kilometres in diameter, making it the third largest alkaline ring complex in the world. The igneous rocks, rich in sodium and calcium, were derived from magma that originated many tens of kilometres below the surface. The geology reflects the roots of an ancient volcano that intruded and explosively erupted about 1300 million years ago. At the time of eruption, the Pilanesberg was one of the largest volcanoes in Africa. The intrusive–extrusive process was complex, and both lava flows and dykes were formed, the latter occurring as a series of intrusions of crystalline rock types called syenites and foyaites (Cawthorn, 1988).

The dominant topographic features of the complex are the major concentric dykes formed by magma that intruded ring fractures created during the collapse of the volcanic caldera. Geologically the complex is a major scientific attraction, and several classic geological sites are marked by roadside plaques while literature on the geosites is available at the park. The once immense caldera has been eroded away, but visitors can still see the remains of ancient lava flows, tuffs and volcanic breccias, as well as an old fluorite-mining site and a non-diamond-bearing kimberlite pipe.

Barberton Mountain Land (1)

Mpumalanga Province, 'the place where the sun rises', encompasses one of the oldest parts of the planet, and some of the earliest and most intriguing rocks on earth can be found and studied there. The 3600-million-year-old volcanic rocks of the Barberton Mountain Land, which scientists call the Barberton Greenstone Belt, and the somewhat younger sedimentary formations provide direct evidence of conditions on the surface of the very early Earth. Scientists, and increasingly tourists, from all over the world come to this scenic part of South Africa to use this window into the Earth's history to obtain information on aspects of the surface of the primitive planet. Close to the Komati River there is still evidence of

3600-million-year-old volcanic activity, such as submarine lava flows that formed pillow-like structures as we see them formed in recent volcanic eruptions. There are very few places on our planet where the ancient ocean floor can be studied in detail. Thus the volcanic and sedimentary rock formations of the easily accessible Barberton Mountain Land represent some of the best-preserved and oldest geology on Earth.

At that time, over 3500 million years ago, the atmosphere was very inhospitable to life and devoid of free oxygen. From this hostile environment, now almost miraculously preserved in layers of chert, are microscopic fossilized remains of primitive bacteria, which are considered to be the earliest evidence of life on Earth. The existence of primitive blue-green algae, their remains now preserved as stromatolites, also indicates that the life-giving process of photosynthesis had already started. These stromatolitic structures are easily accessible in numerous road cuttings in the area. Throughout the Barberton region, small ripple marks in some of the ancient sandstones bear testimony to the existence of tidal currents which migrated back and forth as the tides turned. Now petrified in the rock, they indicate the governing effect of the moon very early on in the history of the planet (Curror, 2002).

Gold mining in the Barberton area started in the 1880s, and some mines are still producing gold from the underground reefs. The historic town of Barberton provides interesting insights into the early days of the gold rush, and some of the old mining shafts have been re-opened to give the visitors a feel for the difficult conditions under which the miners performed their risky activities. The Barberton Branch of the Geological Society of South Africa has compiled a pamphlet which provides a road log and information on a selection of various sites along the scenic route.

Conclusion

These examples illustrate a selection of sites and areas in South Africa where geological, palaeontological and palaeo-anthropological developments have been introduced into conventional tourism ventures. This group could be widened to include lesser known geo-attractions (see Figures 3.4 and 3.5) such as the Cederberg Wilderness Area (9) and the West Coast Fossil Park (Western Cape); Makapans Valley (12) and Mapungubwe (8) (Limpopo Province), Oribi Gorge (32) and Valley of the Thousand Hills (33) (KwaZulu-Natal), and the Magaliesberg Range (35) in Gauteng and Northwest provinces. These and many other examples have been described by Viljoen and Reimold (1999), illustrating the considerable geotourism potential of South Africa. This country needs to market its natural and cultural assets more broadly by addressing the educational tourism market more effectively. South Africa boasts some of the most spectacular geological heritage on our planet. Examples include direct evidence of life in some of the oldest rocks on the Earth in the Barberton Mountains; the transition from reptiles into mammals and some of the oldest dinosaur fossils in the Karoo strata; the transition from ape man to the genus *Homo* in the Sterkfontein World Heritage Site along with some of the oldest stone tools and evidence for the first controlled

Figure 3.4 The Mapungubwe rock formation that was recently declared a World Heritage Site because of the formidable Iron Age Site on its top (photograph courtesy of M. J. Viljoen).

Figure 3.5 The Cederburg Wilderness area (photograph courtesy of David Newsome).

use of fire; and archaeological evidence that some of the first 'modern humans' inhabited South Africa's coastline for more than 100 000 years. Even these very few examples suffice to show that there remains a huge potential in marketing South Africa as a destination which can help us understand our planet's history, the history of life, and the history of mankind.

Acknowledgement

This is University of the Witwatersrand Impact Cratering Research Group Contribution No. 75.

References

Cann, R. L. (1987). Mitochondrial DNA and human evolution. *Nature*, 325, 31–36.

Cawthorn, R. G. (1988). *The Geology of the Pilanesberg*. National Parks Board, Mafikeng.

Curror, W. D. (2002). *Golden Memories of Barberton*, 7th edn, revised and enlarged by Hans Bornman. African Pioneer Mining Ltd, Barberton.

Grünert, N. (2003). *Namibia – Fascination of Geology. A Travel Handbook*, 2nd edn. Klaus Hess Publishers.

Hilton-Barber, B. (2003). Kruger – south to north. *Sawubona Inflight Magazine*, South African Airways, December, 123–128.

Hilton-Barber, B. and Berger, L. (2002). *The Official Field Guide to the Cradle of Humankind*. Struik Publishers.

Laubscher, S. and Reimold, W. U. (2003). *Meteorites – The Sky is Falling*. Council for Geoscience, Pretoria.

Oppenheimer, S. O. (2003). *Out of Africa's Eden. The Peopling of the World*. Jonathan Ball Publishers.

Reimold, W. U. (1999). Geoconservation – a southern African and African perspective. *Journal of African Earth Sciences*, 29(3), 469–483.

Reimold, W. U. (2001). Tourism . . . Ecotourism . . . Geotourism! A case for a new national tourism strategy. *Geobulletin*, 44(4), 20–23.

Reimold, W. U. (2002). South Africa's natural heritage and its potential for geotourism. *Résource*, 4(4), 42–45.

Reimold, W. U. and Gibson, R. L. (2005). *Meteorite Impact! The Danger from Space and Vredefort: South Africa's Mega-Impact*. Chris van Rensburg Publications.

Reimold, W. U., Brandt, D., De Jong, R. and Hancox, J. (1999). *Tswaing Meteorite Crater – A Natural and Cultural History of the Tswaing Crater Region Including a Description of the Hiking Trail*. Popular Geoscience Series 1, Council for Geoscience, Pretoria.

Sawubona (2003a). Talking tourism. *Sawubona Inflight Magazine*, South African Airways, October, 36–38.

Sawubona (2003b). The power of tourism. *Sawubona Inflight Magazine*, South African Airways, September, 4.

Sawubona (2004a). Meet Mr Tourism. *Sawubona Inflight Magazine*, South African Airways, September, 113.

Sawubona (2004b). Hit the heritage trail. *Sawubona Inflight Magazine*, South African Airways, September, 61–74.

Schlueter, T. (1999). Conservation of geological sites in East Africa. *UNESCO Bulletin*, 34(1), 4–6.

Schlueter, T. and Kibundjia, M. (1999). Conservation of geological sites in East Africa. *NMK (National Museums of Kenya) Horizons*, 3(3), 21–23.

Schneider, G. (2004). *The Roadside Geology of Namibia*. Sammlung Geologischer Führer, Gebr. Bornträger.

Schutte, I. (2003). Documenting geosites in the Kruger National Park: Part I. *Geobulletin*, 46(4), 19–21.

Schutte, I. (2004). Documenting geosites in the Kruger National Park: Part II. *Geobulletin*, 47(1), 10–13.

Viljoen, M. J. and Reimold, W. U. (1999). *An Introduction to South Africa's Geological and Mining Heritage*. Geological Society of South Africa, Johannesburg, and Council for Mineral Technology (MINTEK), Randburg.

Websites

www.africadream.org

www.earthworks.fsnet.co.uk/geopark.htm (provides an explanation of the geopark concept and links to other relevant websites)

www.europeangeoparks.org (provides information about already established European geoparks)

www.freedompark.co.za

www.nsf.gov/od/lpa/news/02/pr0202.htm

www.openafrica.org

www.primeorigins.co.za/news/236136.htm

www.sahra.org.za (website of the South African Heritage Resource Agency)

www.southafrica.net

www.unesco.org/bpi/science/content/news/upress/99-21e.htm (an announcement of the intention of UNESCO to launch the official geopark label in 1999)

4

Geotourism in Australia

Jane James, Ian Clark and
Patrick James

Introduction

Since the latter part of the last century, Australia's
tourism industry has experienced enormous growth
in both domestic and international tourists. In the
late 1970s Australia received less than a million international tourists each year. Since that time there has
been significant growth, with the development of
both traditional and emerging markets. One of those
latter areas is geotourism. Both international and
local tourists are attracted to a number of sites where
Australia's unique geological heritage is exhibited.

The size, age, antiquity, scale and variety of
Australia's landscapes and continent mean that a
great range of scenic and outstandingly unique geological features is displayed from all States and
Territories and from across its many climatic and
geographic zones. From the tropics in the north to
the temperate forests of the south, from mountains
to deserts, and from barren, seemingly featureless
landscapes to wide vistas, Australia reveals many of
its most famous and fascinating tourist destinations
and attractions as icons of rock, stone and soil.

In 2003, over 4.7 million international visitors
travelled to Australia – only a slight drop from the
peak of 4.9 million visitors in 2000, the year of the

Sydney Olympics. This minor reduction reflects the adverse impact of global events such as 11 September 2001, the SARS health epidemic and the influence of the war in Iraq. Visitor numbers have been on the increase since mid-2003, with traditional markets (UK, USA and Europe) showing steady recovery rates and emerging markets (e.g. China and India) indicating strong growth (DITR, 2004). Annual growth is predicted at 4.8 per cent, with 7.3 million visitors expected by 2010 (Tourism Forecasting Council, April 2004). Domestic travel, whilst remaining relatively static, also shows an increase in both bed nights and expenditure since 1999.

Tourists today are frequently more demanding and sophisticated than travellers of the past. The primary offerings of food, drink and shelter that form the basis of Maslow's hierarchy of needs (Maslow, 1954), and that were the basis of travel in earlier centuries, have taken on an entirely new meaning. Tourist centres and leisure facilities have not only been built to provide service, but also to entertain, educate, inform and attract tourists. Many offer the latest in design, luxury and technology (e.g. the Wonambi Interpretive Fossil Centre at the World Heritage site of Naracoorte Caves in South Australia), and whilst these physical facilities can be an initial attraction to a destination, there is still a degree of wonder associated with the vast uniqueness of Australia. Much of that natural landscape is a reflection of its underlying geology.

Many of these modern tourists are experiential visitors, often identified as 'cultural or ecotourists' (Leader-Elliott, 1996) and have been targeted by both State and Federal tourism campaigns, such as *Brand Australia* (Australian Tourist Commission, 1998, 2004), *Australia into the New Millennium* (Australian Tourist Commission, 1999), and the *SATC Tourism Plan 2003–2008* (SATC, 2002), which illustrate various aspects of Australia's diverse landscape and culture. These images are reinforced by marketing campaigns from State tourism offices, as with the South Australian Tourism Commission (SATC, 1998) and the Northern Territory Tourism Commission (NTTC, 2003), both of which have identified critical platforms in their marketing strategies as being nature-based tourism for visitors interested in 'natural heritage and icons', 'unspoilt nature' and 'uniqueness'. It would be a rare national or international advertising campaign that did not include two of the three 'R's of tourism icons – the Rock (Uluru or Ayers Rock) and the Reef (the Great Barrier Reef). The third one is 'Roos' – for kangaroo, Australia's national wildlife icon.

The Australian Federal Government's recent 'Medium to Long Term Strategy White Paper on Tourism' (Australian Government, 2003) comments at some length about 'Australia as a land of unique and spectacular landscapes' and the significance of this to the growth of nature-based and ecotourism.

Australia's geological heritage

Australia's rocks are remarkable for a number of reasons. They cover the range of geological eras, representing geological time from some of the oldest rocks on the planet, in the ancient continental fragments of Western Australia, through to the relatively recent and well-preserved remains of the megafauna at Naracoorte Caves (Figure 4.1F), where the forerunners of Australia's unique marsupial fauna, the giant kangaroo, are fossilized.

Figure 4.1 Location of geotourism sites in Australia: A, Uluru (Ayers Rock); B, Great Barrier Reef; C, Blue Mountains; D, Sydney Harbour; E, Tesselated pavement; F, Naracoorte Caves; G, Remarkable Rocks; H, Wave Rock; I, Shark Bay stromatolites; J, Mt Gambier Blue Lake.

The recent landscape evolution of Australia has been strongly influenced by both its geographic position and its unique island status. Not only have the flora and fauna evolved in isolation, but the landscape itself has also been influenced and moulded by changing climates and weather patterns, fluctuating sea levels and gradual but increasing isolation. This follows the break-up of Gondwana in the Mesozoic sea, culminating with the separation of Australia from Antarctica 50 million years ago. Since that time Australia has drifted slowly north (at a rate of 5 cm per annum) towards Asia, where its ultimate destiny lies in forming a major mountain range which in 50 million years' time will rival the Himalayas!

The Earth's three major groups of rocks – igneous, metamorphic and sedimentary – are all represented in Australia. In addition, the major geological eras are represented, as evidenced by the diversity and evolutionary history of the landscape. Stromatolites, some of the earliest known evidence for life on Earth, are found in the rocks of northwest Western Australia. By coincidence, these can be compared with modern forms that exist as 'living fossils' at Shark Bay in Western Australia – a living remnant of a complex past (Figure 4.1I).

The juxtaposition of this great variety of rock types and gentle continental rising and falling 'see-saw' movement during the northwards drift has led to the development of the Great Artesian Basin, which underlies much of eastern central Australia. Beneath the sands that form part of the 'red centre' of Australia, the aquifers that provide access to water in one of the driest continents on Earth are sandwiched between older impermeable basement rocks and the overlying impermeable sediments.

65

Australia also has great mineral wealth. There is gold in Victoria and Western Australia, there are diamonds in the north and great coal reserves in the east in New South Wales, and oil and gas both inland in the basins and on the continental shelf to both the south and west of the Australian landmass. There are opals and 'tigers' eye' for jewellery, and lead and aluminium for the manufacturing industry. The Australian economy is fuelled as much by this resource richness as by the wheat and wool that are traditionally recognized as producing wealth.

Much of the cultural and industrial heritage of Australia is associated with mineral discoveries following colonization in the 1800s, with mines like Burra forming the largest copper mine in the southern hemisphere and the Chinese gold trails of the Victorian goldfields being exemplified by the successful recreation of life there at Sovereign Hill in Ballarat. The built and archaeological heritage associated with these and other sites across Australia provide a cultural dimension to Australia's geology that presents another view of the remarkable rocks of this land.

Geotourism sites

Australia is well endowed with a number of outstanding geological sites that underpin the country's geotourism. Some examples include the Great Barrier Reef, Uluru (Ayers Rock), Shark Bay, Wave Rock, the Remarkable Rocks, the Naracoorte Caves, Sydney Harbour, the Blue Mountains, tesselated pavement and volcanic landforms.

Great Barrier Reef

The Great Barrier Reef (Figure 4.1B), in the Coral Sea off Australia's north east coast, is one of the wonders of the natural world. It is World Heritage listed, and is one of Australia's – and the world's – premier holiday destinations. It is a beautiful and awe-inspiring feature, visible from space. Home of countless marine species, the reef is the largest complex of coral in the world, stretching for approximately 2000 km along the coast of Queensland, forming a natural breakwater. It is separated from the mainland by shallow lagoonal seas that range in width from 16 to 161 km. In some places the reef is more than 122 m thick. The Great Barrier Reef system is the largest UNESCO World Heritage Area, covering more than 300 000 square kilometres (Lucas *et al.*, 1997). It comprises more than 3000 individual reefs that range in size from 1 hectare to over 10 000 hectares in area, and includes many islets, coral gardens and unusual marine life. The area is protected by the Great Barrier Reef Marine Park, which encompasses most of the reefs and inter-reef areas as well as the neighbouring lagoon and a large section of the continental shelf (Kelleher, 1986).

The corals that make up the various reefs and cays, and provide the basis for the great variety of sea and animal life, consist of individual coral polyps – tiny living creatures that join together to form colonies. Each polyp is a tiny jelly-like blob crowned by tentacles, and looks like an anemone but much smaller. Each polyp lives inside a shell of aragonite, a type of calcium carbonate which is the hard shell-like material that is commonly called coral. The polyps join together to create 'forests' of coloured coral in interesting fan-, antler-, brain- and plate-like shapes.

There are many different types of coral; some are slow growing and live to be hundreds of years old while others are faster growing. The colours of coral are created by algae. Only live coral is coloured. Dead coral is white. The form and structure of the individual reefs show great variety that may be subdivided into two main classes: platform or patch reefs, resulting from radial growth; and wall reefs, resulting from elongated growth, often in areas of strong water currents. There are also many fringing reefs where the reef growth is established on sub-tidal rock of the mainland coast or continental islands.

The Capricorn-Bunker Group National Park is a Queensland State Park that encompasses a terrestrial section consisting of four islands: Fairfax Island, a coral cay consisting of two small islands on an egg-shaped reef; Hoskyn Island, which is similar to Fairfax but is not a cay; Heron Island, made up of sand and broken coral on a coral and rock basement; and Lady Musgrave Island, a cay surrounded by extensive coral reefs.

The ideal environment for coral is shallow warm water where there is a lot of water movement and plenty of light, and the water is salty and low in nutrients. Reefs are sensitive to climate change, to changes in patterns of water movement and to physical damage – so problems like global warming, El Niño and the building of moorings or breakwaters can cause damage. Water circulation in and around the Great Barrier Reef is very complex, being governed by properties of the Coral Sea, land run-off, evaporation, the southeast trade winds, and forced up-wellings due to strong tidal currents in narrow reef passages and coastal waters, including mangroves. Tides are generally semi-diurnal, with diurnal inequality towards the north, becoming almost diurnal in Torres Strait. The maximum tidal range is about 3 m along most of the coast, increasing to 6–9 m in the Broad Sound area between 21° and 23° S. Water is vertically well-mixed for most of the year, with stratification occurring due to freshwater input during the wetter months from January to April. Freshwater run-off can be localized causing significant physical and biological effects. The often nutrient-rich water resulting from both agricultural and domestic land-use on the adjacent mainland may have a negative effect on the reef system, and thus on the sea and land animals which depend upon it for survival.

Tourists visit the Great Barrier Reef in large numbers; there are numerous resorts and reef destinations. They come to see the beauty of reef life, the tropical island flora and fauna; to play in the lagoons, swim, surf, ski, paraglide and sail; and to get close to the coral by snorkelling, reef walking, scuba diving and going out in glass-bottomed boats. The fascination of the reef is that it is alive, yet dead. Marine life is abundant, both in and on the water – all there because of the geological structure.

The reef, like many natural wonders, has its own problems, including issues related to the visitor experience. Tourism in the region is intensive, over-fishing is a problem, and oil exploration from the lucrative continental shelf is sometimes touted. Whilst in some ways the reef is resilient, in others it is fragile and requires comprehensive and wide-ranging site and visitor management.

Uluru

Uluru, previously known as Ayers Rock (Figure 4.1A), the world's largest monolith, and Kata Tjuta (The Olgas), a series of 36 dome-like rock formations, are remarkable geological and landform features set in a contrasting, relatively flat, sand-plain environment 450 km southwest of Alice Springs. Undoubtedly Uluru is Australia's most well-known and well-recognized icon. It is a geological landform more correctly known as an *Inselberg*.

Uluru and Kata Tjuta are also part of an important cultural landscape that makes up the World Heritage listed Uluru–Kata Tjuta National Park in the Northern Territory of Australia. Also in this enormous park are many Aboriginal sacred sites, spectacular scenery, and famous rock formations (ANPWS, 1982). The rock formation of Kata Tjuta stands up to 546 m high and covers an area of 3500 hectares and, like Uluru, produces an incredible light show at sunset, with crimsons turning to rusts, and pinks to mauves.

Uluru–Kata Tjuta National Park was inscribed on the World Heritage List in two stages, initially for its outstanding universal natural values and then for its outstanding universal cultural values. Its natural values are recorded as an example of ongoing geological processes; and as an example of exceptional natural beauty and a combination of natural and cultural elements. Its cultural value is described as an outstanding example of traditional human land use, being directly associated with living traditions and beliefs of outstanding universal significance (ANPWS, 1986).

The Park is situated on the southern margin of the sedimentary Amadeus Basin and comprises extensive sand plains, dunes and alluvial desert, punctuated by the Uluru monolith and Kata Tjuta some 32 km to the west. Uluru is composed of steeply dipping, feldspar-rich arkose sandstone, and has been exposed as a result of folding, faulting, the erosion of surrounding rock, and infill. The monolith has a base circumference of 9.4 km, smooth sloping sides with a slope of up to 80°, and a relatively flat top. The rock has been sculpted by weathering and sheet erosion, with layers 1–3 m thick, parallel to the existing surface, breaking away. Deep parallel fissures extend down the sides from the top of the monolith, where weathering has exploited the softer and less resistant layers of sedimentary rock. A number of caves, inlets and overhangs at the base, formed by chemical degradation and sandblast erosion, are sites of rock art and engravings that are evidence of the enduring cultural traditions of the Anangu people.

Kata Tjuta, covering about 3500 hectares, comprises 36 steep-sided rock domes of gently dipping Mount Currie conglomerate consisting of clasts of fine-grained acid and basic igneous rocks and metamorphic gneiss in an epidote-rich matrix. Kata Tjuta tends to have hemispherical summits, near vertical sides and steep-sided intervening valleys, and has been exposed by the same process as Uluru. Lithosols, gravelly red earths, red earthy sands and calcareous red earth soils are derived from weathered Mount Currie conglomerate, and are found as isolated pockets on scree slopes and alluvial fans. Gently sloping sand plains of medium-textured red earths, sandy loams and red earth sands are separated from dune formations of red siliceous sand and red earth sands by a transitional zone comprising largely of very coarse siliceous sand. Dunes up to 30 m high are characterized by mobile crests, vegetated flanks and swales riled and gullied by water. These and the sand plains occupy the bulk of the Park. Surface water is largely restricted to seasonal pools fed by short, shallow watercourses from the monolith. Defined watercourses do not exist in the dune formations, although swales are moister and ponding may occur after rain.

Tourists come to Uluru to witness the colour changes, particularly at sunrise and sunset. Australians come in their thousands, as it epitomizes 'the outback' experience, and most tourists marvel at the contrast of this single isolated mono-lith that towers above the vast inland plains of the central Australian deserts.

Shark Bay

Shark Bay is located more than 800 km north of Perth in Western Australia, at the most westerly point of the Australian continent. The islands and the land surrounding it have three exceptional natural features: vast sea grass beds that are the largest (4800 square kilometres) and richest in the world; a dugong (sea cow) population; and stromatolites. These ancient relic, pre-history stromato-lites (Figure 4.1I) are colonies of algae which form hard, dome-shaped deposits that are rare modern examples of the oldest forms of life on Earth. Shark Bay is also home to five species of endangered mammals (http://whc.unesco.org/sites/578.htm).

The spectacular 1500-km coastline of Shark Bay is made up of a series of east–west peninsulas and islands which separate inlets and bays from each other and the Indian Ocean. The coastline includes some of the highest cliffs of the Australian coastline, including the 200-m high Zuytdorp cliffs (DCLM, 1989). There are three distinct landscape types: the Gascoyne-Wooramel province, which comprises the coastal strip along the eastern coast of the bay and consists of a low-lying plain backed by a limestone escarpment; the Peron province, which comprises the Nanga/Peron peninsulas; and the Faure Island/sill, which com-prises undulating sandy plains with gypsum pans or birridas, and ancient inter-dune depressions filled with gypsum. The seaward margin of this province terminates in a scarp 3–30 m high and narrow sand beaches; Edel province, which comprises Edel Land peninsula and Dirk Hartog, Bernier and Dorre Islands, is a landscape of elongated north-trending dunes cemented to loose limestone. The province terminates to the west as a series of spectacular cliffs.

The oldest rock in the area is Late Cretaceous Toolonga limestones and chalk. The most extensive younger rocks are Peron sandstones and Tamala limestones (the offshore islands are composed of the latter). These rocks are often overlain by a series of longitudinal Middle to Late Pleistocene dunes. The extensive supratidal flats of Gladstone Embayment, Hutchison Embayment and Nilemah Embayment are comparable to the coastal 'Sabkhas' off the coast of the Arabian Gulf. Gypsum has been formed as a result of evaporation of saline groundwaters within the sediments of broad tidal flats adjacent to areas such as Hamelin Pool (DCLM, 1989). Shell beaches occur at the southern end of Lharidon. The inland terrestrial landscape of Shark Bay is predominantly one of low, rolling hills inter-spersed with birridas (inland saltpans that are at sea level). Shark Bay itself is a large shallow embayment, approximately 13 000 square kilometres in area, with an average depth of 9 m (maximum of 29 m). The Bay is partially enclosed by a series of islands. Influx of oceanic water is through the wide northern channel, the Naturaliste Channel, between Dorre and Dirk Hartog islands, and the South Passage, between Dirk Hartog Island and Steep Point.

A significant feature of the Bay is the change in salinities from oceanic (salin-ity 3.5–4.0 per cent) in the northern and western parts of the bay through meta-haline (salinity 4.0–5.6 per cent) to hypersaline in Hamelin Pool and Lharidon Bight (salinity 45.6–47.0 per cent) (DCLM, 1989). The salinity gradient has a marked influence on the distribution of marine organisms within the Bay. The area is also affected by the Leeuwin Current which sweeps past in the Indian Ocean.

Shark Bay is a complete marine ecosystem containing many important and fascinating features, including the Wooramel Seagrass Bank, the Faure Sill and ecosystems dominated by benthic microbial communities which flourish in the hypersaline embayments. The discovery of stromatolites at Hamelin Pool was a major factor in Shark Bay being declared a World Heritage Area, and has helped to unravel the history of life on Earth. Hamelin Pool's stromatolites are internationally renowned as the most extensive examples on Earth of growing marine stromatolites. They have attracted a great deal of public attention, both in Australia and overseas, and are of major scientific interest to biologists and geologists. The discovery of growing stromatolites in the Hamelin Pool in 1954 has enabled scientists to gain a better understanding of the oldest form of life on Earth, dating back to at least 3.5 billion years ago.

The warm, shallow waters at the southern end of Hamelin Pool favour the growth of simple single-celled micro-organisms known as cyanobacteria, where more than 50 species, formerly known as blue-green algae, can be found. Microbial mats built from cyanobacteria and other microscopic organisms trap sediment to produce rock-like structures called stromatolites. The cyanobacteria communities build stromatolites by trapping fine sediment with a sticky film of mucus and binding the grains together with calcium carbonate, which is chemically extracted from the water in which they grow. Because the cyanobacteria need sunlight to grow and have the ability to move towards light, their growth keeps pace with the accumulating sediment.

Stromatolites grow in Hamelin Pool because of the extreme salinity of the seawater, the limited circulation of the water, and the presence of calcium carbonate. This environment, which has evolved over some 10 000 years, is perfect for cyanobacteria. It depends on the Faure Sill, a sand barrier at the entrance of Hamelin Pool that restricts the flow of seawater into the Pool. Coupled with high temperatures and increased evaporation, it produces water that has more than twice the salinity of normal seawater. In such an environment most other living organisms, particularly predators of the microbes, cannot survive.

Another feature of Shark Bay is the millions of small white shells that have accumulated on Shell Beach. They are the bivalve Cardiid Cockle (*Fragrum erugatum*). The proliferation of this particular species, which lives in the coastal waters between Dampier and the Abrolhos Islands, is thought to be the result of high water salinity (salt concentration), and has led to the accumulation of millions of these tiny shells along the shore of Lharidon Bight and Hamelin Pool.

Shark Bay also contains the largest reported seagrass meadows (4000 square kilometres) as well as some of the most species-rich seagrass assemblages in the world. They are of international importance because of their rich biodiversity and high organic productivity. The Wooramel Seagrass Bank is the largest reported structure of its kind in the world, covering some 1030 square kilometres. The bank is one of the largest bodies of carbonate sediment formed by an organic baffle (stabilized carbonate sediment bound by seagrass beds) yet recorded from a modern environment. The only deposits of comparable origin and size are the seagrass beds on the Mediterranean coast of France.

Wave Rock

Wave Rock (Figure 4.1H) is a much-photographed natural wonder located 350 km southeast of Perth. The rounded wavelike formation is actually an overhanging wall on the northern side of a large granite outcrop named Hyden Rock, after the nearby town in the middle of the Western Australian wheatbelt. Wave Rock is an outcrop of granite about 15 m high and 110 m long.

Hyden Rock is an example of an Isenberg, an outcrop of rock that stands above the surrounding land surface. Isenbergs are the result of erosion by water and wind over long periods of time. They are usually composed of rock that is more erosion resistant than the surrounding rock. This may be because of small differences in composition or grain size.

The West Australian Goldfields are underlain by large granite plutons that formed deep below the Earth's surface more than 2700 million years ago. The upper surfaces are irregular in shape, and in some parts are closer to the surface. Where these parts are exposed by erosion of the overlying rock and soil, the original country rock is exposed. There are dozens of these outcrops in the district. Hyden Rock, Camel Peaks, The Humps and King Rock are the largest. The higher of them stand about 50 m higher than the valley floor, which is about 300 m above sea level. Hyden Rock is a mixture of medium- and coarse-grained porphyritic granite and adamellite. The Humps is composed of a variably textured, medium- and coarse-grained granite and adamellite that is in part porphyritic.

There are varying opinions about the origin or the wave-like shape of Wave Rock. It has been suggested that the exposed rock surface of the lip of the Wave is harder than that below, allowing water to erode the softer rock below into a wave shape. Another suggestion is that the wave on Hyden Rock was formed by the more thorough weathering of granite underneath an old, higher soil surface. This would have taken place over a long period of time. As the weathered and decomposed granite material at and near the soil surface is eroded away, it undercuts the upper exposed surface. This process of producing flared forms can be seen elsewhere on Hyden Rock and is common in other granite terrains of the world, including the Eyre Peninsula in South Australia (Twidale, 1982). However, none are as spectacular as Wave Rock. The vertical bands of red, ochre, greys and browns that accentuate the wave shape have been caused by water, carrying dissolved minerals such as iron, running down its face.

Remarkable Rocks

The spectacular outcrop of eroded granite tors known as Remarkable Rocks (Figure 4.1G), on the southern coast of Kangaroo Island, is another example of a popular tourist destination that has been formed by the weathering of granite over millions of years. Sitting atop a smooth granite dome on the cliff face, the impressive Remarkable Rocks forms what appears to be a cluster of precariously balanced boulders. This remarkable geological feature is located within Flinders Chase National Park. Geological phenomena are major attractions in the Park. The naturally sculptured aeolianite cliffs formed during the Pleistocene lie on top of much older Cambrian age granites and metamorphic rocks. Admiral's Arch displays the ability of the ocean to carve and shape the coastline. The nearby Kelly Hill Caves offer a visually stunning example of limestone caves and cave formations.

Remarkable Rocks is part of a large suite of granitic rocks that formed during the Cambro-Ordivician Delemarian Orogeny which produced the ancestral Flinders and Mount Lofty Ranges in South Australia. At this location the exposure of the granite to millions of years of weathering and erosion has modified them into strange and interesting shapes. Contraction resulting from cooling of the granite as the overlying sediments were removed by erosion caused a widely spaced set of rectangular joints to form. When the granite was exposed at the surface, weathering exploited the joint sets and produced large rounded boulders, which have further weathered and eroded to form the shapes that we see today. Remarkable Rocks is probably the major tourist drawcard on Kangaroo Island, being both spectacular and photogenic. The rocks are also dangerous, with steep and slippery slopes that lead down to the major swell and waves of the Southern Ocean and have led to some tourist mishaps and even deaths.

Naracoorte Caves

Naracoorte Caves National Park is the only World Heritage Site in South Australia. It is located 300 km southeast of Adelaide in the Limestone Coast tourism region of the State. The system of 26 caves, south of the township of Naracoorte, is part of the extensive karst topography of the region. The caves are significant because they contain an extensive fossil record of the terrestrial fauna that have inhabited the region for at least the last 500 000 years. Small openings at the surface to the caves (known as sinkholes) have acted as traps, collecting animals and preserving the most complete fossil record known for this period of time. The bones of animals such as *Thylacoleo carnifex* (marsupial lion) and *Thylacine, Zygomaturus* and sthenurine kangaroos are found within the 20 fossil deposits discovered so far (Figure 4.1F). Naracoorte Caves contain clues to help interpret the geological and unique evolutionary history of Australia.

Thousands of bones of animals that lived in the area during the Pleistocene Epoch (1.8 million years to 10 000 years ago) have been found in the caves. By studying these bones it is possible to determine the range of species that made up the ancient animal communities of the region. Reconstructed skeletons of a number of Australia's extinct megafauna have enabled geologists to interpret both their appearance and their habitat.

So far, over a hundred species of vertebrate animals representing four of the major vertebrate groups (amphibians, reptiles, birds and mammals) have been recorded. This fossil record covers several ice ages and the arrival of humans on the Australian continent. It is well known that during the latter portion of the Pleistocene Epoch the giant mammals known as the 'megafauna' became extinct. In Australia, practically all of the large mammals (and some large reptiles and birds) died out around 45 000 to 50 000 years ago, but the cause is not known. It is hoped that by systematically studying the evidence from the Naracoorte Caves the answer to this and other questions about the ancient world of the megafauna will be revealed.

The caves and other karst features of the region are formed in a thick layer of limestone comprising of shells, bryozoa and calcareous bodies of other marine creatures deposited during the Oligocene to Miocene periods (25–5 million years ago). During this time the Southern Ocean extended over 100 km inland from the current coastline. As the sea began to retreat to its present position during the Pliocene and early Pleistocene periods, high groundwater stands dissolved the limestone to form the caves at Naracoorte. The present land surface features a system of stranded dunes parallel to the present coastline, which have formed during a series of marine transgressions and regressions. The oldest of these is the 800 000-year-old Naracoorte East Range, which contains the Naracoorte Caves. Visitors to Naracoorte are able to see reconstructions of past environments, including the megafauna in the Wonambi Fossil Centre, to take guided tours both above and below ground of the various cave features, and, for the more adventurous, to undertake caving which introduces real speleology in some of the narrowly connected parts of the extensive cave system. The interpretive centre at the World Heritage site also has a computer link to Bat Cave, where visitors get a real-time image of the local bat colony.

Sydney Harbour

Sydney Harbour is an example of a major drowned river valley system, referred to as a ria (Figure 4.1D). This feature shows the bays and headlands topography that typifies flooded river valleys, and explains the reason behind the construction of that other Australian icon, the Harbour Bridge. Crossing the well-sheltered and indented harbour was easier by bridge than travelling the long distance around its shores.

The rocks around the shores of Sydney Harbour are mostly sandstone and shale formed during the Triassic Period (about 220 million years ago). At that time, Australia was part of the Gondwana super-continent and the Sydney region was a large freshwater lake. This was slowly filled in by deposits of sand, mud, silt and pebbles washed in by large rivers. Over the millions of years that followed, these sediments were gradually overlain by others. They were compressed into sandstone, mudstone and shale. These formations were later raised by earth movements, starting in the Jurassic Period (200 million years ago). During this time great cracks formed and molten lava rose up through the rocks to form volcanic vents; these then cooled and hardened to form dykes of basalt. Remains of basalt dykes can still be found around Bradleys Head, North Head and Nielsen Park. Two to twelve million years ago, the Sydney plateau was uplifted by movements in the Earth's crust. The Parramatta River and its tributaries flowed across this plateau, gradually cutting deep V-shaped valleys into it and leaving narrow sandstone ridges behind. About 6000 years ago, when the sea rose to its present level, the Parramatta River valley was drowned and Sydney Harbour, with its coastline of inlets and headlands, came into being.

The landscape around the harbour is one of steep hills, long narrow ridges, deep rocky valleys and intricately eroded cliffs. The eastern part of the harbour is predominantly Hawkesbury sandstone. Sandstone is a very hard rock that tends to break away in large blocks, leaving the boulders and vertical cliffs that characterize the Sydney coastline. To the west the harbour is predominantly made up of

Ashfield shale. Shale is not as hard as sandstone, and tends to weather and erode without forming boulders or cliffs. As a consequence, the western shoreline of Sydney Harbour tends to be much flatter and devoid of rocky outcrops.

Along some parts of the harbour there are some low-lying areas of sand that have been deposited by water (alluvium) running between hills of sandstone. Particularly high areas such as North Head and South Head, which were once islands, are now joined to the mainland by sand spits such as the Corso area of Manly and the low sandy area between Bondi and Rose Bay. Smaller amounts of sandy material have been deposited by streams where they enter bays on the southern side of the harbour, such as Rushcutters Bay, Darling Harbour and Homebush Bay.

Along with Macquarie Harbour and the Hawkesbury River to the north, Sydney provides one of the safest and sheltered ports for ships of all sizes, and a city location that is enviable. The former convict settlement that grew into Australia's largest city, is made up of buildings that hug the undulating landscape, surrounding the bays and coves that border this unique geological feature – the ria.

The Blue Mountains

The Greater Blue Mountains Area of New South Wales consists of 1.03 million hectares of sandstone plateaux, escarpments, rock ramparts, buttresses and gorges dominated by temperate eucalypt forest (Figure 4.1C). The site, comprising eight protected areas, is noted for its representation of the evolutionary adaptation and diversification of the eucalypts in post-Gondwana isolation on the Australian continent. Ninety-one eucalypt taxa occur within the Greater Blue Mountains Area, which is also outstanding for its exceptional expression of the structural and ecological diversity of the eucalypts associated with its wide range of habitats. The site contains a wide and balanced representation of eucalypt habitats – wet and dry sclerophyll, mallee heathlands, as well as localized swamps, wetlands and grassland. It also provides a significant representation of Australia's biodiversity, containing 10 per cent of the vascular flora as well as significant numbers of rare or threatened species, including endemic and evolutionary relict species, such as the Wollemi pine (*Wollemia nobilis*), which have persisted in highly-restricted microsites (Costermans, 1983).

The rocks in the Blue Mountains fall into three main groups. The rocks that dominate the scenery belong to a structure known as the Sydney Basin which extends south along the coast from Newcastle to Batemans Bay and westwards to Ulan and Lithgow. The marine and freshwater sandstones and shales that were deposited during the Permian and Triassic periods have undergone little deformation other than slow vertical uplift of around 100 m. The oldest rocks in the Sydney basin are marine shales and mudstones. These are overlain by coal measures that contain the coal and oil shale that is mined at Lithgow and Clarence. There are three broad subdivisions of the rocks above the coal measures: the Narrabeen Group (the oldest), the Hawkesbury Sandstone (middle), and the Wianamatta Group (the youngest). The landscape of the western Blue Mountains is dominated by sandstones of the Narrabeen Group. The Hawkesbury Sandstone dominates the eastern Blue Mountains and extends to form the cliffs around Sydney Harbour. The Wianamatta Group, being softer shales, is easily eroded and is found mostly in the central part of the Sydney Basin, from the mountains almost to the city centre (Pickett and Alder, 1997).

Underlying the Sydney Basin rocks are the folded rocks of the Lachlan Fold Belt. These can be seen at the bottoms of the deeper gorges, where erosion has cut down through the Sydney Basin sediments. The younger rocks overlying the Sydney Basin are found in small patches on top of some of the higher points. These are basalts that formed part of an extensive sheet that covered the area before the erosion of the gorges. The basalts have been dated as 14.6–17.7 million years old.

Tesselated pavement

The tesselated pavement on the south east coast of Tasmania (Figure 4.1E), adjacent to Eaglehawk Neck and the Port Arthur Peninsula, is part of a spectacular section of coastline. High cliffs have formed from erosion by waves along horizontal and vertical cracks or joints. Undercutting and collapse of the high cliffs have produced a variety of rugged coastal landforms that form part of a well-known interpretive geotourism coastal trail. The most well-known coastal landforms include the Blowhole, Tasmans Arch, the Devil's Kitchen (a spectacular gash-like cavernous slot that forms an apparently boiling cauldron for foaming and surging water) and finally the offshore Lanterns (coastal stacks). All of these highly scenic features were formed by wave erosion along joints in dark-coloured Jurassic dolerite (165 Ma) and its dominant host, almost horizontally layered Permian sandstone (250 Ma).

At the base of the cliffs the wave-cut platform produces a spectacularly smoothed pavement that has been eroded from a sequence of horizontal inter-layered sandstones and shales, which are intensely jointed at right angles to the horizontal layering. The joints are planar fractures in the rocks, formed during uplift, and form parallel sets in two directions at right angles to each other. This has resulted in the rocks being divided naturally into large rectangular blocks. The joint planes are lines of weakness in the rocks, making them susceptible to erosion by the waves as they break across this wave-cut platform. The result is a large, natural hopscotch pitch, with a brick-like or mosaic pattern of 'tiles' (tesselated) formed from the eroding sandstones.

Volcanic landforms

Australia is a relatively stable and aseismic continent, but volcanic activity has occurred in the Mount Gambier area of South Australia in relatively recent geological time and has been recorded as an important part of local Aboriginal cultural recollections. The outbursts, which would have been spectacular, took place along a northwest–southeast trend line in southwestern Victoria and southeastern South Australia. The most recent volcanoes, Mt Gambier and Mt Schank (Figure 4.1J), are well known scenic attractions. Both show crater-like collapse structures on their summits that are the result of explosive eruptions, which included super-heated steam from aquifer water in contact with hot magma and associated with ash clouds and basaltic lava flows. The earliest volcanic activity occurred 1.5 million years ago, with the more recent volcanoes of Mt Gambier and Mt Schank forming only 5000–10 000 years ago. The crater at the top of Mt Gambier sits below the water table and forms the Blue Lake. It is aptly named, as the water is a distinctive blue colour for many months of the year as the result of its high dissolved calcium content, which reflects the blue colour of sunlight that is refracted and reflected from its surface. The volcanoes of this region are significant sites (Clayton, 2004) and are part of Australia's most extensive volcanic province, rated the sixth most significant, and the third largest, in the world. There is a visitor Discovery Trail that provides an opportunity for tourists to learn about both the natural and cultural history of the area.

Conclusion

The geology of Australia is diverse, unique and remarkable. The diversity is related to the complexity of rock types, mineral deposits and fossils, and the uniqueness is related to its geological evolution, from the earliest beginnings with the formation of the ancient cratons that form the basis for the present-day continent, to the relatively recent break up of Gondwanaland. The subsequent drift of the island continent northwards, through a range of climatic zones and geographic locations, has resulted in a unique flora and fauna, as isolation served to protect the diversity that was captured at the moment of break-up. The landscapes of Australia range from mountains to valleys, deserts to coasts, and its very variety is a reflection of the rocks that make up its foundations.

References

Australian Government (2003). A Medium to Long Term Strategy for Tourism: Tourism. White Paper, Commonwealth of Australia, Department of Communications, Information Technology and the Arts.

Australian National Parks and Wildlife Service (ANPWS) (1982). *Uluru (Ayers Rock-Mount Olga) National Park: Plan of Management.* ANPWS.

Australian National Parks and Wildlife Service (ANPWS) (1986). *Nomination of Uluru (Ayers Rock–Mount Olga) National Park for inclusion on the World Heritage List.* ANPWS.

Australian Tourist Commission (1998). *Brand Australia* (video). Australian Tourist Commission.

Australian Tourist Commission (1999). *Australia into the New Millennium* (video). Australian Tourist Commission.

Australian Tourist Commission (2004). *Brand Australia.* Australian Tourist Commission.

Bureau of Tourism Research (2001). *Statistics: Datacard: Expenditure.* At http://www.btr.gov.au/statistics/datacard/dcexpnite.html (accessed 7 May 2004).

Clayton, D. (2004). *Discover the Limestone Coast.* Limestone Coast Tourism, Hansen Print.

Costermans, L. (1983) *Native Trees and Shrubs of South-eastern Australia.* Weldon Publishing.

DCLM (1989) *Shark Bay.* Western Australian Department of Conservation and Land Management, Como WA.

DITR (2004). *Impact April 2004: A Monthly Fact Sheet on the Economic Impact of Tourism and the Latest Visitor Arrival Trends.* Australian Government, Department of Industry, Tourism and Resources (available at http://www.industry.gov.au/impact, accessed 15 April 2004).

Kelleher, G. (1986). The Great Barrier Reef: A World Heritage Site. *Educating for the Environment: Proceedings of a Seminar and Workshop.* Australian Government Publishing Service, pp. 60–64.

Leader-Elliott, L. (1996) *Cultural Tourism Opportunities for South Australia.* South Australian Tourism Commission.

Lucas, P., Webb, T., Valentine, P. and Marsh, H. (eds) (1997). *The Great Barrier Reef as a World Heritage Area.* Great Barrier Reef Marine Park Authority, pp. 31–42.

Maslow, A. (1954). *Motivation and Personality.* Harper & Row.

Mulvaney, J. and Kamminga, J. (1999). *Prehistory of Australia.* Allen & Unwin.

NTTC (2003). *Northern Territory Tourism Commission Strategic Plan 2003–2007.* Darwin: NTTC.

Pickett, J. and Alder, J. (1997). *Layers of Time: The Blue Mountains and their Geology.* New South Wales Department of Mineral Resources.

South Australian Tourism Commission (1998). *Corporate Plan 1998–2005.* South Australian Tourism Commission.

South Australian Tourism Commission (2002). *South Australian Tourism Plan 2003–2008: Inspiring Partnerships for Sustainable Tourism.* South Australian Tourism Commission.

Twidale, C. R. (1982). *Granite Landforms.* Elsevier Publishing Company.

5

Geotourism resources of Iran

Alireza Amrikazemi and
Abbas Mehrpooya

Introduction

Iran has a rich culture and civilization as well as an outstanding natural environment. Its natural and cultural diversity specifications have caused it to be listed as one of the top ten tourist countries in the world (Francesco Frangialli, Secretary General of the World Tourism Organization, 2004), and its archaeological, cultural and natural attractions form an excellent basis for developing geotourism. For years its geological features have been studied by researchers from around the world. The country has been labelled a 'geologists' paradise' or 'the 1.5-million-km^2 geological museum'. While Iran has a great range of geological phenomena, geotourism is just emerging and taking its first developmental steps. This chapter presents general information about Iran's geology and places where it occurs, as well as some examples of geotourism products. However, it is clear that the future development of geotourism requires comprehensive planning.

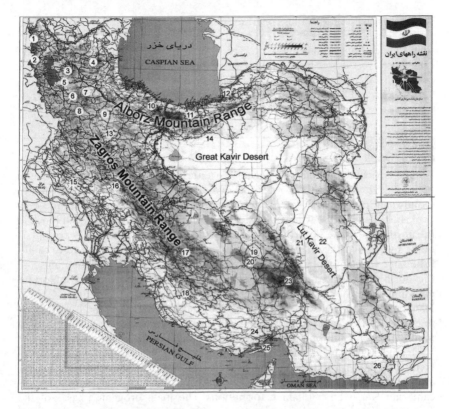

Figure 5.1 Geographical features of Iran. (1) Ropy lava, Maku; (2) columns of basalt; (3) Sahand Volcano, craters; (4) Sabalan Volcano, Shirvan Valley, Sarein hot springs; (5) Travertine Springs, Kandovan Village; (6) Takht-e-Soleyman; (7) erosion columns, Mahneshan; (8) Karaftoo Cave; (9) Kataleh khor Cave; (10) Alamkûh Peak; (11) Damavand Volcano; (12), (26) mud volcanoes; (13) Alisadr Cave; (14), (24) salt domes; (15) Kabirkûh, landslide; (16) Gahar Lake, OshtoranKûh mountain range, waterfalls; (17), (18) canyons, valleys; (19) sinkhole; (20) Meymand Village; (21) sand pyramids; (22) yardangs; (23) Rayen Craters; (25) Qeshm Island.

Iran

Iran is a large Middle Eastern country bounded by the Caspian Sea in the north and the Persian Gulf in the south (Figure 5.1). The 500-km northern coastline and the 1500-km southern one are both formed by water boundaries, while there are numerous lakes throughout the country. Iran also shares borders with Iraq, Turkey, Armenia, Azerbaijan, Turkmenistan, Afghanistan and Pakistan. It has an area of more than 1 500 000 km^2 and a population of over 65 million people. In the north it is bounded by the Alborz (sometimes shown as Elburz) Mountains, with the Zagros Mountains in the west. Together they cover half the country, while the remainder comprises forests and fertile plains. The highest point in Iran is Mount Damavand (5671 m) and its lowest part is the Caspian coast, 28 m lower than sea level.

Iran lies in the temperate zone but, owing to its large latitude and altitude ranges, the difference between temperatures in various parts of the country at the same time is often as much as 40°C. This is due to the existence of its mountain ranges and vast desert lands, both of which have a big influence on the climatic conditions of the country. The geographical features of Iran include high peaks, vast deserts and Kavirs, large rivers and permanent glaciers.

Geology

Iran belongs to the Alpine–Himalayan orogenic belt, extending from the Atlantic to the Pacific Ocean. It separates the two regions of Eurasia in the north and Gondwana in the south. The political boundaries of Iran approximate the orogenic belt between the Arabian–African unit in the south and the Asian block in the north. Due to the closure of an ocean located between these blocks around 65 million years ago, the main geological features of the Iranian region were established. Two huge mountain ranges, the east–west trending Alborz Mountains and the northwest–southeast trending Zagros Mountains, are the most important ones and dominate the tectonic and stratigraphic features of the country. Central Iran, bearing the Iranian basement and the Makran Plain, and the East Iranian region, both have interesting geological records. Together they have created a mountainous region which covers about 50 per cent of the country's area.

The oldest rock unit, which forms the basement of Iran, is exposed in Central Iran. The Pan-African orogeny is a significant event in Iran's geological history, and formed the Iranian basement. Outcrops occur in Alborz, and include precambrian Kahar and Soltanieh formations. The main orogenic phases of the Palaeozoic Era have not influenced the Iranian region as much as in other areas in Europe and North America. However, during the Middle to Late Triassic Period an important compression phase affected the Iranian region, resulting in the closure of a Late Palaeozoic ocean situated between Iran and Turan. In the Early Tertiary Period, the Laramide orogeny in the Iranian region was marked by the closure of the sea between the Iranian and Arabian plates during the Late Cretaceous Period and the Early Palaeocene Epoch. This north–east trending movement led to the uplift of the Zagros Mountains, which are still rising today.

The Lower to Middle Eocene Epoch was a period of extensive volcanism in most of Iran. Volcanism occurred in the Uromiyeh–Dokhtar zone as a long volcanic-plutonic part of the Zagros Orogeny. It started during the Cretaceous Period and reached its peak during the Eocene Epoch of the Tertiary Period. The tectonism leading to the present physiography of Iran occurred during the Alpine Orogeny, which started in the Late Tertiary Period and continues to the present time.

Landforms and related processes

Iran's geomorphic features lend themselves to geotourism, with the size and diversity of the landforms and related processes. These include features related to mountains, volcanoes, water and other factors, as well as Qeshm Island.

Mountainous features

Mountains cover half of Iran's area, and because of this they are among the most important tourist attractions in the country. There are 1500 mountains higher than 3000 m and 600 peaks higher than 4000 m in Iran. Particular mountains which hold significance for geotourism include Mounts Damavand, Alamkuh, Sabalan and Taftan. Mount Damavand is a young volcano that formed in the late Tertiary and early Quaternary Periods. Its 5671-m summit is the highest peak in the Middle East, and it is considered to be one of the world's highest conical peaks. It is located in the north of Iran near the capital, Tehran. In addition to natural tourism and sporting attractions, the mountain displays some geological features and related phenomena of relevance to geotourism. They include its basalt columns, permanent glaciers and hot mineral water springs, as well as a wide variety of volcanic features. One of its most significant features is the possibility of direct observation and accessibility to its internal basement. The deep valley, which is located on its northeast sector, provides opportunities for geotourism as well as volcanological research.

Mount Alamkuh (4850 m), Iran's second highest peak, is located in northern Iran. The mountain is a huge granite mass which has led to the metamorphism of its surrounding layers. There are over 200 mountains in this region with peaks higher than 4000 m. Its main tourist attraction is a vertical cliff which is 500 m high with a base at an elevation of 4300 m. It attracts lots of professional rock climbers from Iran and other countries around the world every year. Another outstanding feature of the mountain are its large glaciers, which are up to 5 km long.

Mount Sabalan (4815 m), a volcano located in the northwest, is Iran's third highest mountain. Three important phenomena distinguish it for tourism: a crater lake, a valley and a mineral spring. On the highest point of the mountain lies a scenic freshwater lake, one of the highest in the world. It was formed during the final volcanic phase, and is the result of the volcanic dome's downward collapse. The lake is approximately 7000 square metres in area, and it is between 25 and 35 m deep. The surface of this lake is usually covered with ice throughout the year, and only in summer time does the ice turn to water. To the north of the mountain lies the long and deep Shirvandarreh Valley, which has a wide variety of scenic landscapes. It has been formed as the result of flood erosion in pyroclastics and tephra. A range of scenic landforms occurs, including erosion and conglomerate columns as well as a variety of other structures. The valley's profile and its walls show well-beddings in pyroclastics. Surrounding the mountain there is a concentration of hot-water mineral springs. They are traditionally used in the northern region for bathing and water therapy, and in the Sarein Region, in the south, some modern facilities have been built for therapeutic use.

With more than 50 000 visitors per year, tourism is growing rapidly in the region. This has created a demand for visitor accommodation, facilities and services. Located on the western side of the mountain, in the Meshkin-Shahr region, is Iran's hottest mineral spring, the temperature of which rises to 86°C. An interesting point here is that there is another cold spring just a few metres away where temperature hovers around 0°C. In the same region, geothermal energy is being developed.

Mount Taftan (4100 m), in southeast Iran, is the country's only semi-active volcano. There are some traces of volcanic activity on the peak and its surroundings, including sulphur fumaroles. The mountain can be accessed by a main road and it has two hiking trails toward the peak, by which approximately 2000 tourists climb to the top each year.

In northwest Iran a diversity of volcanoes and small craters have formed the Sahand mountainous region, among which the highest peak is 3600 m. The set of craters in the area has its own unique features, including Lake Uromiyeh.

Canyons

There are three large canyons in different parts of the country. In the southeast of Fars Province, a 4-km long spiral canyon has its origin through tectonic activity, karst and erosion, and in some places it is over 300 m deep. In the north of the Alborz Mountain range, facing the Caspian Sea, there is one other large canyon, which is covered in dense forest. The depth of this canyon is between 350 and 400 m, and its formation is through intense flood erosion at a time of mountain uplift. In the southeast region, a long canyon has been created in weak formations from flood and storm erosion. Due to large anticlines and calcareous formations there are many canyons and narrow capes in the southern regions of Zagros, of which the most beautiful examples are in Fars Province.

Landslides

The world's largest landslide occurred in the west of Iran at the foot of Mount Kabirkûh. The huge sliding mass traversed a distance of 50 km, and it is so large that it covers the area of a standard topographic (1 : 50 000 map). The complete shape of this landslide can only be observed from the air, as from land the whole scope of the slide cannot be fully comprehended. At the foot of Kabirkûh, and also in other areas in the Zagros mountain range, there are many landslides of different dimensions.

Volcanic features

As well as the large number of volcanic mountains in Iran, there are also several other features related to volcanoes or igneous activity. They include lava flows, lava rivers, basaltic columns, craters and volcanic villages.

Lava flows

Pahoehoe lava flows are fluid basaltic flows. They flow very fast because of their low viscosity. They are not thick, generally being less than 1 m deep. As a pahoehoe flow moves it develops a thin, glassy crust, which is moulded into billowy surfaces resembling coils of rope – hence they are often referred to as ropey lava. The other major type of lava flow is called an aa flow. These are generally slow moving, and are usually between 3 and 10 m deep. The surface of the flow cools and forms a crust while the interior remains molten. As it continues to move, the hardened crust is broken into a jumbled mass of angular blocks and clinkers (Hamblin, 1992).

In northwest Iran, at Maku City, there is a large area covered by pahoehoe and aa flows. These flows are partly the result of the Mt Ararat volcanic eruption, but are also due to magma rising up to the surface through faults and fractures and then flowing across a vast plain. Mt Ararat is located in Turkey on the border of northwest Iran, but most of its basaltic lava flows toward Maku in Iran. In this region another flow has exposed light and porous basaltic rocks. These are formed when gas within the fluid interior of the flow migrates upward. Although Maku is the best site to view these lava features, they also occur in other locations around the Damavand and Sabalan volcanoes.

Lava rivers

The basaltic flows of Mount Ararat have created another particular phenomenon in the Maku area; a river of lava. During the eruption the lava flowed down a valley, and afterwards water erosion carved a channel inside the cooled lava and rebuilt the river's bed. The walls of this valley are dark and glossy, and the flow of the river down it creates a scenic vista. The river resembles a large black snake, and its local name is *Zangmar* ('black snake' in Persian).

Basaltic columns

Hexagonal columns of basalt occur in many parts of Iran. The most important and interesting ones are located near Maku City, Ploor Town in northern Iran (this is related to the Damavand Volcano), and Birjand City in the east. The columns are usually formed by contraction when lava cools, with their long axis being approximately perpendicular to the cooling surface (Bates and Jackson, 1982). The Maku columns are situated along a valley and are approximately 50 m high with sharp joints and clear surfaces. The Damavand columns are widely spread along the eastern side of the mountain, and are not arranged in the same way as those in Maku. Sarbisheh (Birjand) is another typical example of these columns.

Craters

Iran has a number of volcanic craters, including a set in the Rayen region that comprises fourteen craters of oval and circular shapes. The largest has an opening with a diameter of 1200 m and a depth of more than 300 m. It is considered that these craters are not volcanic but meteoric in origin, and considerable research is being undertaken to establish their true origins.

In the Ghorveh region, a set of craters includes some in the shape of a set of rosary beads. In the area there are many pumice and volcanic foam mines as well as volcanic bombs. The biggest bomb is 3 m long with a diameter of 1 m, and is perfectly spindle-shaped.

Volcanic villages

The two villages of Kandovan (northwest Iran) and Meymand (southeast Iran) comprise houses cut into the volcanic rocks. Kandovan is located at the foot of Mount Sahand, where the shelters have been dug out of hardened ashes or lahar beds (Figure 5.2). The houses have been carved into the steep slopes of the mountain and are now supplied by electricity, running water and a wastewater system. Some have two stories with staircases inside, and all are still inhabited.

Meymand village is located at the foot of Mt Mozahem, and it is approximately 2000 years old. Here the house walls are built of volcanic conglomerate and hardened ashes. The carved structures include a mosque (which is the largest opening), a school, a public bath, and a structure that seems to have been used as a fire

Figure 5.2 The village of Kandovan (northwest Iran) comprises houses cut into the volcanic rocks.

temple. The Meymand Village differs from that of Kandovan; the area is not so steep, and also the houses are no longer inhabited.

Water features

These include numerous lakes, waterfalls and mineral springs.

Lakes

There are many lakes in Iran, which have different sources and characteristics. The most important is the Caspian Sea, which forms the 500-km long northern boundary of the country. It is the largest lake in the world ($436\,000\,km^2$) and is one of the remnants of the old Sea of Paratethys. Because of its size and unique characteristics, the lake is considered to be a sea (Shahrabi, 1994).

Along the coast are large deltas which originate from the mouths of rivers flowing down from the Alborz Mountains. On the north coast lies the Anzali lagoon, which has a special place in environmental geology in relation to its land-forms, plants and migratory bird species.

The Gorgan Gulf lies on the far eastern coast of the Sea. The strip-like penin-sula of Miankaaleh separates it from the Caspian Sea and has made it similar to a half-closed small basin. This Gulf enjoys special research importance due to issues related to its deposition, submarine flows and streams. Being a protected area in Iran, the peninsula has great potential for geotourism development.

Lake Uromiyeh is Iran's largest lake ($5000\,km^2$) with super-saturated salt water. Salt crystals cover the shallow coastal parts of the lake, and it is home to the unique Arthemia crustacean. The 'ooze lands' in the coastal part of the lake are of special interest to the many health tourists who travel to the area for therapy for skin diseases and arthritic pain. A few other islands provide scenic attractions on the lake.

Lake Gahar is an excellent example of a lake formed as the result of a landslide. It is located in the OshtoranKûh mountain range, and resembles a glacial lake. The lake is 2.5 km long and 500 m wide, and is fed by the streams and springs flowing down from the mountain range. It was formed by a large landslide (with a volume of about 20 000 000 m^3) blocking the mouth of the valley and making a natural dam. The gradual collection of water behind this dam has led to the formation of the lake. Some rivers flow from this lake, giving an indication of its large volume of water.

Waterfalls
Most of Iran's waterfalls are in the Zagros and Alborz mountain ranges. The highest waterfall (80 m) occurs in Lorestan Province. However, the Bisheh, Shevie (Talezang) and Margoon waterfalls also attract many visitors and are important ecotourism destinations.

Mineral springs
There are over 400 mineral and hot-water springs in Iran. These springs are divided into four groups depending on their average temperature: subthermal, hypothermal, homothermal and hyperthermal. There are different ideas regarding the spring's sources of heat, but most are related to magmatic sources. The springs occur mostly in volcanic areas or areas with geodynamic activity. Their compositions are different, but usually include carbonate, sulphur, sodium and iron compounds (Shahbeyg, 1993). The majority and also the most important mineral and hot-water springs in Iran are in Azarbayjan, Ardabil and Tehran Provinces.

The hottest mineral spring is located in the Meshkin Shahr region at the foot of Mount Sabalan volcano, and its temperature rises to 86°C. Since the spring is 2200 m above sea level, the water temperature is near boiling point. There is one other spring in central Iran, on the margin of Kavir, whose temperature rises to 75°C. Iran's hot springs form key attractions for Iranian and international tourists. Other areas that have hot-water springs include the Sarein region (south of Mount Sabalan), Larijan (East of Mount Damavand), Geno (in southern Iran) and Ramsar (northern Iran). There are some interesting formations in the area of the springs, which produce travertine deposits. These include cone shapes, shield-like shapes, travertine terraces and strip-like spiral walls of different colours.

In the Azarshahr region, near Mount Sahand, there is a collection of these formations, including conical and shield-like forms, which are the remnants of old springs. Also, several active springs along a fault have turned this region into a 'Travertine Park'. The colours of the deposits are varied, and include yellow and shades of brown caused by different combinations of iron in the spring waters. In the Salmas region, on the northwest border, there is another colourful collection of these springs, which have created many white or milky-coloured travertine terraces. Inactive springs in the forms of circles and hollow hemispheres have turned the region's surface into a lunar landscape.

In the Damavand and Larijan regions there are many springs comprised of sulphur. They have traditionally been used for many years, and have led to tourism prosperity in the region. The travertine deposits have created a variety of interesting shapes on the natural features of the region, as well as on the leaves and branches of the shrubs and bushes, thus making the whole region a geotourist's wonderland.

Case study 5.1 describes the Takht-e-Soleyman Complex.

Other features

There are a range of other landforms with geotourism potential in Iran (e.g. see Case study 5.1). They include mud volcanoes, salt domes, caves, sinkholes, deserts and chimney rocks (erosion columns).

Mud volcanoes

There are two mud volcanic regions in Iran: in Chahbahar region near the Oman Sea, and in the surroundings of Bandar-e-Tourkmen, near the Caspian Sea. Chahbahar's numerous mud volcanoes are the bigger and more active, and it is believed that their formation is related to geodynamic movement and uplift. The mud volcanoes on the margin of the Caspian Sea are more related to oil and gas fields, and in the region smells of crude oil. Their mud is less viscous, and because of this their bubbles blow out quickly. In the Caspian Sea some large mud volcanoes have been reported where the mud has erupted above the sea surface. However, the duration of their activity has been brief, although they probably continue to be mildly active under the water.

Salt domes

There are over 200 active and inactive salt domes of various sizes concentrated in the southern part of the country. In central Iran and south of Alborz there is also a considerable number of these domes. These large masses of salt have risen upwards due to their difference in weight from surrounding rocks, and where their crust has reached the surface of the earth they have formed large hills and mountains. This mass has led to a change of position in the surrounding formations, thus altering the region's morphology. Through dissolution after rain, some minerals that accompany salt (such as calcite, hematite and sulphur) remain in the vicinity, forming dense deposits.

In the southern Zagros Mountains there is an extremely scenic area due to the folding and formation of salt domes. These have been formed as a result of the pressures put on the Iranian Plate by the Arabian Plate. The salt domes also outcrop in three islands in The Persian Gulf on Qeshm, Larak and Hormoz Islands. The latter is entirely a salt dome, with many interesting landforms due to a variety of rocks and ores having been brought up to the island's surface by the salt mass. These have given the Hormoz Island a colourful appearance, representing an outdoor museum of lithology and mineralogy. In parts of the dome that are in direct contact with the sea, vertical walls have been formed. Extraction of ruddle (red ochre) has turned the southern part of the island reddish, and this red hue stretches out over a large part of the surrounding sea.

In the south of the Semnan Province, at the northern margin of the Great Kavir Desert, there is a collection of about 40 salt domes which are considered to be the best in the world (Jackson, 1990).

Case study 5.1: The Takht-e-Soleyman Complex, Iran

Takht-e-Soleyman is a UNESCO-listed World Heritage site which includes a natural lake, a collection of ancient buildings, the Dragon Stone (Sang-e-Eghdeha) and Zendan-e-Soleyman Mountain (Figure 5.3). The oldest buildings date back to the first millennium BC, and the most important one is the Azargoshab Fire Temple which, based on historical records, is considered to be Zoroaster's birthplace. The lake is in fact a large perennial travertine spring taking its water from deep below the earth's surface. It has an oval shape with diameter of up to 115 m and a depth of between 50 and 70 m. Travertine deposits have made a large plate, 20 m high, around the lake, on which ancient buildings are situated, and the lake is located in its centre. The water flows downward through a few streams and has led to the formation of a structure that is called Sang-e-Eghdeha. This is a long, spiral wall made of early travertine deposits, and it has gradually increased to its current height of 1.5 m.

Around the main site there are other hot water and travertine springs, some of which are used for bathing and water therapy by both local people and tourists. There is another phenomenon in this complex, 2 km away from the main site, named Zendan-e-Soleyman, which is a cone-shaped mountain. This is the remnant of a former large travertine spring, and a rupture in the walls (the result of a fault) has been created by water drainage from the lake now becoming inactive. The view of the inner side of the hollow mountain gives rise to the mountain called Zendan-e-Soleyman (Prison Mountain).

Figure 5.3 Takht-e-Soleyman is a UNESCO-listed World Heritage site that includes a natural lake, a collection of ancient buildings, the Dragon Stone (Sang-e-Eghdeha) and Zendan-e-Soleyman Mountain.

Caves

There is a wide variety of caves in Iran, including calcareous (karst), salt, ancient and human-made caves. The calcareous caves are in diverse forms of multi-storied, river, lake and well caves. Examples include:

1. *The Kataleh Khor Cave.* Located about 150 km from Zanjan city, Kataleh Khor Cave is the longest and most scenic in Iran. Its formations date back to the Oligo-Miocene Epoch. About 3000 m of this cave's route has had walkways installed, and these are illuminated for tourists. The reception and accommodation facilities are well developed, and it has a diversity of simple and compound stalactites and stalagmites, mushroom-like calcareous columns, deposits, strip-like formations, calcareous bodies and a variety of other scenic phenomena. So far three floors of this cave have been discovered, and a vast area (20 km in length) has been explored. However, not all of the cave has yet been discovered.
2. *Alisadr Cave.* Iran's largest lake cave is located in the vicinity of Hamadan city. The cave is 2.5 km long, with the depth of water reaching 8 m in some parts. The lake water is pellucid and fresh, and the cave contains many caveroneous phenomena including a range of colourful stalactites. It has excellent reception facilities, and tourists explore the cave by pedal boat and on foot. The presence of nearby accommodation adds to this established geotourism product, which is a major natural attraction.
3. *Karaftoo Cave.* Located between Takab and Divandareh cities, Karaftoo Cave is Iran's biggest ancient cave. This four-storey cave was created in limestone formations dating back to the Oligo-Miocene Epoch. Some parts of this cave have also been excavated by humans, and based on archaeological excavations, as well as signs and objects discovered in the cave, researchers believe that the history of its inhabitation dates back to Arsacides' period (250 BC). At other times in the past the cave has been the residence and place of worship for different tribes. A wide array of hand tools in the cave is related to the pre-historic period, which suggests that early humans lived in the cave. One of the most scenic parts of the cave is the roof of the fourth floor, which is reminiscent of a theatre ceiling. There, some bowl-like holes and convex (lens-like) protrusions cover the surface of the roof, displaying a beautiful morphology. These holes are the result of karst erosion in the limestone formations.

Sinkholes

The largest doline or sinkhole occurs in the Rafsanjan Region, Kerman Province. This sinkhole is like a gigantic funnel, with the diameter of its entrance being 60 m. It is of an unknown depth as, so far, measurement has not been possible. The hole was formed by uncontrolled overuse of underground waters in the region. This created a hollow space in a fragile rock formation, and hence the weight of the upper layers led to their sudden collapse into the space beneath. Among other karst sinkholes there are interesting examples in eastern Alborz and also in the surroundings of Hamedan city (near the Alisadr Cave region).

Kavirs and deserts

Desert areas and kavirs cover about 25 per cent of Iran's area. These regions have a collection of all the geomorphologic phenomena related to deserts. Iran's two great deserts are Lut Kavir and Great Kavir. Lut Kavir is a vast, relatively

Figure 5.4 Chimney rock created by erosion in conglomerate beds, which alternate with soft layers of clay and marl or hard layers of sandstone.

unexplored region in the eastern part of central Iran. It includes three of the world's unique phenomena (Ahmadi, 1998):

1. Ghourd – the world's highest sand pyramids, which are huge sand dunes 2000 m long and 500 m high
2. Yardang or Kalut – an area 150 km long, 70 km wide and 80 m high, which comprises long, deep moats (ditches) created by storms and floods
3. The hottest point in the world, as recorded by satellite images (Kardavani, 2003).

Iran's vast deserts also contain wide ergs with a variety of sand deposits, such as Seif, Barkhan, Yardang, sand pyramids (Ghourd), sand channels and Nebka in a variety of different forms. Vast clay and saline lands as well as salt polygons are other ubiquitous features of its deserts (Zomorrodian, 2003).

Chimney rocks (erosion columns)

Erosion in conglomerate beds, which alternate with soft layers of clay and marl or hard layers of sandstone, creates interesting landforms. Where there are vertical joints, the result of this heterogeneous erosion is the formation of columns or wall-like column ranges. The top columns have a huge rock or a remaining part of a layer, and are usually called chimney rocks (Figure 5.4). In the Mahneshan region there is a collection of these columns with the different forms and sizes that appear predominantly in Pliocene conglomerates. Locally the columns are called Sang-e-Adam (Adam's Rock) because of their physical similarity to a human profile with a large head, narrow neck and cylindrical body. Besides

89

Mahneshan, formations such as this can be viewed in several other parts of Iran in the southeast, along the southern coast and on Qeshm Island.

Qeshm Island

Qeshm Island is located in southern Iran in the Persian Gulf. It is 120 km long, and has an average width of 20 km. The island is part of the Zagros Mountains, and it is the largest island in the Persian Gulf. From the point of view of natural phenomena, the island enjoys a special status. Harra mangroves are located in the northern part of the island, and form the habitat for many rare and endangered species of plants and animals. On the southern part, there is a large sea-turtle nesting habitat. The island's phenomena have been recorded as part of UNESCO's Man and the Biosphere (MAB) Program. There is also a wide variety of geological phenomena on Qeshm Island. These include a range of landforms.

The Kharbas coastal caves have been formed in clay and marl beds. Originally they were formed as the result of wave action, and they are deep and interconnected. They have been extended by humans, and were probably used by the ancient residents of the island as a shelter against enemy attacks.

Across the whole of the island there is a wide variety of landforms created by erosion. An example of a scenic vista caused by erosion is found at Darreh-e-Setarehha (the Valley of Stars) on the southern side of the island. Due to the variety of geological formations in the area, especially a limy sandstone whose amount of calcite varies in different parts, the erosion has created many heterogeneous and dissimilar forms. There is a main valley with some tributaries where columns, strip-like walls and arches are abundant, and other landforms create an unusual picturesque landscape. The valley is an ideal place for the study of different types of erosion. The Queshm Roof is a high plateau that stretches along the north–central area of the island. It is predominantly made up of limestone, and is more resistant to erosion than its surrounding formations. The short-term growth of plants after rainfall creates novel scenery in this hot and dry region.

The Chahkuh valley and a similar one nearby have U-shaped profiles. The mouth of the Chahkuh Valley is wide and surrounded by high walls, but its width gradually decreases until it becomes very narrow. The walls are very high and there is little light. Water erosion and dissolution have created long and deep clefts in the shape of concave, spoon-like spherical holes. At the mouth of the valley there are some shallow wells, forming a place for the rain to be stored, and because of the hot and dry weather the stored fresh water has a high value. It seems that this valley and similar vales nearby are related to a large anticline, which has played a key role in the formation of the Namakdan salt dome. This dome, in the southern part of the island, has created various phenomena, and has had a big influence in shaping the morphology of the area, largely through its deposits of iron compounds such as hematite and oligist. The walls of this mountain are rough and jagged, and consist of a variety of stones and ores. In part of the mountain there is a salt cave, which has been formed as the result of salt dissolution. The cave is about 200 m long, with cavernous phenomena such as saline stalactites and columns. Beside the cave there is a spring of saturated salty water, which deposits salt and hematite in its path and has formed a red and white strip in the area. Other phenomena on the south coast include vast and flat coastal lowlands covered in long ripple marks with bright, thin particles of oligist. In addition there is a rocky coastline and colourful coral reefs.

Conclusions

Iran has many geological wonders and considerable geotourism potential. While, according to the Iran Tourism Organization, over a million tourists visited Iran in 2002, only a small number of these visitors is attracted by the country's natural phenomena, due to absence of adequate information. However, the existence of the geological phenomena described in this chapter makes a strong argument for developing geotourism in Iran. From the point of view of both general and specialized visitors, such tourism would have the capacity to attract large numbers of tourists. To achieve such an aim, there is an urgent need to undertake a comprehensive geotourism development plan. This should include:

1. Preparing a scientific inventory of geological attractions.
2. Reporting on each particular phenomenon in order to classify and rank them from the point of view of 'value' and 'importance', as well as compiling information for each site based on the existing data.
3. Formally registering each site in the list of the country's national sites.
4. Ensuring appropriate protection and conservation of the sites to prevent any kind of harm and/or loss resulting from civil, economic and other human activities – i.e. minimizing any adverse impacts of local people's activities.
5. Establishing an organizational plan for sustainable geotourism development under the total supervision of the country's official authorities, namely the Geological Survey of Iran (GSI) and the Environment Protection Organization (EPO).
6. Registering the country's geotourism sites as geoparks and introducing specific limits included in the definition of a geopark by UNESCO in order to acquire support by this organization.

While nature-based tourism has enjoyed a long history, geotourism is a new and specialized branch of tourism, not only in Iran but also throughout the world. Its establishment may lead to some initial resistance in justifying its related benefits and advantages to governmental authorities or the private sector, as it is difficult to provide the budgets to develop and advance the industry. There is also another problem that can be observed mostly in developing countries; that is, the lack of protection and conservation of geological phenomena. However, writing books and papers and holding meetings and conferences in this regard can contribute to the introduction of this new branch of tourism and its related values.

In conclusion, we wish to suggest a few examples of appropriate protection, conservation and development measures in relation to geotourism:

1. Due to the fragile nature of many caves, visitation should be under the supervision of tour guides. Other issues to be taken into account include creating trails and making visitors use these paths, and the provision of proper electric lighting for visual effects as well as paying attention to the phenomena's changing colour because of moss growth effects. Finally explanatory signs, incorporating plans and schematic maps, should be provided.

2. Visiting geological features such as erosion forms and phenomena, mineral springs and travertine cones should be allowed, provided visitors are kept at a minimum distance from the geo-attraction in order to prevent any potential adverse impacts.
3. In order for mountains, valleys and canyons to be developed as geotourism attractions, a thorough study should be carried out before any development occurs. Infrastructure such as footpaths should be constructed in a safe manner so as to allow easy tourist access without adverse environmental impacts on the geotourism attractions under observation. The provision of cable cars in such regions could be useful.
4. The use of local and traditional facilities in different geological sites will enhance their attractiveness. This may include sports and/or recreational facilities for the tourists – for example, the inclusion of camels in desert regions, visiting local communities, and the provision of easy access to the traditional facilities of life in the same regions. All of these are vital elements of sustainable geotourism development.

The recognition of 'geo' in natural features is the first achievement of geotourism. This should be followed by a study of the direct and indirect economic, scientific and cultural benefits. Finally, research should be undertaken into geotourism's mental and health benefits, which are related to being close to nature.

Acknowledgements

The authors would like to acknowledge their colleagues – Behrouz Farhatjah, Syed Abbas Fazeli, Mohammad Hasan Nabavi, Jafar Omrani and Jafar Sabouri.

References

Ahmadi, H. (1998). *Applied Geomorphology.* Tehran University Publications.

Bates, L. R. and Jackson, J. A. (1982). *Glossary of Geology.* American Geological Institute Press.

Hamblin, W. K. (1992). *Earth Dynamic Systems.* Macmillan Publishing Company.

Jackson, M. P. A. (1990). *Salt Diapirs of the Great Kavir (Central Iran).* Geological Survey of America Press.

Kardavani, P. (2003) Lut Kavir Desert. *Iranian Cultural Heritage News Agency*, 11 September, p. 1.

Shahbeyg, A. (1993). *Mineral and Thermal Waters of Iran.* Geological Survey of Iran Press.

Shahrabi, M. (1994). *Seas and Lakes of Iran.* Geological Survey of Iran Press.

Zomorrodian, M. J. (2003). *Geomorphology of Iran*, Vols I & II. Ferdowsi University Press.

Part Two: Geoparks

6

Geoparks – a regional, European and global policy

Marie-Luise Frey, Klaus Schäfer,
Georg Büchel and Margarete Patzak

Introduction

Geoparks have been promoted in Germany since the beginning of the 1990s, especially in the Vulkaneifel region. Their institution is a direct result of geological public relations work. Under this general heading a new sector called 'geotourism' developed gradually in the Eifel region, out of the link between geological knowledge transfer activities and the tourist industry (Frey *et al.*, 2002). The key geopark elements are especially evident in this sector and they form the basis for the local strategy, which can be applied at a range of levels – regional, national, international and global. This strategy is explained in the following sections, using exemplary data and results as well as perspectives for a sustainable future from the Geopark Gerolstein, and concept and projects realized within the Geopark Vulkaneifel.

To understand better the approach taken, which leads to a special geopark profile, it is necessary to explain the chronological development of the

Vulkaneifel, since this reveals the decision-making processes required for creating perspectives relating to sustainability. In this case, the decisions were not made on a purely geoscientific level but involved a close association between decision-makers from politics and business, scientists and regional managers. In order to clarify this aspect, this chapter will present the experience gained with the 'learning by doing' implementation in the Geopark Gerolstein and Geopark Vulkaneifel, as well as the scientific approach for structuring. The chapter also shows that the practical results and evaluation of the operative level in geoparks are a necessary part of the structural political hardware needed for the ideal as well as financial security in the future. This concept is supported by UNESCO programmes. In conclusion, the chapter establishes that geoparks are not necessarily mutually competitive, especially if they are located in different tourist regions. However, they must develop their own profile in accordance with the specificity of their geology, local traditions, and political, administrative and economic conditions.

Geotourism – what does it mean?

'Geotourism' has been recognized as a discipline within the German geoscientific community since the late 1990s (Frey, 1998). The topic emerged during the process of establishing geoscientific public relations as a discipline within the geosciences and the conception of geological trails in the Eifel region in 1984 (Kasig, 1993). The basis for this development was the longstanding cooperation with the associated Hillesheim community established in the light of university geological mapping courses which first resulted in the establishment of geo-trails (Kasig, 1993). In a pilot project within the Vulkaneifel, the associated Hillesheim community and their mayor, A. Pitzen, instituted a geological trail at the end of the 1980s. The successful completion of the geo-trail (Kasig *et al.*, 1989) and its acceptance by guests fast-tracked the existing endeavours of the neighbouring communities to make use of their landscapes for tourists (Brauers, 1993; Frey, 1993; Bell and Koziol, 2000).

The Destination Eifel (Figure 6.1) was created in 2004, and consists of the Nature Reserve Eifel, the German–Belgian Nature Reserve Hohes Venn–Eifel, the German–Luxemburgian Nature Reserve and the Geopark Vulkaneifel, which is accredited as a European Geopark and is a member of the Global UNESCO Network of Geoparks. The Geopark Vulkaneifel covers an area of approximately 120 000 hectares and is located between Koblenz and Trier, north of the Moselle River (Figure 6.2). The Geopark Vulkaneifel comprises 15 geo-centres and 257 field locations that are open to visitors.

The political decisions made by the individual structures within the Geopark Vulkaneifel are carried independently by five associated communities and two districts that have joint responsibility for the park. By founding their own centres as well as the Vulkaneifel Geopark Limited Liability Corporation (Ltd) in Daun, which is affiliated with the Daun economic development agency, these communities and districts maintain the long-term financial security of the Geopark.

As part of geological public relations, geotourism remains a challenge – particularly where the use of modern communication media is concerned. This challenge must be faced for the continuation and progress of the geosciences, for public benefit and for the sustainable development of regions on a worldwide

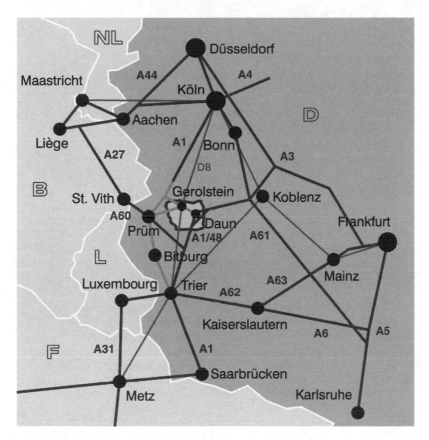

Figure 6.1 Map of the Eifel region – Germany–Luxembourg–Belgium.

scale. The sustainability aspect affects the maintenance and creation of jobs in the regions, the securing of the tourism sector, the acceptance and integration of geological and natural heritage conservation in parallel with protection of the biosphere, and regional planning schemes.

Understanding and implementing sustainability in this form opens new perspectives which comply with sustainability as put forward in Agenda 21, but seen from a different angle. The interconnectedness of these simple new approaches, and their transfer from the regional to a European and global scale, give the geoparks a special value. This leads to a higher regional acceptance combined with an increased professional quality. As a result of this, geoparks are fundamental for enhancing the image of the geosciences. Consequently, UNESCO activities to establish a 'Global Network of Geoparks' for the global benefit were positively supported from the outset.

The term 'geotourism' was defined by Frey in the 1998 meeting of the German Geological Society as follows:

> Geotourism means interdisciplinary cooperation within an economic, success-oriented and fast-moving discipline that speaks its own language.

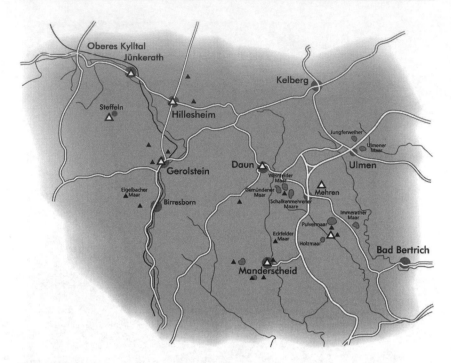

Figure 6.2 The Geopark Vulkaneifel comprises 15 geo-centres and 257 field locations that are open to visitors.

> Geotourism is a new occupational and business sector. The main tasks of geotourism are the transfer and communication of geoscientific knowledge and ideas to the general public.

Thus geotourism is based on the interaction between politics, geoscience, universities and the tourist industry. It achieves a quasi-balance between regional value and sustainable use and development by using the potential of the landscape and its established infrastructure. The sustainable protection and safeguarding of the geological heritage of a region is the fundamental principle behind geotouristic activities. Due to communication problems, the interaction between academics and politics usually results in direct conflict for the local actors in the geotourism sector. In spite of using the same terms and motives primarily, this is due either to a lack of objectives or to having disparate objectives. Politicians deal mainly with the general public (and not with scientists) and one of their main interests is in being re-elected, whereas scientists focus mainly on research and pay particular attention to detail. Another problem is that although they use the same language, they mean different things. Successful collaboration requires open discussion between the parties, a high degree of creativity and a constant exchange of information.

In Germany, the geosciences have set the course for a completely new direction embracing both economic and socio-political dimensions. The cooperation with the tourism industry, with its well-established structures and professional procedures that include suitable marketing structures, adds a success factor for geoscientific public relations. With regard to the fast-moving information society, technological as well as social changes, the task of transferring knowledge from the geosciences to the various target groups has only just begun. One of the duties of modern geosciences is to accept and further develop this task (Frey *et al.*, 2002). The tourism industry labels a development that has been continuing over a number of decades a 'trend' which has a positive effect on the economy and integrates social changes. In view of this background, the geosciences are compelled to engage with 'ordinary people', since they are the main economic drivers – especially in regard to tourism.

The Gerolstein Geopark

In order to increase the importance and value of the geological heritage of the Gerolstein district, the concept of a geopark was based on providing information/education, tourism and geoscientific research. It secures the constant supply of actual information on the multidisciplinary activities in the region, once the established internal network between geoscience, tourism/economy, politics and society is functional. This focuses the attention of the local population as well as visitors on their environment while involving them in the future planning and development of their region. To fulfil this objective, greater emphasis is placed on the aspect of beauty and the extraordinary geological setting of the landscape, which can lead to a continual increase in the appreciation of the geological heritage. Parallel to this, geologists impart the value and significance of geoscientific work to visitors, using relevant university study results and topics.

The geopark concept is supported by the following pillars:

1. Safeguarding the geological heritage
2. Transferring the regional value to the general public, linking directly to tourism
3. Establishing a sustainable economic future
4. Creating a regional geological identity
5. Increasing the appreciation of geological objects and processes
6. Cooperating actively with universities and other European and international institutions such as the Réserve Géologique de Haute Provence (France).

The Geopark Gerolstein comprises four geological trails. Their itineraries reflect a range of aspects including political (villages and communities, integration of the local population), touristic (e.g. duration of stay of visitors, or prolongation) and scientific (focus on specific geological themes such as volcanism). The aim is to increase visitor awareness of the landscape, and prolong the duration of their stay by providing interesting information about geological phenomena. The opening of the first trail in the Geopark resulted in an increasing demand for professionally guided tours along the trail.

Thus, the concept pillars are directly linked to the development of educational concepts for promoting geoscientific knowledge among children and students, the training of tourist guides and the creation of new job types. Furthermore, the concept also leads to the participation and support of universities and the local community in regional research projects. In this way, the geopark structure has an active effect on regional development. At the local political level, the mayors of Gerolstein in the Vulkaneifel Region, and the elected representatives of the local communities, have been promoting the institution of the geopark since 1990. The Eifel Association coined the name 'Geopark Gerolstein' in 1989.

The local natural history museum in Gerolstein is intensively involved in the Geopark activities as an 'indoor facility'. This facility is central to the task of promoting the philosophy of geological heritage conservation and the necessity for safeguarding and archiving these sites. The museum also plays an important role in serving as a centre for programmes suitable for children.

The marketing of the Geopark was placed in the professional hands of the tourism and business development company, TW Gerolsteiner Land GmbH (Ltd). National projects were carried out in cooperation with the Eifel Tourismus GmbH (Ltd) in Prüm, especially those related to realizing the LEADER IIC project of the European Union: 'Development of Geotourism in Europe'. The new model for directly linking the geosciences to tourism opened up fresh approaches especially for national marketing concepts. The UPS (Unique Point of Selling), which is the Vulkaneifel image, is being successfully promoted. The thematic content of this relationship has highlighted the importance of supplementary geoscientific products for touristic marketing.

Levels for geoscience transfer

The communication of geoscientific issues and 'geo-knowledge' is not trivial (Frey *et al.*, 2002). Geoscientific topics must be presented in an interesting manner and use the associated landscape experience in order to enhance the holiday and recreational value. This cannot work in one direction only. In the case of the Geopark Gerolstein, these pillars are also the transfer levels. To facilitate the transfer between and within the levels instruments or media are also required, including on-site explanatory signposts, print media, programmes such as guided tours, special events such as conferences, persons such as geopark guides, portable multimedia devices, advertising materials, souvenirs, and television and radio coverage.

After completing a number of trails in 1997 and producing flyers for the Geopark, it became apparent that various target groups require different levels of geological information – in other words, the transfer intensity varies between target groups. This is closely correlated to the level of education and the interest of the visitor. The experiences gained in the Gerolstein Geopark are described through five transfer levels, including the intensity of transfer obtained. They are:

1. General public
2. Science
3. Economy
4. Media
5. Society.

Transfer level 1 – general public

Instrument: information

The target group for the instrument information consists of adults, local residents, individual visitors and visitor groups. Texts and sketches were selected for this group, which is assumed to be interested in nature and landscapes. Explanatory signs have an informative character and are visually and emotionally appealing. For technical reasons and UV-resistance, a maximum of four colours were selected for the signs in the Geopark Gerolstein, all of which were produced by screen-printing. Experience shows that coloured signs combined with brief informative texts have a high positive acceptance among walkers, irrespective of their content.

The design of each of the 81 signs and 84 locations of the Geopark Gerolstein follows a uniform concept. As a rule, a sign will contain three or four illustrations of objects of which one can be seen directly by the observer in the landscape. Each designated location is used to explain a self-contained issue, and visitors are not compelled to read each sign during their walk. Each of the four trails deals with one main theme. The combination of geological topics and others has led to a high acceptance of geology. In response to visitor demands, the informative signs of each trail were reproduced on paper and are compiled into geo-reports.

As a first instrument for information, flyers were used. The transfer intensity of geological knowledge was reduced from the informative signs to the promotional flyers. This reduction, away from pure geological information in the landscape, constitutes a move towards meeting the needs of the human recipient and confirms the basic need to see beautiful landscapes and nature, thus creating an emotional stimulus. This illustrates that the instrument 'information' comprises two components – attracting attention, and information. The interaction between stimulation and fulfilment depends on the social development and the needs of the recipient visitor. Equally important is the potential of the Gerolstein staff and infrastructure to translate geological facts into coherent and graphically appealing content, and to produce and distribute the product through professional design and marketing. This characterizes the basic factors for geological knowledge transfer intensity.

Instrument: education

The role of the education sector in the geopark concept is an additional transfer level related to the general public. Among the instruments available for this transfer level are events such as excursions for school classes and teachers, seminars, and scientific lectures for the environmentally and culturally interested public and for residents who enjoy introducing their landscape to visitors. The character, type and intensity of the geological knowledge vary according to the recipients or the target groups.

Teacher training seminars are organized in cooperation with the Pedagogic Centre in Daun for teachers interested in geoscientific topics. Between 1993 and 2003 three training seminars were held for Geopark guides, two concerning regional projects. The concept and content of these seminars were based on the first one held by the Geopark Gerolstein, in 1993. The seminar tutors are renowned scientists from university institutes and the civil service, as well as independent university lecturers, and the course participants have to pass tests. With the support of the Business Development Company Daun, two new companies were founded which provide professional guides for excursions.

Transfer level 2 – science

Instrument: university collaboration

Scientific studies are the basis for the geological knowledge transfer process and therefore for geotourism, through which this knowledge is transferred. The development towards the IT society is such that the general public can generally access the same opportunities for obtaining information about published study results as the scientist. Consequently a prerequisite for geological knowledge transfer is the integration of the rapid changes achieved by improved technology, and simplified and accelerated access to information. This ensures that old scientific concepts are not transferred to the general public without prior filtration and comment. Integrating the universities into the process of geological knowledge transfer is time consuming and labour intensive. In fortunate circumstances, a geopark is the object of long-term research carried out by universities and the results of these studies are readily available. These can then be incorporated in the communication of geological knowledge in order to keep it up to date and to ensure success with visitors.

Since the establishment of the Geopark Gerolstein there has been close cooperation with the co-initiator, Professor Dr. W. Kasig from the Geological Institute at the Technical University (RWTH) Aachen. A close working relationship also exists with other local and national universities in Bonn, Jena, Cologne and Dortmund, and is evident in mapping projects and other research work (e.g. Zine, 1993; Witt, 1996; Hesse, 2002; Jaspers, 2002; Klinkenberg, 2002). In addition to pure geologic topics, a thesis on the subject ('The Pedagogic and Geological Foundation for providing Endo/Exodynamic and Regional Geologically-based Lessons in the Aachen Region') by Heer (1998) has now been completed and includes findings on touristic topics (Baumgart, 1997; Körnig, 1997).

Further projects have developed from the positive cooperation between university departments and communities. These projects have investigated particular aspects – for example, 'water'. All named activities have strengthened the general confidence in geological topics, brought science, politics and the general public closer together, and stabilized the established institutions.

Transfer level 3 – economy

Instrument: tourism

Geotourism is built on the foundations of information, education, science and research, and the general aim of the trail itineraries – e.g. 'Getting to know the beauty and richness of the landscape through, for example, hiking' (Frey, 2000).

An important objective in tourism is to adapt flexibly to the desires and needs of guests. Their satisfaction and positive feedback leads to more than just an image boost. Guests will tend to spend their money in places where they feel contented.

A personal approach is highly regarded by guests, and specially trained geopark guides or geopark rangers are excellent instruments for communicating geological topics. The inclusion of the geopark guide's personality and the requirement to make the whole group actively participate are important factors for successfully communicating geological themes to the public. In addition to this, providing a touristic programme adapted to the needs of the visitor is of great importance.

Establishing tourist routes of between one and four days in the Geopark Gerolstein has led to the creation of standardized short tours for guests. Since the opening of Route 1 in 1994, the acceptance of the geological excursion programme along the trail has been high. The later routes and the associated half-day tour programmes have also been widely accepted, with a number of them starting at hotels and inns.

Modern society has increased the need in people to experience authenticity of rocks and landscape (Opaschowsky, 1989; Grauvogel, 1994). This requires targeted geological and educational processing of the various geological topics and fields, as well as for the tourism industry.

Transfer level 4 – media

Instrument: television, radio, print media
In the modern IT-society, the whole population can be addressed quickly and attractively via television, radio and the press, in that order. This is a task for the tourist organizations. The success of the product depends not only on the contents of touristic programmes and the provision of competent professional and logistic support for the visitor, but also on the personal contact with media representatives, be they journalists, documentary makers or the decision-makers for series contributions and overall concepts. This work proved to be extremely important during the course of the development of Geopark Gerolstein. For example, the number of tourists visiting the region increased two to three days after the broadcast of television reports about the Geopark Gerolstein, which included spectacular images of the Munterley Reef, the Rockeskyller Kopf Volcano Complex and the Maars of Daun, and provided considerable information about these tourist destinations. A three-day hike with the SWR (Südwestrundfunk) Broadcasting Corporation in 2000 not only attracted approximately 600 guests, but also had the effect that many of these guests subsequently extended their stay in the region.

Continuous public relations, professionally handled for the Geopark Gerolstein and the Natural History Museum Gerolstein by the local and national tourist organizations, are the basis for public awareness among the population. This task requires full-time staff and long-term financial assurance. Maintaining contacts with media representatives is an important investment for future projects.

Transfer level 5 – society

Instrument: geological heritage
At first glance, it may seem that the protection, safeguarding and evaluation of the geological heritage is at odds with the aspiration of a region to achieve

sustainable development of tourism. Geoscientists are also unused to facing a known area of conflict, namely the securing of raw materials, as a positive means for communicating geological knowledge and topics. However, it is often overlooked that there still remains a close relationship between the population and 'their' landscape; people do not want their own landscape-shaping activities, carried out to maintain modern living, to been seen in a negative light. There is a desire to experience this landscape in an intact state, and safeguarding the landscape (and therefore the home of the population) is of major importance. The general public know that they are responsible for protecting and safeguarding their 'home'. Positive development begins when this responsibility is linked to positive economic outcomes. Because of the changing economic structures that this development entails, the level of acceptance for protecting the regional geological natural heritage is relatively high among the general public. In this process, geological knowledge is conveyed not only on a rational but also on an emotional level. The dissemination of geological knowledge creates a new awareness or a new geological identity, or reactivates subconscious feelings. People can actively shape their landscape again, protect and learn about it. A new form of regional pride is born, which enables the public to identify themselves with their unique landscape.

Case study 6.1 describes the educational programmes of the Geopark Gerolstein.

Case study 6.1: Education in the Gerolstein and Vulkaneifel geoparks

One of the objectives of these geoparks is to establish long-term job perspectives for professional, dedicated people as conveyors of geological knowledge – the so-called 'Geopark Rangers'. Although the persons concerned do not have a formal degree in geological science, their training must lead to professional, highly motivated guides. The training seminars consist of various modules, including:

1. General and applied geology
2. Geological methods
3. Geology-related communication tools
4. Geological natural heritage and geotourism.

All content is based on the current situation, and the objective of the course is not primarily concerned with imparting details and specialist knowledge. Instead it is to introduce the participants to the world of geosciences as a whole, as well as to the basic landscape phenomena and the processes of landscape evolution and modification. Participants are expected to learn to visualize in three dimensions, as well as in space and time.

Continual, professional support of the guides is important for two reasons: first to make sure that they are up to date with the latest university regional research results, and secondly to comply with the need of the participants to be a part of the geopark developments. This type of training has aroused the interest of the project 'lernEXPERT', Learning in the 3rd Life, of the Federal Ministry of Education (Berlin).

Collaboration with teachers and schools

In collaboration with the Daun District Pedagogic Centre, the Geopark Gerolstein prepares educational courses in the form of half-day and full-day geological excursions. This cooperation with professional colleagues at the university who are involved in the everyday workings of the Geopark has proven successful. Particular emphasis is placed on the presentation of experiments for explaining geological phenomena and processes. In addition to this, the introduction and explanation of the current scientific views plays an important role. The combination of a visit to geopark locations and the presentation of the latest regional research results, as well as the introduction to useful experiments for the classroom, has a very high resonance among the participants.

In response to a request by the Gerolstein Elementary School, Geopark Gerolstein carried out project days on 'The Gerolstein Reef' and 'Volcanism'. The geopark philosophy excludes programmes such as collecting fossils as a means to 'promote physical activities', which poses a challenge in how to prepare geological topics for children in a different way. For example, in a project carried out in 2003, children were encouraged to keep an event diary of geological issues combined with geological card games. In half-day units spread over a period of three days, various topics were explained through drawing, colouring and crafts. A combination of such programmes with hiking tours is especially effective, since this age group is extremely keen on 'discovering'. Both approaches have resulted in new elements for touristic children's programmes.

The Vulkaneifel family – innovative experience with educational toys

There is no doubt that children are important in spreading information and promoting a region. The examples mentioned above and the touristic work have revealed a need for child-appropriate 'entry level' elements in Earth matters, since at their stage they hardly exist. As a rule, adults determine what children should like. Consequently, children will set other priorities. They enjoy playing with rocks and splashing about in water. Water and rocks, together with time, are central geological topics. Today time is scarce, even for children, which makes it even more important to provide them with the opportunity for getting to know their Earth and the natural world that surrounds them. This should occur as early as possible, since an understanding of the earth is existential for all people.

One way of introducing kindergarten children to Earth-related topics is through the development of an appropriate family of characters, such as the 'Vulkaneifel family'. This approach is based on observations of the region called the Vulkaneifel, a region famous for its volcanoes. There are many stories involving the Dauner Maars (low craters formed by explosive eruptions) known colloquially as the 'eyes of the Eifel' (Figure 6.3). The positive image associated with the name 'Vulkaneifel' made it an ideal name for a popular figure, and thus a key task was to make the name 'child friendly'. The children of today like dolls and figures that go on expeditions and experience adventures, and this can be used to develop a system for familiarizing children with geological topics. The following objectives must be taken into account:

1. A regional geo-family name, which creates an identity and presents a family relationship to the geological world

Figure 6.3 Geopark Vulkaneifel – Maar volcano craters, known colloquially as the 'eyes of the Eifel'.

2. Promotion of awareness of the time spans involved in landscape development
3. Selection of regionally typical and important geological phenomena and processes that represent geological topics and can be simply translated into images and figures
4. Use of a geological relevant surname and a regionally typical first name

5. Choice of a central figure as a popular representative of the whole family
6. Copyright protection of the illustration of figures
7. Creation of adventurous stories about geological topics and processes involving the figures
8. Stories that communicate information about the selected and suitably adapted geological topics both correctly and in a child-appropriate manner
9. Use of the figures in geological games, such as Memory and geo-card games, where illustrations of the figures help to increase the acceptance of geological topics.

The Vulkaneifel family, with Willi Basalt as the central figure, has existed in the Geopark Gerolstein since 1994 (Frey, 1995; Figure 6.4a). This character and the Vulkaneifel family were officially launched in the spring of 1996. The trade label is protected by patent laws. To date, eight members of the Vulkaneifel family have been developed, their names being ordered according to the geological areas and the existing geological phenomena (Table 6.1).

The figure of Willi Basalt can be used for the indirect transfer of geological topics. The body of the figure is the typical polygonal cooling structure of basalt rocks, and the head symbolizes a piece of limestone. This can be explained logically, because as magma ascends it can transport fragments of the country rock upwards. This has happened to Willi Basalt. Since the ascent of magma in the Western Eifel was very fast, the arms of the figure are metallic green and represent olivine crystals. The four fingers indicate that there was not enough time during the rapid ascent for crystal growth. In order to integrate the figure into modern life, sneakers were chosen as the most suitable footwear. The figure is involved in a story called *Willi Basalt and the World of Mineral Water* (Frey, 1995), with cut-out figures for children. There is also a book containing illustrations of the whole family, for colouring and drawing by numbers.

The response to the Vulkaneifel family has been positive with both adults and children. Continuous public relations work and the association of nature tour offers for children with the figure, as in the 'Willi Basalt tour', or 'On our way with Willi Basalt' have led to a high degree of identification of the population with the character. The future task and perspective is to increase the awareness and understanding of the figure and his family members so that children can take part in their 'geo-world'.

Socio-economic results: Gerolstein Geopark and Vulkaneifel Geopark

The socio-economic success of geotouristic projects is founded in their acceptance among the population and the associated life of the projects or philosophies. The geopark philosophy is the perception, protection, stewardship, sustainable development and evaluation of the geological heritage. The success of this philosophy requires the cooperation of local and regional authorities, and of the communities and involved actors from business and science. From the scientific standpoint, the integration of the European and global level is viewed as a challenge and an additional opportunity for assuring the future.

Figure 6.4a Willi Basalt – a geotourism product used in the interpretation of geological features and/or phenomena for children.

Figure 6.4b An example of a geotour location: Giant's Causeway, Northern Ireland (photograph courtesy of Patrick Mc Keever).

Target-group adapted field trips – geotouristic products

The field trips on offer in the Gerolstein and the Vulkaneifel geoparks have achieved a high acceptance among visitors. Between 1993 and 2003, approximately 30 000 adult visitors booked geo-tours along Route 1 of the Geopark

Table 6.1   Geological members of the Vulkaneifel family

Era	Geological name of family member
Palaeozoic	*Oscar Dolomit* (rock type of the Gerolstein Limestone Basin) *Anna Sandalina* (Palaeozoic coral) *Rudolpho Phacops* (Trilobite)
Mesozoic	*Hansi Sandstein* (red bunter sandstone) *Frank Eisenstein* (iron ore)
Cenozoic	*Willi Basalt* (typical volcanic rock) *Gabi Pyroxen* (mineral in basalts) *Lisa Maar* (important type of volcano in the Vulkaneifel)

Gerolstein. Taking into account all 15 facilities, this means that the geopark guides have guided at least 300 000 persons through the Vulkaneifel in 10 years. Route 1 is therefore the 'star' of the Geopark. Group bookings are evenly distributed in the time between April and October. Since the opening of the Geopark Route 1 in 1994, about 100 groups have booked a guided geological tour per year. Similar numbers are recorded for the other Vulkaneifel facilities. Most groups come from the direct vicinity of the Geopark, up to 100 km away. Thus, the philosophy of the Geopark is to sustainably shape its future.

Analysis of the age groups of tourists visiting the Geopark indicates that there is no evidence of a group specialization having developed over its 10-year existence. In the beginning, the impression was that the main users were only primary-school classes and adult groups. However, over the years it has also attracted classes from secondary, comprehensive and junior high schools, as well as vocational schools. The advantage of Route 1 is that a tour can be linked to a visit to another tourist attraction – the Fortress Kasselburg, which contains an eagle and wolf park. This combination of the two offers constitutes a satisfying day trip for the visitor.

All geo-facilities of the Vulkaneifel offer geo-excursions for interested guests. In 1994, the tourist organization began publishing a joint geo-programme containing all regular geo-activities provided by the various geo-facilities. The scheduling of the geo-activities is such that guests may participate in a different geo-activity on each day of their stay in the Vulkaneifel. This arrangement of activities was developed and realized by the touristic decision-makers. Over the years, various programmes have been provided for different visitor groups. These events include geo-tours along geopark routes or geo-trails, special interest offers, geological seminars, geo-weekends, geology talks, 'Geo on a bike' and 'Geo for kids'.

The number of geo-excursions in the Vulkaneifel is high, and every weekday a different geo-facility has a geo-tour on offer. Two or three geo-talks are held in each facility per year, but in view of the high costs involved, special interest offers for hobby geologists are no longer organized. Dedicated geopark guides accompany each activity, and there has also been an increase in the number of specialist tours.

Tourism marketing and Vulkaneifel image wins

The publication of the geo-magazine *GeoLife Vulkaneifel* (recently changed to the *Vulkaneifel Magazine*) replaced the numerous flyers that existed before the year 2000. The magazine, available in German and Dutch, contains information about regionally relevant topics, a schedule of geo-excursions for booking purposes, and lists of available souvenirs. Between 2001 and 2004, the distribution of the magazine varied between 30 000 and 50 000.

Geopark souvenirs (such as notepads with geological motifs, postcard sets or replicas of trilobites from Gerolstein) have been developed together with local companies, and form an important economic contribution. Further developments include the production of candles with geological motifs, Willi Basalt dolls, and Vulkaneifel family colouring books. Involving companies from the Eifel region in the creation of these products has proved to be a positive strategy, which has already caused other companies to think along new lines.

From the professional and political points of view, the founding of the Geo and Nature Park Company Vulkaneifel Geopark GmbH (Ltd) in 2004 is another step in the sustainable development of the Geopark. Before this event, the political committees had begun with the national marketing and standardization of the guest services through information, guidance and assistance by founding the Eifel Tourismus GmbH (Ltd) in Prüm in 2002. The continual close cooperation between these two companies is the basis for a further positive development of this region.

Innovative geotourism project examples in Vulkaneifel, and European collaboration

Long-term project work with various cooperative partners and the presentation and information exchange on a professional level has led to a growing acceptance of geotourism in Germany among geoscientists since 1998. However, this does not impact much at the regional level. Here, the prime interest lies in the direct effectiveness of the investments, which is reflected in the number of guests or the earnings. Thus, effectiveness depends on the geo-products, the demand, positive resonance and acceptance. Over a fifteen-year period, a large number of investments were made in the region's infrastructure, museums, geo-trails and geo-routes. The institution of the geo-facilities resulted in increased support for additional activities in order to foster their effectiveness. This is apparent in the production of 'software', meaning tourist-relevant products. These not only include geo-excursion products but also the sale of print media etc. The demand for souvenirs by the guests and the realization that the selection of typical souvenirs is very limited led to the development of new geo-touristic approaches in cooperation with EU partners in EU supported projects (Eschghi and Frey, 1998). The projects in the Vulkangarten Steffeln provide an example (Eschghi, 1999; Pickel *et al.*, 2001).

The Vulkangarten Steffeln was created as a measure for revitalizing the former lava quarries near the Steffelnkopf volcano. The state authorities coordinated the project as a model for the follow-up use as a geo-touristic facility (Frey and Büchel, 2000). As a result, a centre was built in 2000 from which vantage point visitors can view the West Eifel volcano fields. It attracts 6000 visitors annually, and has had a significant impact on the village of Steffeln. The capacity of the existing hotel has been increased and the small shop, which was about to close down, is still in existence. The village community identifies itself with the Vulkangarten, and the centre is now operated by a local group of the Eifel Association in Steffeln.

Apart from these visible results, there have also been important image wins. These include a boost to the image, development of geological consciousness (or geo-identity), acceptance among the general public, and international recognition through cooperation with neighbouring European regions. The successful completion of the regional and European community project 'Development of Geo-tourism in Europe' resulted in the production of the *GeoLife Vulkaneifel* magazine and geo-souvenirs from the Vulkaneifel, as well as the creation of the European Geoparks Network and the establishment of the qualifying trade label 'European Geoparks'.

Continuation of European cooperation has allowed the Volcano House in Strohn to take the first steps, in 2003, towards twinning with the Irish partner community Bunmahon in the Coppercoast Geopark.

The European Geoparks Network

The development of networks is an innovative concept that goes beyond local boundaries. In this case it is the European Geoparks Network, which was created by the Geopark Gerolstein and the Vulkaneifel Geopark in cooperation with neighbouring European regions in France (Réserve Géologique de Haute Provence, Digne les Bains), Greece (Petrified Forest Lesvos, Sigri) and Spain (Parque Cultural del Maestrazgo-Terruel) (Frey and Bauer, 2001). These are the founders of the European Geoparks Network, and are the owners of the trade label 'European Geoparks', which has been officially registered as a trade name. The first project aimed at building the Network was begun in 1998, and was initiated by the French partner in the Réserve Géologique de Haute Provence. This cooperation began in the form of a pilot study carried out in the LEADER programme of the European Union. As a direct result of the project, the founding regions achieved the qualification of the network regions as 'European Geoparks' supported by UNESCO (Anonymous, 2001a). The organizational units of the network are the Advisory Committee, the Coordination Committee (which has the authority to make decisions) and the administrative Cellule de Coordination. The European Geoparks Network has two coordinators, which have equal representation on the Network.

A wide range of instruments is utilized by the Network. These include a charter, accepted by all Network members, which defines the criteria and requirements of the geological heritage philosophy. There are also two symposia per year for aligning and realizing common project work, as well as an annual convention for exchanging current developments (Zouros *et al.*, 2003). The Network also has an Internet presence for informing members and cooperating with and admitting interested, high-quality regions. It also displays promotional materials (stickers etc.) and retail products (e.g. a four-region notepad with geological motifs, a geo-postcard set with motifs from four regions, etc.). In 2004, the Network comprised twenty-three regions from nine nations.

The German and European-wide cooperation between geoscience and tourism has produced positive results for the geoscientists and established a range of requirements and perspectives. All geoscientists and politicians as well as tourism specialists are involved in implementing these. The future of geological knowledge transfer to the general public has begun and has achieved far more than many geoscientists initially had hoped for. Change, movement, continuous innovation and communication with other actors are of the essence! Forge ahead, having in mind that Planet Earth is not dead – and follow Gallileo's words: 'Yet it moves!' The insight of this policy is evident in the Global Network of Geoparks, set up by the UNESCO Division of Earth Sciences in February 2004. The technical aspects and fundamentals of this development are described in the following section.

The UNESCO Global Network of Geoparks

To disseminate globally the local experience gathered in the Gerolstein and Vulkaneifel geoparks, the United Nations Educational, Scientific and Cultural Organization (UNESCO) is currently establishing an international network of geoparks to promote territories around the world which integrate significant examples of the Earth's geological heritage in a strategy for regional economic development. Geoparks in this network are defined as territories where the geological heritage of the Earth is safeguarded and sustainably managed.

Geoparks:

1. Educate and teach the broad public about issues in geology and environmental matters (education)
2. Provide a tool to ensure sustainable development (tourism)
3. Preserve geological heritage for future generations (conservation).

The Global Network of Geoparks assisted by UNESCO

In response to the decision of UNESCO's Executive Board in June 2001 (Anonymous, 2001b) and in harmony with the recommendation of an International Group of Experts, as well as of the Scientific Board of the International Geoscience Programme (IGCP) at its 29th session in February 2001, the Division of Earth Sciences of UNESCO was invited to pursue the general objective 'Education in Earth Sciences' by promoting geoparks as multidisciplinary activities, providing UNESCO's assistance to national initiatives. UNESCO's involvement in the geopark concept was considered crucial in raising public awareness for geological heritage issues, achieving the fullest international recognition, and having an effective political impact.

Together with an International Advisory Group for Geoparks (consisting of geoscientists representing governmental and non-governmental organizations from the Americas, Africa, Asia/Oceania and Europe, as well as the International Geoscience Programme (IGCP), International Union of Geological Sciences (IUGS) and International Geographical Union (IGU)), UNESCO has developed Operational Guidelines (Anonymous, 2004) to provide directing principles for National Geoparks requesting to be included in the international Network.

A geopark seeking UNESCO's assistance is a territory with well-defined limits that has a large enough surface area for it to serve local economic development. It comprises a certain number of geological heritage sites (on any scale), or a mosaic of geological entities of special scientific importance, rarity or beauty, representative of an area and its geological history, events or processes. It may not solely be of geological significance but also of ecological, archaeological, historical or cultural value. A National Geopark is run by a designated authority with an adequate management infrastructure, which adopts its own territorial policy for sustainable regional socio-economic development. This has a direct impact on the area involved by improving human living conditions and the rural environment, thus strengthening identification of the population with their area and triggering cultural renaissance. Respectful of the environment, it shall stimulate, for example, the creation of innovative local enterprises, small business, cottage industries and new jobs by generating new sources of revenue (e.g. geotourism, geoproducts). This should provide a supplementary income for the local population and attract private capital. It also serves as a pedagogical tool for environmental education, training and interdisciplinary research related to geoscientific disciplines, broader environmental issues and sustainable development.

An international meeting was held at the UNESCO headquarters in Paris on 13 February 2004, where the final version of the *Operational Guidelines for National Geoparks seeking UNESCO's Assistance* (Anonymous, 2004) and recommendations were presented. A Global Network of Geoparks assisted by UNESCO was established, and the aim of this Network is to provide a platform of cooperation and exchange between experts and practitioners in geological heritage matters under the umbrella of UNESCO. The Network spans all regions of the world, and shall bring together groups that share common values, interests, or backgrounds. The Global Network shall serve to develop models of best practice and set standards for territories, which integrate the preservation of geological heritage in a strategy for regional economic development. Thirty-three National Geoparks were evaluated and are now members of the Global Network of Geoparks assisted by UNESCO (Table 6.2).

Throughout the years, and previous to the current UNESCO Network, the Division of Earth Sciences has established close links with the European Geoparks Network. Both work on the same guiding principles, although UNESCO offers its sponsorship to interested territories of Member States at the global level whereas the European Geoparks Network builds up a network of European Member regions. Following assessment, regions that are part of the European Geoparks Network will become part of the Global Geoparks Network.

Table 6.2 Global geoparks

Country	Geopark
PR China	Mount Lushan
PR China	Wudalianchi
PR China	Songshan
PR China	Yuntaishan
PR China	Danxiashan
PR China	Stone Forest – Shilin
PR China	Zhangjiajie Sandstone Peak Forest
PR China	Huangshan
PR China	Xingwen National Geopark
PR China	Hexigten National Geopark
PR China	Yandangshan National Geopark
PR China	Taining National Geopark
Ireland	Copper Coast European Geopark
Northern Ireland	Marble Arch Caves and Cuilcagh Mountain Park
Scotland	North West Highlands
Germany	Naturpark Terravita European Geopark
Germany	European Geopark Bergstrasse-Odenwald
Germany	Vulkaneifel European Geopark
Germany	Geopark Swabian Albs
Germany	Geopark Harz Braunschweiger Land Ostfalen
Germany	Mecklenburg Ice Age Park
Greece	Psiloritis Natural Park
Greece	Petrified Forest of Lesvos
Germany	Vulkaneifel European Geopark
United Kingdom	Abberley and Malvern Hills Geopark
United Kingdom	North Pennines AONB Geopark
France	Réserve Géologique de Haute Provence
France	Astroblème Châtaigneraie Limousine
France	Park Naturel Régional du Luberon
Italy	Madonie Natural Park
Italy	Rocca di Cerere Cultural Park
Austria	Nature Park Eisenwurzen
Austria	Kamptal Geopark
Spain	Maestrazgo Cultural Park

Conclusions

The practical experience gathered locally through years of innovative work and the successful cooperation between geosciences, local and regional community management, tourism agencies and the involvement of the local population must be made available to all. This should be done while taking into account and respecting the local situation regarding the political and management structures, traditions and culture of each country concerned. The acceptance and mutual cooperation of the geoparks concept has now begun, following the guidelines drafted by UNESCO. This has occurred despite the persistence of minor differences between the activities undertaken (e.g. concerning the question on collection/selling of fossils). A further long-term objective will be to stimulate the formation of regional networks on all continents, such as Africa or Asia, for local activities and to reach out to local politicians. Africa is a very important target area for geological heritage, and has enormous potential for sustainable economic development.

The history of Earth is inscribed in its landscapes and in the rocks beneath our feet. Only here can we trace the cycles of change and renewal that have shaped the Earth in the past and will continue to do so in the future. Too easily, we forget that the geological history of the Earth; its rocks, minerals, fossils and landforms are not only an integral part of our natural world, but are also inextricably linked to the evolution of life, cultural development itself and the ascent of humanity.

As a fundamental part of the natural world, geology and landscape have had a profound influence on society, civilization, and cultural diversity, especially in regard to the formation and location of mineral and energy resources, without which modern societies could not function. Our use of land for agriculture, forestry, mining, quarrying and for building homes and cities is intimately related to the underlying rocks, soils and landforms.

This record of the Earth's history is surprisingly fragile. It must be conserved so that future generations can enjoy it and improve our understanding for the benefit of the planet and humanity. We should strive to conserve this geological heritage because it is of scientific, cultural and aesthetic significance, as well as having potential for economic development. The safeguarding of the Earth's diversity must go hand-in-hand with respect for the cultural diversity that has arisen over time.

The establishment of geoparks should be based on a strong concept, political will with financial long-term support, and professional management structures. All of these are demonstrated through the two German examples. Although rather small and rural, those regions have an enormous potential for sustainable development, which is inextricably linked with the preservation of our environment. The examples illustrate how local action generates feedback which can lead to global action.

Acknowledgements

We would like to express our special gratitude to all participating institutions and persons mentioned in this chapter. Cooperation between groups with different mind-sets, such as tourism, science and economy, requires openness, understanding, constructive criticism, compromise and the willingness to change. Our special thanks go to Klaus Schäfer for his patience, understanding, constructive contributions in discussions and support for the 'geo-thing'. We would also like to thank Professor Georg Büchel for his commitment to bringing 'geological public relations' into the university. The first three authors wish also to thank our co-author, Dr Margarete Patzak, for the professional support given to us by the UNESCO, Division of Earth Sciences.

References

Anonymous (2001a). *European Geoparks Network Magazine*, Issue 1.
Anonymous (2001b). *161 EX/Decisions, 3.3.1*. Executive Board, in June 2001, UNESCO.

Anonymous (2004). *Operational Guidelines for National Geoparks seeking UNESCO's Assistance.* UNESCO.

Baumgart, K. (1997). Die touristische Inwertsetzung von Lehrpfaden aufgezeigt am Beispiel des Geoparks in der VG Gerolstein. Unpublished thesis, Trier University.

Bell, W. and Koziol, M. (2000). Das Maarmuseum in Manderscheid. *Die Eifel*, 95(1), 15–18.

Brauers, J. (1993). *Die Geo-Route Manderscheid.* VG Manderscheid.

Eschghi, I. (1999) *Geo-Infoband Vulkaneifel.* Geo-Zentrum Vulkaneifel und Landkreis Daun.

Eschghi, I. and Frey, M.-L. (1998). Projekte der Landschaftsinterpretation in der Vulkaneifel. *Die Eifel*, 93(3), 141–142.

Frey, M.-L. (1993), Der 'Geo-Park' in der Verbandsgmeinde Gerolstein: Planung und Realisierung. *Die Schöne Eifel, Gerolstein.* Eifelverein, pp. 106–113.

Frey, M.-L. (1995). *Willi Basalt in der Welt des Sprudelwassers – Eine GEO-Park Geschichte*, Issue 1. VG Gerolstein, p. 9.

Frey, M.-L. (1998). Geologie – Geo-Tourismus – Umweltbildung: Themen und Tätigkeitsbereiche im Spannungsfeld Ökonomie und Nachhaltige Entwicklung. *Terra Nostra, Schriften der Alfred-Wegener Stiftung, 98/3, 150 Jahre Dt. Geol. Ges., 06.-09.10.1998, Technical University Berlin.* Programme and Summary of the Meeting Contributions, Technical University Berlin.

Frey, M.-L. (2000). Geotourism, a new perspective for public awareness on geology: Case study Geo-Park Gerolstein & Geo-Centre Vulkaneifel, Germany. *3rd International Geoscience Education Conference, Sydney* (Abstract), pp. 156-157.

Frey, M.-L. and Bauer, A. (2001). European Geoparks, Geowissen, Tourismus, Ökonomie und nachhaltige Entwicklung. *LEADER Forum*, 1, 10–11.

Frey, M.-L. and Büchel, G. (2000). Nachhaltige Nutzung – Inwertsetzung vulkanischer Zeugnisse in der Westeifel vor den Aspekten Landschaftsschutz, Abbaugeschichte, Rekultivierung, vulkanologische Diversität und geotouristische Inwertsetzung am Beispiel des Vulkangarten Steffeln. *1. Int. Maar Conf., Daun, Vulkaneifel, Germany, Terra Nostra*, (6), 196.

Frey, M.-L., Schäfer, K. and Büchel, G. (2002). Geowissenschaftliche Öffentlichkeitsarbeit – eine Option für die Zukunft. *Scriptum*, 9, 17–37.

Grauvogel, B. (1994). Tourismuspädagogik. *Trier Tourismus Bibliographien*, 5, 1–150.

Heer, A. (1998). Pädagogische und geologische Grundlagen zur Durchführung eines endo-/exogendynamsich und regionalgeologisch fundierten Geologieunterrichts in der Gegend von Aachen. Unpublished thesis, RWTH Aachen, Geological Institute.

Hesse, G. (2002). Hydrogeologische Erkundung von Maar-Diatrem-Vulkanen am Beispiel des Geeser Maares (Westeifel). Dissertation, Friedrich-Schiller-University of Jena, Chem.-Geowiss. Fak.

Jaspers, K. (2002). Das Paläozoikum zwischen Büdesheim und Duppach (Eifel). Unpublished mapping project, RWTH Aachen, Geological Institute.

Kasig, W. (1993). Der Eifel-Geo-Pfad zwischen Aachen und Daun als Beispiel geologischer Öffentlichkeitsarbeit. *Eifeljahrbuch.* Eiferverein, pp. 57–69.

Kasig, W., Eschghi, I. and Laschet, C. (1989). *Begleitheft zum Geo-Pfad Hillesheim.* Verbandsgemeinde Hillesheim.

Klinkenberg, M. (2002). Das Paläozoikum zwischen Gerolstein und Büdesheim (Eifel). Unpublished mapping project, RWTH Aachen, Geological Institute.

Körnig, N. (1997). Konzeptioneller Ansatz zur Neugestaltung von Museen im ländlichen Raum am Beispiel ausgewählte Museen im Fremdenverkehrsgebiet 'Gerolsteiner Land'. Unpublished thesis, Fachhochschule Kempten-Neu Ulm, Hochschule f. Technik & Wirtschaft.

Opaschowsky, H. W. (1989). *Tourismusforschung – Freizeit- und Tourismusstudien* (3). Leske & Büdrich.

Pickel, W., Frey, M.-L., Hennig, M. and Schäfer, K. (2001). *Erlebnistipps Vulkaneifel – z.B. Auf den Spuren des Eisens.* Publ. Verkehrsverein Oberes Kylltal.

Witt, K. (1996). Geochemische Untersuchungen der Gesteine, Böden und Wässer ausgewählter Bereiche der Gerolsteiner Mulde, Westeifel, Deutschland. Unpublished thesis, RWTH Aachen, Inst. f. Mineralogie und Lagerstättenkunde.

Zine, N. (1993). Die Geologie des Gebietes zwischen Gerolstein, Hinterhausen, Müllenborn und Niederbettingen auf Blatt 5705 Gerolstein. Unpublished mapping project, RWTH Aachen, Geologisches Institut.

Zouros, N. K., Martini, G. and Frey, M.-L. (2003). 2nd European Geoparks Network Meeting. *Proceed. International Symposium Geological Heritage Protection and Local Development, 3–7.10.2003, Lesvos Island, Greece.* Lithografia.

7

Geotourism: a perspective from southwest Germany

Christof Pforr and
Andreas Megerle

Introduction

The aim of this chapter is to provide a brief overview of the development of geotourism in southwest Germany, focusing in particular on the Swabian Alb, which represents an ideal geotourism destination. In this context geotourism is understood as being more than just geological tourism (e.g. fossicking or visiting caves), and embraces the identification of geo-objects, landscape marketing and interpretation of the geological heritage of a region in a sustainable manner. Collaboration, coordination, effective communication and transfer of know-how are hereby discussed as important mechanisms to achieve sustainable outcomes. The Network History of the Earth (*Netzwerk Erdgeschichte*) is presented as a successful example of regional collaboration to promote sustainable geotourism.

Sustainable geotourism

Geotourism is an expression of a growing trend to experience the natural and cultural landscape in contrast to the common urbanized lifestyle – a contemporary phenomenon that has become evident worldwide since the late 1980s. This appreciation of nature and heritage is fast becoming a new impulse generator for the tourism industry. In recent years geotourism has therefore developed into a very appealing concept, attracting a variety of people with diverse interests – particularly from the tourism industry, but also governments as well as environmental and conservation groups (see, for example, Megerle, 1999; Megerle and Pauls, 2003). The increasing demand for 'geo' has led to the development of geotourism attractions based on geological formations such as caves, volcanic craters, thermal springs, karstification and waterfalls. These resources, transformed into geotourism products, have made many regions unique geotourism destinations. They attract increasing numbers of tourists, with the consequence that in some areas geotourism has already been described as a mass phenomenon (TIA, 2003) – in particular where the term is only understood as yet another market segment, but there is also general agreement that geotourism poses an enormous potential for many regions.

Since the mid-1990s geotourism has been increasingly debated by the tourism industry, politicians, conservationists, geographers, geologists and academics alike (Clement, 2003; Frey, 2003; Granitzki and Buddenbohm, 2003; Megerle and Pauls, 2003; Zellmer and Röber, 2003). Very little has, however, been written about the promotion of the landscape as a tourism product with a specific emphasis on geo-objects and their socio-cultural, economic and ecological contexts. In fact, only a few studies have been devoted to geotourism as an important mechanism for geo-conservation and sustainable development (Patzak, 2000; Megerle and Megerle, 2002; Buckley, 2003; Kraus, 2003). As geotourism is complex and multidimensional, there is no generally accepted agreement about its conceptual and practical boundaries and a definitional approach appears problematic. Multiple stakeholders with sometimes conflicting interests make geotourism not only an academic and technical discourse but also, and more so, a socio-political question, which is influenced by its specific regional and local context.

The tourism industry regards geotourism as a new, growing market segment with a prosperous future, particularly so in the light of the ever-increasing demand by tourists around the world for the ultimate nature experience. A recent large-scale study conducted by the Travel Industry Association of America (TIA) and *National Geographic Traveler Magazine*, for instance, explored the current standing and future potential of the geotourism market in the USA. It claimed that 55 million Americans can be classified as geotourists, and that nearly 100 million more are prepared to support this new market segment with their travel dollars (Schiller, 2002; TIA, 2003).

With clever marketing strategies the tourism industry therefore promotes 'geo' to capitalize on this new trend. The growing economic significance of geotourism can, however, make it tempting to ignore any potential negative ecological and socio-cultural impacts. There is, for instance, the danger of overuse of the often rather fragile ecosystems on which the geotourism experience relies. Although geotourism offers great opportunities for economic development, in particular for many regional and remote areas, it should therefore not be understood narrowly as a new tourism product or niche market only.

Its potential as a job and income generator, particularly for local communities and therefore as an effective means of regional development, has seen geotourism also being strongly pushed by governments through the development of policies and strategies (e.g. BMBF, 2001, 2002; Weber and Eckhardt, 2003). Too often, however, governments in partnership with the industry adopt only a narrow product-centred perspective, without accepting geotourism as a mechanism to contribute to a more sustainable approach to tourism development in natural areas. Some governments have taken a different direction by adopting a more inclusive approach, reaching out to other relevant stakeholders and not only the industry. Such an initiative is, for instance, evident in the 'Year of the Geosciences', proclaimed by the German Government in 2002. As part of an intensive dialogue on geoscience issues involving all parts of society, geotourism was promoted for its potential to contribute to a more sustainable use of resources. This Science in Dialogue, under the umbrella of the German Ministry for Education and Research, (Bundesministerium für Bildung und Forschung) offered a variety of events, such as geoscience exhibitions, lectures and fieldtrips, and also led to the establishment of four National Geoparks (BMBF, 2001, 2002; Granitzki and Buddenbohm, 2003; Megerle and Pauls, 2003; Weber and Eckhardt, 2003; Zellmer and Röber, 2003). The initiative was well received by the general public and has highlighted the enormous interest in and awareness of geoscience issues, which needs to be met with appropriate information and education. Geotourism plays a crucial role in this context, as it provides an opportunity to experience geology while at the same time contributing to geoconservation by facilitating a more sustainable use of resources through usage and knowledge.

This approach is congruent with the view of many environmentalists and conservationists who advocate geotourism as a vehicle to promote conservation and a sustainable management regime. They hope that this idea of protection through usage will generally lead to more sustainable outcomes and an increase in ecological and socio-cultural awareness and behaviour. Thus, the symbiotic relationship between tourism and geoconservation and its potential to contribute to the sustainable development of a region is recognized (see, for example, Reimold, 1999; Patzak, 2000; Megerle and Megerle, 2002).

Considering all these diverse approaches to geotourism, it is not surprising that some discrepancy over its objectives exists. A definition is always a matter of perspective, interests and values, which ultimately leads to distinct and often conflicting perceptions of a complex and dynamic concept such as geotourism. With the academic discussion becoming increasingly refined, a prevalent understanding of geotourism has emerged as the intersection of nature-based tourism focusing on geo-objects and sustainable tourism (Buckley, 2003; Lang, 2003). The term 'geotourism' is therefore often promoted as a much broader concept – not only as a new market segment, but also as a normative direction contributing to geoconservation and sustainable development. In this context geotourism therefore cannot simply be used synonymously with geological tourism, as it embraces the values of sustainability. Hence geotourism should be consistent with the principles of sustainable development, balancing economic, ecological and social aspects as an integrated whole. Megerle and Megerle (2002), for instance, suggest that geotourism should be viewed as part of a holistic management approach to the broad field of geological and landscape history, including its interconnected-ness with flora and fauna, the cultivated landscape, and present land use. Sustainability and environmental education are seen as integral parts.

The debate about definitions and how the concept of geotourism can be translated into the real world remains often highly technical and academic, neglecting the consideration of values and interests of the various stakeholders involved. In the search for compromise, the struggle of who gets what, when, where, how and why (Lasswell, 1936), they determine the interpretation and implementation of geotourism. Consequently, to ignore these interactions and power arrangements would mean to omit a highly political phenomenon – a process that governs how the concept of geotourism is defined and translated into action or non-action.

Collaboration – coordination – information exchange

A socio-political goal like sustainability facilitated through the development of geotourism relies on the support and commitment of all affected parties. This entails a process of transparent collaboration involving all relevant stakeholders, particularly from the tourism industry, government and the community. To make geotourism a sustainable reality, transparent collaboration is an essential component as it will not only create greater acceptance of the consensually established aims and objectives for geotourism but also assist with its implementation in a region.

Collaborative and partnership approaches have been frequently discussed in tourism analysis in recent years (Bramwell and Sharman, 1999; Hall 1999, 2000; Selin, 1999). Bramwell and Lane (1999: 180) argue that 'collaborative arrangements for sustainable tourism are part of the conflict resolution, problem solving and capacity building processes that are central to sustainable development'. The literature on collaborative arrangements is also characterized by a great diversity in its terminology, encompassing everything from coalitions, alliances, task forces and networks to public–private partnerships (Bramwell and Lane, 2000). Here, the term 'collaboration' is used to refer to a mechanism that involves all the relevant stakeholders in dialogue structures and information networks to negotiate a region's future development through consensual agreements on common objectives. This is regarded as an important and powerful tool for sustainability in general and therefore also for the development of geotourism, which contributes to geoconservation and sustainable regional development (Robinson, 1999; Hall, 2000; Megerle and Pauls, 2004a).

Despite the acknowledgement of the benefits of collaborative arrangements in tourism policy and planning, a successful collaboration of all relevant stakeholders is rarely found. 'Perhaps the most startling point in many regions' as Pipkin (1996: 796) remarks, 'is how often people who care about the region's destiny have simply never sat together and talked about where the region was going, what changes they would like to see, or what tools are available to shape the future'. Visiting a geo-object, for instance, might for some be an exercise driven by scientific interest only; to others it might be a welcome business opportunity, and to still others this might ring in the beginning of the end – a sell-out of the natural and cultural heritage of the region. Moreover, geotourism might also be welcomed as an engine for the regional economy and a new employment generator which at the same time is also able to contribute to geoconservation, as the geo-object in question might otherwise be more endangered by an alternative usage.

There are certain problems associated with a collaborative approach, which often result from existing conventional power structures and political processes (Ladkin and Bertramini, 2002). For example, the common business–government alliance can impact negatively on the inclusiveness of network structures. This often neglects stakeholders representing socio-cultural and environmental community interests (Hall, 1999; Jenkins, 2001; Pforr, 2001, 2002, 2004). Selin (1999: 271), in a more critical review, therefore states that 'it will take a concerted effort from many sectors to ensure that current and emerging tourism partnerships contribute to the sustainable future of the field'. The appropriate inclusion of all relevant stakeholders shaping the future direction a region takes forms the basis for consensus and shared decision-making, which in turn leads to a greater legitimacy of political decisions, democratic empowerment as well as equity, and therefore fulfils aspects of the social dimension of sustainability (Hall, 2000). Collaboration is therefore an important mechanism 'for achieving sustainable outcomes and as symbolic of new ways of working' (Robinson, 1999: 393). However, some questions still remain unanswered (Hall, 1999; Jenkins, 2002; Ryan, 2002) – how can the process of consensus-building be organized best? Who is allowed to participate, and who gives that permission? What happens to those who are not allowed to participate? How is the process entrenched in existing political structures? Thus, the debate about collaboration in tourism policy and planning is inherently political and shows the political nature, in particular the distribution of power, involved in shaping the approach to tourism development. Case study 7.1, Network History of the Earth (discussed in more detail later in this chapter) is a good example where, despite some difficulties, a successful partnership between various regional stakeholders has emerged. It also highlights the importance of coordination and the transfer of know-how in such a network structure.

Coordination is another significant element of a collaborative process (Ladkin and Bertramini, 2002). It aims to bring together the core actors to better organize their communication effectively through appropriate structures and processes, encompassing 'the formal institutionalized relationship among existing networks of organizations, interests and/or individuals' (Hall, 2000: 83).

Geotourism mirrors the highly fragmented nature of the tourism system, with its complex network of stakeholders, diverse structures and processes, disjointed and divided competencies and the unclear allocation of responsibilities that warrant the establishment of an effective and efficient coordination regime (Edgell, 1990; Hall, 1994, 1998; Pauls and Megerle, 2002; Pforr, 2004). Since 'there is no other industry in the economy that is linked to so many diverse and different kinds of products and services as is the tourism industry' (Edgell, 1990: 7), a unique coordinating role emerges to oversee and develop opportunities, to provide leadership, to bring relevant stakeholders together, and to plan as well as to enhance the relationships among the key stakeholders from the private and the public sectors (Hall, 2000). Thus coordination is a complex political activity of consensus building (Hall, 2000), and at the same time, can establish important dialogue structures and information networks.

To develop geotourism as a mechanism for sustainable regional development and geo-conservation requires an adequate knowledge base and a sufficient exchange of information and know-how between the relevant stakeholders.

In this context, information is understood broadly to encompass 'monitoring, research, databases and information systems, communication, dissemination and ownership of information describing natural systems and human interactions with them' (Dovers, 1995; 142). In order to achieve sustainable outcomes the expertise and knowledge of the relevant actors from the public and the private sector, community groups and academia are essential, as is their willingness to collaborate (Bramwell and Lane, 1999, 2000; Hall, 2000). Thus, the establishment of communication networks and adequate exchange of this information are important to implement geotourism successfully in the region. Research activities are, furthermore, crucial in the attempt to implement regional sustainable development through geotourism. Communication and collaboration between academic researchers and other stakeholders must therefore be ensured through appropriate coordination efforts. Research outcomes translated into information comprehensible to the general public must be made available to the wider community. This provision of adequate information through geo-education and interpretation programmes can foster greater awareness for the issue of sustainability in general, but also its translation into a regional and local context. Geo-education and training can create a better understanding and acceptance for the changes needed to ensure a more sustainable future in the region.

Nevertheless, the question remains whether this rather academic discourse is reflected in geotourism operations on the ground, and whether the concept is able to overcome the traditional conflict line between economy and ecology and to contribute to a new common ground for the benefit of the entire community.

Geoparks as a suitable framework for geotourism

Geoparks, a fairly recent development focusing in particular on geotopes of regional and national geoscientific importance, can be seen as instruments to coordinate the many stakeholders towards the common purpose of regional sustainable development. In Germany, for instance, four National Geoparks were established in 2002–2003; Nationaler Geopark Schwäbische Alb (Megerle and Pauls, 2003), Nationaler Geopark Mecklenburgische Eiszeitlandschaft (Granitzki and Buddenbohm, 2003), Nationaler Geopark Braunschweiger Land (Zellmer and Röber, 2003), and Nationaler Geopark Bergstrasse-Odenwald (Weber and Eckhardt, 2003). The certification *Nationaler GeoPark*, awarded by the Alfred Wegener Foundation for the Advancement of the Geosciences for a period of five years on behalf of the Federal Ministry of Education and Research (BMBF), does not, however, signify a protected area category. The associated logo, *planeterde – Welt der Geowissenschaften*, has to be seen as a quality label which is linked to three core objectives: environmental protection, sustainable regional development and geo-education (Huth and Junker, 2003; Mattig, 2003). In essence, geoparks aim to foster regional identity, create greater awareness for local conservation issues through geo-education, and act as a framework for regional sustainable development by bringing together a wide range of stakeholders.

This National Geopark movement is also linked to International Geopark initiatives such as the UNESCO Global Network of Geoparks, a Programme which intends to promote a worldwide network of geoparks, as well as the Network of

European Geoparks (Clement, 2003; Huth and Junker, 2003; Mattig, 2003). The latter is a conglomerate of various European geoparks established with the aim of increasing public awareness of geoheritage and geosciences as the foundation for regional sustainable development. This European network initiative, founded in 2001, was initially based on four geoparks in France, Germany, Greece and Spain (Clement, 2003).

All these National and International Geopark networks promote a better understanding of the importance of a sustainable usage of resources. An underlying philosophy common to all these initiatives is the view that geoparks play an important role in creating awareness for the importance of preserving the Earth's natural and cultural geo-heritage. Taking a holistic approach, geoscientific, cultural and socio-economic elements are brought together to achieve sustainable development (Megerle and Megerle, 2002; Mattig, 2003). Thus, the establishment of geoparks makes an important contribution to the aims and objectives of Agenda 21, a plan for action to implement sustainable development agreed upon at the UN Conference on Environment and Development in Rio de Janeiro in 1992. It is argued here that geotourism as a suitable vehicle for regional sustainable development can play a significant role in supporting this process of rethinking development in a regional context. The motto 'protection through usage and education' can lead to a wide range of outcomes, including:

1. Enhanced visitor satisfaction through nature-based experiences by direct interaction with geo-objects as well as geo-heritage interpretation (Figure 7.1)
2. Nature and heritage conservation through sustainable management regimes
3. Socio-economic benefits for the communities in the region by transforming geo-resources into geotourism products.

Figure 7.1 Know-how transfer to Japan: recently trained field guide simulating geo-interpretation work (Network Partner Tuebingen; photograph courtesy of Andreas Megerle).

Geotourism in southwest Germany: the case of the National Geopark Swabian Alb

Southwest Germany is characterized by a distinct and diverse landscape, based on over a billion years of geological history. The area can be subdivided into three main landforms. The first is the Upper Rhine Graben (*Oberrheingraben*) in the west, which is bordered by the Black Forest (*Schwarzwald*) in the east and the Vosges Mountains (*Vogesen*) on the western, French side. The second is the south-western cuesta landscape (*Schichtstufenland*), gently sloping towards the south-east, while the third is the Alpine piedmont (*Alpenvorland*) (Figure 7.2).

The formation of the Alps and the subsequent caving in of the Upper Rhine Graben caused the uplift of the Black Forest as well as a slope in the surface rock, which led to the formation of the cuesta landscape as the main characteristic geological feature. Except for the Cretaceous period, the full stratigraphic sequence is presented as heritage of the southwest's fascinating geo-history of tectonical and erosive forces. Beside this typical cuesta landscape, the geology of southwest Germany offers rich mineral deposits, with evidence of silver, iron and lead mining in the Black Forest (of Roman and, in the north, even Celtic origins), thermal springs (Bad Urach) and remnants of volcanic activity (Kaiserstuhl, Schwäbische Alb, Odenwald). In addition, it has craters caused by meteoroid impacts (Noerdlinger Ries, Steinheimer Becken), and fossil-bearing deposits (*Holzmaden, Dotternhausen*) as well as archaeological evidence of prehistoric activities (*Homo erectus heidelbergensis*, *Homo erectus steinheimensis*, the world's oldest musical instrument and work of art). Finally, it also has many caves, dolines and springs as a result of intense karstification (Borcherdt, 1993; Schwäbische Alb Tourismusverband, 2001, 2003; Huth, 2002).

This richness, marketed as 'a one billion year journey of geological history', provides plentiful geo-objects in southwest Germany. From a geological point of view the most interesting region here is the Swabian Alb, which features, for instance, in an area of approximately 6000 km^2, a total of 2588 caves registered by the German Speleological Association, making it the region with the highest cave density in Germany. Many of the southwest's resources have been developed into more than 200 diverse geotourism attractions. These include 19 abandoned mines, 32 geoscience museums, 27 geo-trails and 18 caves open for visitors, numerous of them featured in the National Geopark Swabian Alb (Huth, 2002).

Network History of the Earth

The Network History of the Earth (Megerle and Pauls, 2004b) was initiated by the Chair of Applied Geography (University of Tübingen) at a conference on sustainable tourism in 1997. During a first get-together in Stuttgart, the Chair of Applied Geography put forward the idea of developing high-quality sustainable tourism based on the unique geo-resources of southwest Germany. Soon joined by other parties, the newly formed network decided to promote a 'one billion year journey through the history of the Earth' as a sustainable geotourism product package. As a framework for this cooperation, common guidelines for sustainability were developed. This so-called Network History of the Earth initiative

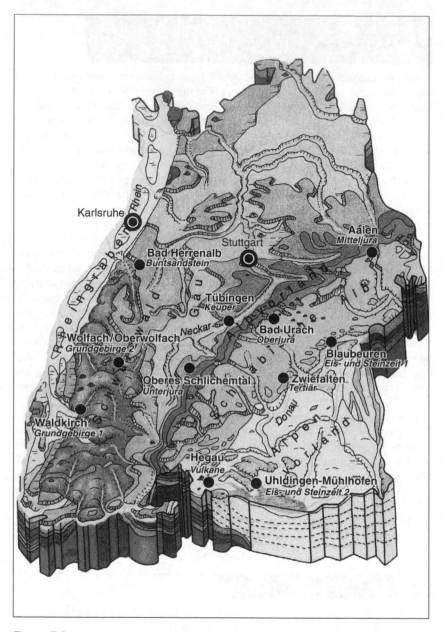

Figure 7.2 Geological block diagram of southwest Germany (source: Landesamt für Geologie, Rohstoffe und Bergbau Baden-Württemberg, 2000).

served mainly as a tool to develop a common language and shared aims and objectives, to create trust, and to explore its strength, available resources, competencies and capacities as well as the anticipated win–win scenario for each network partner (Borkenhagen *et al.*, 2004).

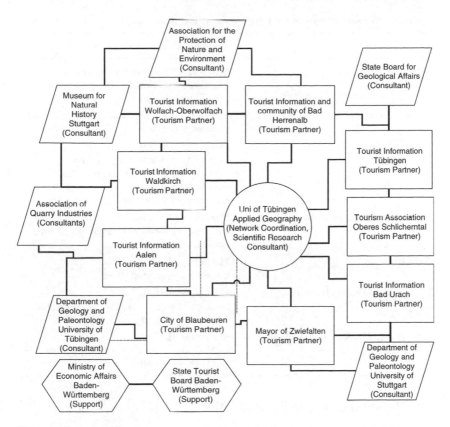

Figure 7.3 Organogram of the Network History of the Earth (source: Megerle, 1999, amended and updated).

Consolidation through cooperation

Soon it became clear that only close cooperation of all participants would allow the realization of such an initiative. This included effective coordination of the diverse range of tourism products and the establishment of quality control mechanisms to ensure conformity to best practice recognized by all partners. Furthermore, it was also considered crucial to ensure adequate cooperation of all relevant stakeholders to be able to line up endorsement and strong support for the network projects at the local level. Next to tourism stakeholders, members from environmental groups, industry associations, museums, government authorities, universities and interested individuals, all-in-all a fragmented and heterogeneous network (Figure 7.3), were brought together by a common interest and attracted by a 'win–win' scenario (Table 7.1).

Such a strategic approach to sustainable tourism based on geo-resources required strategic programmes to achieve its set objectives. One of these projects was the initiation and development of sub-networks at a regional level, covering specific natural areas such as the National Geopark Swabian Alb, which is discussed here in more detail.

Table 7.1 Network History of the Earth: partners and their objectives

Network partner	Anticipated win–win scenario
Chair of Applied Geography	New and exclusive research field Marketing platform for academic discipline Individual benefits
Scientists (geologists)	Marketing platform for academic discipline Individual benefits
Tourism partners	Marketing platform Cost-cutting effects (e.g. joint brochure, shared label) for tourism products New tourism products Exchange of know-how and information
NGOs (environmental lobby)	Marketing platform Increase in awareness of issues concerning environmental protection
Consultants	Marketing platform Contacts to potential clients
Association of Quarry Industries	Marketing platform Increase in awareness of issues concerning the quarry industry
Authority for Geology, Raw Materials and Mining	Marketing platform Increase in awareness for geotope protection and other Authority themes

The National Geopark Swabian Alb

Considering the density of its geological and archaeological attractions, the Swabian Alb is unique on a global scale. Thus it comes as no surprise that this region is one of the classic geotourism destinations, already having been visited in the eighteenth century by one of the most famous geotourists, Johann Wolfgang von Goethe. Today, with fifteen caves open to visitors, fourteen geoscientific-technical museums, six archaeological museums, twelve geoscientific and four archaeological interpretation trails, one visitor mine and hundreds of geotopes of state-wide importance (Huth and Junker, 2003), the Swabian Alb is one of the most significant geotourism destinations in Germany and Europe alike and was therefore a pioneer in the German geopark movement (Figure 7.4).

From a geological park to a National Geopark

The name 'Geological Park Swabian Alb' first appeared on the title of a tourist brochure in 1999 (Hauff *et al.*, 1999) given to the representative of UNESCO, who proposed a UNESCO Geopark Programme during a congress in Wiesbaden, Germany (Eder, 1999). Being familiar with the Swabian Alb from an earlier study period in Tübingen, he encouraged the representative of the Network History of the Earth to develop a geopark on the Swabian Alb and to participate in the UNESCO Programme.

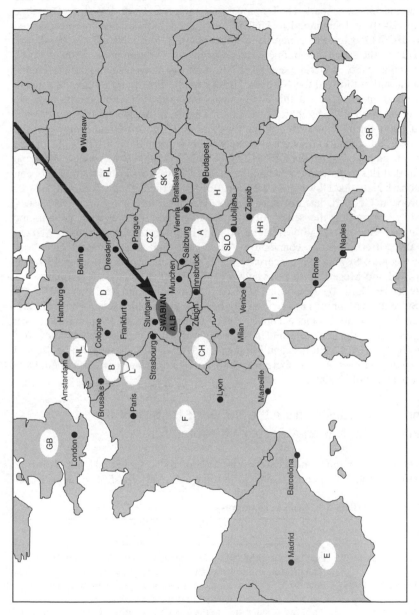

Figure 7.4 The Swabian Alb (source: Schwäbische Alb Tourismusverband, 2003).

An opportunity to initiate such a process arose during the First German Geo-tourism Symposium in Bad Urach (Megerle, 2000), concluded by a round-table meeting organized by the Network History of the Earth. In follow-up meetings this forum was institutionalized as the 'Round Table Geopark Swabian Alb', with the task of establishing a geopark. The framework for the project was developed (Jaeschke *et al.*, 2000) and submitted to UNESCO as a letter of interest for the planned UNESCO Geopark Programme, one of the first proposals UNESCO received.

Due to the strong commitment to this project by 29 communities, the geopark became a reality in December 2001. These pioneers made a small financial contribution and authorized the Network History of the Earth and a regional tourism organization to represent this new geopark network. Under moderation of the Chair of Applied Geography, University of Tübingen (Speidel and Megerle, 2000) and the financial sponsorship of the Swabian Alb Tourism Organization and the Association of Quarry Industries, the Network History of the Earth then elaborated the official proposal for the UNESCO Geopark Programme. As soon as it became clear that this Programme could not be realized, it was forwarded to the European Geopark Network. However, to date, certification of the Geopark Swabian Alb as a European Geopark has not been achieved as there are still unresolved issues, mainly concerning the selling of fossils. Meanwhile, the German programme 'National Geoparks' had been launched and the proposal was therefore also sent to the Alfred Wegener Foundation. Among the first four National Geoparks, the Geopark Swabian Alb, incorporating 29 communities and covering 1364 km^2 (Speidel and Megerle, 2000) was subsequently labelled a National Geopark on 1 July 2003 in Berlin by the German Minister for Education and Research (Table 7.2).

Since then, numerous projects have been initiated of which several have already been implemented. One example is the geotourism map 'National Geopark Swabian Alb', the first of its kind in Germany, published in 2000 by the State Office for Geology, Raw Materials and Mining (Landesamt für Geologie, Rohstoffe und Bergbau in Baden-Württemberg), one of the most important geopark stakeholders (Huth and Junker, 2003).

Know-how transfer from the Network History of the Earth to the National Geopark Swabian Alb

As noted earlier, the founding process of the geopark was initiated by the Network History of the Earth and its subnet, Swabian Alb. Various strategic approaches

Table 7.2   GeoPark Swabian Alb: key events

Date	Event
10 October 1999	First contact with UNESCO to further explore its geopark initiatives
4 July 2000	First meeting of the Round Table Geopark Swabian Alb
13 December 2001	First meeting of communities interested in participating in a network with the aim to establish a geopark
16 May 2002	Application submitted to the UNESCO Geopark Programme and the European Geopark Network
1 July 2003	Certification of the Geopark Swabian Alb as one of the first four National Geoparks in Germany

were employed to facilitate the transfer of know-how from this network to the geopark, amongst them the following:

1. *A bottom-up strategy.* The initiation, moderation and promotion of the Round Table Geopark Swabian Alb has brought different stakeholders together. Strong support for the geopark idea could be achieved through the participation of a broad spectrum of different stakeholders, ranging from the Association of Quarry Industries to the Association for the Protection of Nature and the Environment.
2. *A starter project strategy.* The joint elaboration and realization of starter projects (e.g. drafting proposals for the UNESCO Geopark Programme, the European Geopark Network as well as the National Geoparks initiative, participation in training courses for field guides; Figure 7.5) was important for the creation of a common language between the different stakeholders from academia, tourism, government authorities, private enterprises and nature conservation NGOs. This common language has been one of the most important factors in facilitating effective communication, exchanging know-how and achieving efficient ways of working together on joint projects.
3. *A promoter strategy.* The coordination of the geopark-network has been managed through the same methods and techniques as tested in the Network History of the Earth. In short, the network moderator has to act as a network promoter (Borkenhagen *et al.*, 2004). One of the network promoter's most important tasks, therefore, has been the promotion of various win–win scenarios to the different partners; otherwise the enthusiasm of stakeholders to implement the geopark might have waned fairly quickly.

Moreover, this transfer of know-how is not bound to a regional context or the subnational level: information exchange and thus transfer of know-how from one

Figure 7.5 'Barefoot through the history of the Earth' during the *Day of the Geosite* in an active quarry inside the World Geopark Swabian Alb (Network Partner Zwiefalten; photograph courtesy of Carmen Hägele).

network structure to another has also involved other geopark stakeholders, for instance those representing the National Expert Group for National Geoparks (several members from the Swabian Alb act as bridging actors) or the National Geological Society (Geotope Section), which organizes the official regular meetings of the National Geoparks. An effective exchange of know-how has also been supported through conference papers (e.g. First International Geopark Conference in Beijing/China 2004), presentations (e.g. European Geological Conference in Florence, Italy, 2004), consultancies for geopark applicants and other communication techniques.

Contentious geopark issues

To date, only a minority of communities from the Swabian Alb has participated in the Geopark (Figure 7.6). There are several factors contributing to this situation; one main reason is that the state government of Baden-Württemberg has proposed a Nature Park covering more or less the same area as the Geopark. Although the advocates for the establishment of a Nature Park were invited to the first Geopark Round Table meeting, the Geopark project was criticized and even seen as being in competition with the proposed Nature Park. Until now, some communities and also some government authorities and associations have therefore still been reluctant to cooperate with the Geopark stakeholders.

Despite these difficulties, the Geopark Swabian Alb was, as outlined earlier, successfully established, and was even awarded the quality label 'National Geopark'. In contrast, the concurrently proceeding official top-down planning process for the establishment of a Nature Park was unsuccessful. Interestingly, the main reason for this failure was that the main advocates of the Nature Park, particularly the State Ministry for Food and Rural Areas of Baden-Württemberg, were unable to line up sufficient support from key stakeholders (e.g. communities and industry) at the regional and local levels. In this context an ambivalent role was played by the regional tourism organization, which initially rejected the Geopark idea but became a strong supporter after realizing that the Nature Park proposal was going nowhere – to the extent that they even wanted to take complete ownership of the Geopark.

This contentious issue is closely associated with another controversy, where conflicts have emerged from different geopark aims and objectives of tourism partners and stakeholders from academia. The former would like to use the Geopark label mainly for marketing and promotion of their products, whereas the scientific community has a strong focus on quality standards and the need for a research-based Geopark Programme. This conflict of interests escalated as representatives from the regional tourism organization wanted to take over the management of the Geopark. However, it was finally acknowledged that such a move would endanger the quality label 'National Geopark', and as a compromise it was agreed that the Park would be integrated into the regional tourism organization but be managed by an independent Board with an academic as its Chairman (Case study 7.1). This negotiated solution reflects the important role of tourism partners as key stakeholders. However, the compromise was also reached because the regional tourism organization offered its financial support to ease some constraints in the management of the Geopark. Since many communities are unable or unwilling to take up Geopark membership due to a lack of funds,

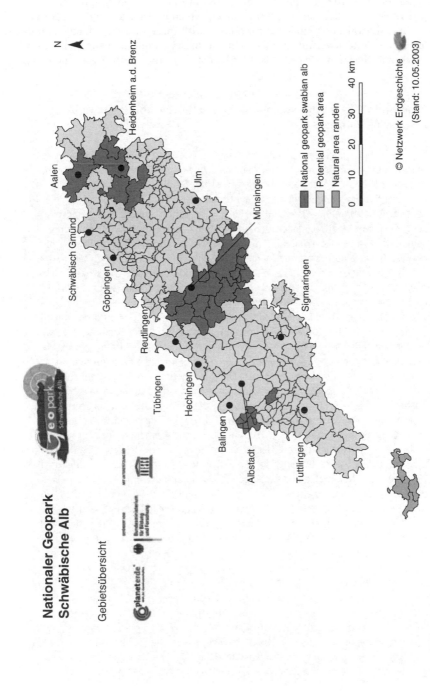

Figure 7.6 National GeoPark Swabian Alb (source: Netzwerk Erdgeschichte, 2003, amended).

seeding funding by the regional tourism organization for the provisional management of the Park was appreciated. This commitment was crucial as, to date, the Park has not yet attracted any state government funds. In contrast, the National GeoPark Bergstraße Odenwald, for instance, which is also classified as a Nature Park, operates on a one million Euro budget with three full-time managers provided by the state government of Hessen – a far cry from the financial means of the Geopark Swabian Alb or the Network History of the Earth (Case study 7.1).

Case study 7.1: Network History of the Earth – networking towards sustainable outcomes

To develop high-quality sustainable geotourism based on the unique geo-resources of southwest Germany, and its promotion as a 'one billion year journey through the history of the Earth', the Network History of the Earth was founded in 1997.

One of the most important elements of the Network History of the Earth is its central network management. To perform successfully, numerous management tasks (e.g. coordination, moderation, mediation, documentation, information dissemination) must be carried out. Particularly crucial, then, is the facilitation of a process to develop a common language which brings together the fragmented network partners and ensures positive cooperation amongst the stakeholders. Another essential task for the network management is to act as the network's engine and steam generator – drafting proposals for common strategies and projects, but also showing emotional leadership particularly when problems are encountered. In this context it is important to identify and promote real and potential future win–win scenarios. A trustful environment facilitates information exchange and the transfer of know-how, and also creates the basis for consensus-orientated decision-making processes. Thus, the network management helps to foster a creative atmosphere, to identify hidden potentials of the various network partners, and to ensure the sustainability of its products and processes. To achieve this ambitious task, personal ties and frequent communication are core elements, and these often emerge from an active involvement in local projects.

As part of a research project (*Lernen im Prozeß der Arbeit*) exploring the development of competencies in networks funded by the German Federal Ministry of Education and Research and the European Community, instruments and tools were developed to examine the transfer of know-how and the creation of competencies within the Network History of the Earth (Pauls and Megerle, 2002; Sydow *et al.*, 2003). Methodologies employed included observations from inside, interviews with network partners, and data analysis. One important finding of this study was the importance of regular face-to-face meetings with their high potential for know-how transfer. It turned out to be less beneficial replacing them with video conferences, e-mail or other communication technologies. Thus, an effectively and efficiently operating network can only function at the regional level, permitting all stakeholders involved to meet with relative ease (a maximum of a two- or three-hour trip to meetings is suggested). Another significant outcome of this research project was the importance of personal ties between network participants. It was found that know-how is mainly transferred outside official meetings during coffee or lunch breaks, and on occasions when the various players participate in a common experience-building event. Consequently, meetings of the Network History of the Earth are now mainly organized more informally – for instance, as excursions.

Despite its successful operation, the Network History of the Earth has also experienced major problems and obstacles. For instance, the economic viability of its tourism products is not yet ensured, mainly owing to limited support by the State Tourism Federation for the Network's promotion and marketing activities. Furthermore, significant barriers to networking activities include the relatively high costs (financial and time constraints) of cooperation and collaboration between network partners, and the often limited capabilities of individuals at the local level, particularly within the tourism domain. Although distance might inhibit some network partners from participating, face-to-face meetings are nevertheless seen as an essential and beneficial activity. Since the creativity and success of the Network History of the Earth relies on the stability and quality of its relational constellations, a high degree of staff fluctuation within the various partner organizations can have a negative impact on the Network's performance. Stakeholder interviews also unveiled insufficient communication and information exchange with staff of visitor information centres, resulting in limited transfer of know-how among tourism partners.

Despite these difficulties, the creative milieu of the Network with its diverse range of actors, combined with an intensive exchange of information and transfer of know-how within its structures but also with external partners, has facilitated the initiation and implementation of a variety of new projects, products and initiatives (PPIs). Examples stemming from the activities of the Network History of Earth include the publication of so-called 'Appetizer Brochures' (designed to stimulate further interest), the organization of congresses and conferences to disseminate information and know-how, and the design and the implementation of training programmes for field guides and interpretive trails (Megerle and Pauls, 2004b). Furthermore, the Network has also actively supported the creation of new networks and sub-network structures, which are promoted and managed by the central Network History of the Earth.

Another interesting activity stemming from the diversity of the Network's partners was the development and implementation of an educational programme (Megerle, 2004) to emphasize landscape as a tool to develop competence, illustrating the Network's activities in the education sector. Similarly, the Network also provides an excellent learning environment for students, allowing them to translate theory into practice – an experience often facilitated through applied research projects. To achieve sustainable outcomes the Network has also developed a best practice framework that is compulsory for all its members. Another important outcome of the Network has been its ability to facilitate personal interaction and learning processes (Fürst, 1994). Research could, for instance, demonstrate that tourism partners became increasingly aware of the special features and unique characteristics of their landscape, but also of the need to protect its geo-resources (Megerle, 1999). Nature conservationists, on the other hand, have begun to understand and accept the necessity for economic activities. On a small scale, Network activities have created some employment opportunities (e.g. development and maintenance of its website, landscape interpretation activities). Moreover, the Network has had a high impact on the discussion of issues concerning sustainable geotourism in Germany – a clear sign of its influence outside its own network boundaries.

To conclude, common products, quality standards, sustainability guidelines and a shared label reflect the Network History of the Earth's capacity to perform effectively. This fact is underlined by a high degree of satisfaction with the Network's organization, management and activities expressed by its partners. Thus, the Network and its activities can be seen as a successful model to develop and promote high-quality, sustainable geotourism.

References

Borcherdt, C. (1993). *Geographische Landeskunde von Baden-Württemberg*, 3rd edn. Landeszentrale für Politische Bildung Baden-Württemberg.

Borkenhagen, P., Jäkel, L., Kummer, A. *et al.* (2004). *Handlungsleitfaden Netzwerke*. Arbeitsgemeinschaft Betriebliche Weiterbildungsforschunge. V/Projekt Qualifikations-Entwicklungs-Management.

Bramwell, B. and Lane, B. (1999). Editorial. *Journal of Sustainable Tourism*, 7(3–4), 179–181.

Bramwell, B. and Lane, B. (eds) (2000). *Tourism Collaboration and Partnerships: Policy, Practice and Sustainability*. Channel View Publications.

Bramwell, B. and Sharman, A. (1999). Collaboration in local tourism policy making. *Annals of Tourism Research*, 26(2), 312–328.

Buckley, R. (2003). Environmental inputs and outputs in ecotourism: geotourism with a positive triple bottom line? *Journal of Ecotourism*, 2(1), 76–82.

Bundesministerium für Bildung und Forschung (BMBF) (2001). *Jahr der Geowissenschaften 2002*. Ministerial Statement 5 November 2001 (available at www.planeterde.de/DasJahr/GeoParks).

Bundesministerium für Bildung und Forschung (BMBF) (2002). *Einrichtung nationaler Geoparks in Deutschland* (available at www.planeterde.de/DasJahr/ GeoParks).

Clement, T. (2003). Umweltbildung in Geoparks – ein Medium zur Besuchergewinnung. In: H. Quade (ed.), *Geoforum 2003: Geotope – Geoparks – Geotourismus*. Deutsche Geologische Gesellschaft, pp. 80–85.

Dovers, S. R. (1995). Information, sustainability and policy. *Australian Journal of Environmental Management*, 2, 142–156.

Eder, W. (1999). Geologisches Naturerbe und UNESCO's Geopark-Programm. In: A. Hoppe and H. Abel (eds), *Geotope – lesbare Archive der Erdgeschichte*. Deutsche Geologische Gesellschaft, p. 33.

Edgell, D. L. (1990). *International Tourism Policy*. Van Nostrand Reinhold.

Frey, M.-L. (2003). Vulkaneifel European Geopark – langjährige geotouristische Erfahrungen. In: H. Quade (ed.), *Geoforum 2003: Geotope – Geoparks – Geotourismus*. Deutsche Geologische Gesellschaft, pp. 61–67.

Fürst, D. (1994). Regionalkonferenzen zwischen offenen Netzwerken und fester Institutionalisierung. *Raumforschung und Raumordnung*, 3, 184–192.

Granitzki, K. and Buddenbohm, A. (2003). Nationaler Geopark mecklenburgische Eiszeitlandschaft – geologische Modellregion und Geotourismuskonzept. In: H. Quade (ed.), *Geoforum 2003: Geotope – Geoparks – Geotourismus*. Deutsche Geologische Gesellschaft, pp. 86–92.

Hall, C. M. (1994). *Tourism and Politics: Policy, Power and Place.* John Wiley.

Hall, C. M. (1998). *Introduction to Tourism. Development, Dimensions and Issues* (3rd edn). Longman.

Hall, C. M. (1999). Rethinking collaboration and partnership: a public policy perspective. *Journal of Sustainable Tourism,* 7(3&4), 274–288.

Hall, C. M. (2000). *Tourism Planning. Policies, Processes and Relationships.* Prentice Hall.

Hauff, R., Megerle, A., Megerle, H. *et al.* (1999). *Abenteuer Geologie.* Touristik-Gemeinschaft Schwäbische Alb.

Huth, T. (2002). *Erlebnis Geologie.* Landesamt für Geologie, Rohstoffe und Bergbau Baden-Württemberg.

Huth, T. and Junker, B. (2003). *Geotouristische Karte Nationaler GeoPark Schwäbische Alb mit Umgebung.* Landesamt für Geologie, Rohstoffe und Bergbau Baden-Württemberg.

Jaeschke, H., Koelbl, S., Kraus, U. and Megerle, A. (2000). *Ein UNESCO-Geopark auf der Schwäbischen Alb! – Bausteine für einen Antrag, Positionspapier des 'Runden Tisches Geopark Schwäbische Alb'.* Runder Tisch Geopark Schwäbische Alb.

Jenkins, J. M. (2001). Statutory authorities in whose interests? The case of tourism in New South Wales, the bed tax, and 'the Games'. *Pacific Tourism Review,* 4, 201–218.

Kraus, U. (2003). Abenteuer Geologie – Chancen für eine nachhaltige Tourismusentwicklung. In: H. Quade (ed.), *Geoforum 2003: Geotope – Geoparks – Geotourismus.* Deutsche Geologische Gesellschaft, pp. 56–60.

Ladkin, A. and Bertramini, A. M. (2002). Collaborative tourism planning: a case study of Cusco, Peru. *Current Issues in Tourism,* 5(2), 71–93.

Landesamt für Geologie, Rohstoffe und Bergbau Baden-Württemberg (2000). *Geologisches Blockbild Südwestdeutschland.* LGRB.

Lang, R. (2003). *Geotourismus und Geotopschutz in Rheinland-Pfalz.* Landesamt für Geologie und Bergbau Rheinland-Pfalz (available at www.lgb-rlp.de/geotop.html).

Lasswell, H. D. (1936). *Politics: Who Gets What, When, How?* McGraw-Hill.

Mattig, U. (2003). Richtlinien zur Ausweisung als Nationaler GeoPark. In: H. Quade (ed.), *Geoforum 2003: Geotope – Geoparks – Geotourismus.* Deutsche Geologische Gesellschaft, pp. 37–41.

Megerle, A. (1999). Planungsnetzwerke als Bewusstseinsbildner für Geotopschutzbelange – das Beispiel Netzwerk Erdgeschichte. In: A. Hoppe and H. Abel (eds), *Geotope – lesbare Archive der Erdgeschichte.* Deutsche Geologische Gesellschaft, p. 72–73.

Megerle, A. (2000) Zukunftsfähiger Geotourismus – ein Baustein zur Agenda 21! *Rundbrief Geographie,* 163, 32–34.

Megerle, H. (2004). *Naturerlebnispfade – neue Medien der Umweltbildung und deslandschaftsbezogenen Tourismus?* (Tübinger Geographische Studien, Heft 124). Geographisches Institut der Universität Tübingen.

Megerle, A. and Megerle, H. (2002). Geotourism? Geotourism! *Attempto,* 13, 16–17.

Megerle, A. and Pauls, K. (2003). Netzwerk Erdgeschichte in Baden-Württemberg. In: H. Quade (ed.), *Geoforum 2003: Geotope – Geoparks – Geotourismus.* Deutsche Geologische Gesellschaft, pp. 48–55.

Megerle, A. and Pauls, K. (2004a). Geotourismusnetzwerke am Beispiel Netzwerk Erdgeschichte. In: J. H. Kruhl (ed.), *Geowissenschaften und Öffentlichkeit* (6th Internationale Tagung der Fachsektion GeoTop der Deutschen Geologischen Gesellschaft, 10–13 April 2002 in Viechtach). Deutsche Geologische Gesellschaft, pp. 59–65.

Megerle, A. and Pauls, K. (2004b). GeoGuides oder Landschaftsguides? – Erfahrungen aus Landschaftsführerausbildungen in Baden-Württemberg. In: J. H. Kruhl (ed.), *Geowissenschaften und Öffentlichkeit* (6th Internationale Tagung der Fachsektion GeoTop der Deutschen Geologischen Gesellschaft, 10–13 April 2002 in Viechtach). Deutsche Geologische Gesellschaft, pp. 12–21.

Netzwerk Erdgeschichte Baden-Württemberg (2003). *Karte Nationaler GeoPark Schwäbische Alb* (available at www.erdgeschichte.de).

Patzak, M. (2000). Tourism and Geodiversity: The Case of Geoparks. Paper presented at the Biodiversity & Tourism Symposium in Port-Cros, France, 20–23 September 2000 (available at http://egis.cnrs-mop.fr).

Pauls, K. and Megerle, A. (2002). Kompetenzentwicklung in Netzwerken – Einblick in das Forschungsprojekt Netzwerk Erdgeschichte. *QUEM-Bulletin*, 3, 17–20.

Pforr, C. (2001). Tourism policy in Australia's Northern Territory – a policy process analysis of its Tourism Development Masterplan. *Current Issues in Tourism*, 4(2–4), 275–307.

Pforr, C. (2002). The 'makers and shapers' of tourism policy in the Northern Territory of Australia. A policy network analysis of actors and their relational constellations. *Journal of Hospitality and Tourism Management*, 9(2), 134–151.

Pforr, C. (2004). On the road to sustainable tourism? Policy diffusion of sustainable development principles. In: C. Cooper, C. Arcodia, D. Solnet and M. Whitford (eds), *Creating Tourism Knowledge*. University of Queensland, pp. 566–576.

Pipkin, J. (1996) 'Biological diversity conservation. A public policy perspective'. *Environmental Management*, 20(6), 793–797.

Reimold, W. U. (1999). Geoconservation – a southern African and African perspective. *Journal of African Earth Sciences*, 29(3), 469–483.

Robinson, M. (1999). Collaboration and cultural consent: refocusing sustainable tourism. *Journal of Sustainable Tourism*, 7(3–4), 379–397.

Ryan, C. (2002). Equity, management, power sharing and sustainability – issues of the 'new tourism'. *Tourism Management*, 23, 17–26.

Schiller, K. (2002). Geotourism takes off. *Travel Agent*, 19 August, 40.

Schwäbische Alb Tourismusverband (2001). *Abenteuer Geologie*. Bad Urach: Schwäbische Alb Tourismusverband (available at www.schwäbischealb.de).

Schwäbische Alb Tourismusverband (2003). *Swabian Alb Info Guide*. Bad Urach: Schwäbische Alb Tourismusverband (available at www.schwäbischealb.de).

Selin, S. (1999). Developing a typology of sustainable tourism partnerships. *Journal of Sustainable Tourism*, 7(3–4), 260–273.

Speidel, W. and Megerle, A. (2000). Bewerbung des Geoparks Schwäbische Alb für die Aufnahme in das Netzwerk Europäische Geoparks und in das International Network of UNESCO Geoparks. Working paper. Geographisches Institut der Universität Tübingen.

Sydow, J., Duschek, S., Möllering, G. and Rometsch, M. (2003). *Kompetenzentwicklung in Netzwerken – eine typologische Studie*. VS Verlay für Sozialwissenschaften.

Travel Industry Association of America (TIA) (2003). *Geotourism: The New Trend in Travel.* TIA.

Weber, J. and Eckhard, C. (2003). Zwischen Granit und Sandstein – Landschaft erleben. Der Naturpark Bergstrasse-Odenwald als Europäischer und Nationaler Geopark. In: H. Quade (ed.), *Geoforum 2003: Geotope – Geoparks – Geotourismus.* Deutsche Geologische Gesellschaft, pp. 100–106.

Zellmer, H. and Röber, S. (2003). Der Geopark Braunschweigerland Ostfalen – Die 'klassischen Quadratmeilen' der Geologie. In: H. Quade (ed.), *Geoforum 2003: Geotope – Geoparks – Geotourismus.* Deutsche Geologische Gesellschaft, pp. 93–99.

8

Geological heritage in China

Jiang Jianjun, Zhao Xun and
Chen Youfang

Introduction

The Chinese people have long realized and enjoyed
geological heritage resources. In their masterpieces
throughout the ages, many great poets and writers
have lauded China's renowned mountains and great
rivers. People can feel that there are paintings in
poems and poems in paintings. Some ancient monks,
Taoists and travellers had a deep love for the mountains and rivers and for embodying themselves into
an integral part of nature. The 5000-year Chinese
history is also a history of the exploration and protection of natural resources, and the recognition,
exploration and protection of natural resources are
being integrated smoothly into the nation's development. In this process the geological heritage has
provided a broad material basis for the advance of
national culture and, in turn, added credit to the cultural connotation of resources. The harmony of the
rich and colourful geological heritage resources
together with the long history of Chinese civilization
is a major characteristic of China's National Geoparks, and it is also an important factor for China to

take a leading place in promoting the UNESCO-sponsored Geopark Programme at a national level.

In 1985, Chinese geologists proposed the establishment of geoparks in geologically significant territories in order to enhance their conservation and improve geoscientific research. In July 1987, the former Ministry of Geology and Mineral Resources (MGMR) issued the 'Circular on Establishing Geological Natural Reserves (Proposed)', this being the first time that the geological heritage protection was proposed in the form of ministerial regulations. In May 1995, the MGMR promulgated the 'Regulations of Protection and Management of Geological Heritage', in which the establishment of geoparks is regarded as a way of protecting geological heritage reserves. In December 1999, the setting up of National Geoparks was further advanced in the National Geology–Geomorphology Protection Conference held by the Ministry of Land and Resources (MLR) in Weihai, Shandong Province. On 3 April 2000, Tian Fengshan, Minister of the MLR, approved the report made by the Department of Geological Environment of MLR for the launch of geoparks in China. In August the same year, the 'Circular on Leading Organization and Staffing of National Geological Heritages (Geoparks)' was issued, and at the same time, the Review Committee of National Geological Heritages (Geoparks) was formed. In September 2000, the MLR issued the 'Circular on the Nomination of National Geoparks', with an attached series of documents on the requirements and procedures for geopark application, establishment, organization and management. The documents included:

1. A National Geopark nomination form
2. An outline of the report on integrated investigation of National Geoparks
3. Guidelines on the overall planning of National Geoparks (proposed)
4. Organizational and operating regulations of the Review Committee of National Geological Heritages (Geoparks)
5. Review standards of National Geoparks.

The circular has advanced the establishment and management of National Geoparks in China through an orbit of legislation and implementation.

At the very beginning of setting up the National Geoparks, a distinct and characteristic emblem was designed. Since 2000, the provinces, autonomous regions and municipalities directly under jurisdiction of the Central Government of People's Republic of China have actively recommended a number of geological heritage sites as geoparks. Through the strict comparison, review and appraisal, a total of 44 National Geoparks have been approved in two batches (in 2000 and 2001).

The establishment of National Geoparks pushed forward the geological heritage protection at the provincial, city and county levels, and already some local governments have approved provincial, city and county level geoparks. Taking the National Geoparks as the core, the network of geological heritage protection at different levels begins to build, and these geoparks become local economic growth points and create new employment positions. At the same time there has been active academic research and geological popularization so that local communities have become more aware of geological heritage protection. The different geoparks have many academic research centres, and the implementation of the geopark programme has been highly regarded and strongly supported by both the local people and governments.

141

China is one of the first countries that have actively joined the promotion of the UNESCO-sponsored Geopark Programme. UNESCO has requested that geoparks should serve as bases of scientific popularization. In this connection, China has launched a holistic improvement in narration preparation, signage, tourist route design, guide book compilation, tour guide training and museum exhibitions. Knowledge of Earth sciences, meteorology, zoology and botany has been included in stories to replace fairy tales and folklores. Scientific popularization has been integrated in tourism, and education in recreation. So far these works have been completed in more than 30 of the 44 National Geoparks. Today, the geoparks movement is widespread in China and has formed the base of public scientific popularization. The establishment of geoparks has helped local governments and inhabitants to be aware of the importance of safeguarding geological heritage resources and the geo-environment, and to participate conscientiously in their establishment and operation. As a result, a new social mode of acknowledging geological heritage and environment is being cultivated. For example, since the founding of Yuntaishan Mountain National Geopark, Henan Province, the inhabitants in the area have taken great care of the woods and geological heritage and today no one is allowed to log the trees. Consequently, the natural resources and geological environment protection have become a common practice among residents of the surrounding areas.

By virtue of the implementation of the conservation of China's geological heritage, local governments have regarded geological tourism as a new economic growth which can alleviate the expenses of geological heritage protection, increase local revenues and enhance employment. The Yuntaishan Mountain National Geopark was approved in 2001, covering an area of 190 km². It is characterized by a combination of cliffs, valleys, forests and waterfalls. By adding both scientific and cultural connotations to tourism, it has become a provincial base for scientific promotion and education and attracts a large number of students and scholars. In 2001, visitor numbers reached 600 000 and income from admissions was 14 million yuan – double the average of previous years. In 2002, the visitor numbers soared to 940 000 (a 68 per cent increase) and the income rose to 27.2 million yuan (up 97 per cent). Thus tourism has powered tertiary industry and enhanced local employment.

In 2002, the revenues of tertiary industry increased by 620 million yuan – 15 per cent above that of the previous year. More than 60 new hotels were built in the country, and approximately 4000 jobs were generated through this rapid tourism development. Meanwhile, the country attracted investment from substantial domestic and foreign enterprises. The projects under construction or negotiation in this aspect totalled 379 million yuan; this will make additional economic growth and provide new employment opportunities. In addition, rapid local tourism pushed forward actions on environmental protection, converting cultivated slope land for recovery of natural vegetation and/or for tree (or grass) planting.

Another example is the Dajinhu Lake National Geopark in Taining County, Fujian Province. This Geopark was constructed in 2000, and is characterized by 'waterside Danxia landforms'. The related tourism projects attracted a large number of visitors. In 2001, the total revenue from tourism reached 202 million yuan – 35.7 per cent above that of the previous year – and accounted for 13.5 per cent of the local GDP. The revenues of tourism-related tertiary industry increased by 450 million yuan, up 12.3 per cent compared with the previous year, accounting for nearly 30 per cent of the local GDP. Tourism has fast-tracked infrastructure development in transportation and cultural recreation, as well as generating employment. The establishment of the geopark and rapid geotourism development has created jobs for a large number of migrants previously in financial difficulty, who now receive pay three to five times higher than before. As a consequence, the instability factor has been reduced and the people now have a higher standard of living.

The establishment of geoparks has also generated a sound social influence. Local authorities and communities now realize that the construction of geoparks conserves geological heritage, optimizes the geological environment, promotes scientific popularization and adds a scientific connotation to tourism. In addition, it is viewed as being beneficial for local economies and employment. It is regarded as a sound way in which geology can advance socio-economic sustainable development.

China's National Geoparks

Since 2000, the provinces, autonomous regions and municipalities directly under the jurisdiction of the Central Government of the People's Republic of China have actively recommended a number of geological heritage sites to be developed as National Geoparks. To date, a total of 44 National Geoparks have been approved (Figure 8.1). In this process of moving from geological heritage protection to geopark establishment, China has cooperated closely with UNESCO. Geoparks have been created in a range of categories, including stratigraphic, palaeontological, structural geology, geological–geomorphic, glacial, volcanic, hydrogeological, engineering and geological disaster. Examples of each are briefly described here.

Stratigraphic heritage

Fuping National Geopark, Hebei. The major geological heritage is the type section and Archaean Longquanguan Formation. The controlling geological setting is the pediment fault system and fault-block mountain masses, and the relevant natural conditions are waterfalls and warm springs.

Songshan National Geopark, Henan. The major geological heritage is the three clear unconformity boundaries of the Archaean/Proterozoic, the Proterozoic/Mid-Proterozoic and Neoproterozoic/Palaeozoic ages. This Geopark is the naming place of the three boundaries listed above. The controlling geological setting is the differential elevation brought about by block movement on the North China Platform. The relevant natural conditions are steep cliffs, perilous peaks and dense forest.

Jixian National Geopark, Tianjin. The major geological heritage is the Mid-Upper Proterozoic section (1.8–0.8 Ga), yielding rich fossils, especially the macroscopic algae earlier than 1.7 Ga. The controlling geological setting is the old gentle stratigraphic section on the North China Platform, and the relevant natural condition is carbonate peak cluster landform.

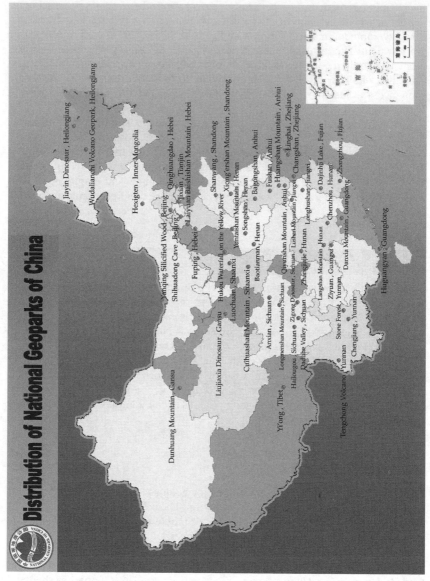

Figure 8.1 Distribution of National Geoparks of China.

Qinghuangdao National Geopark, Hebei. The major geological heritage is the complete stratigraphic sequence on the North China Platform, marine-erosion landforms and granite peak hills. The controlling geological setting is the territories affected by the tectonomagmatic belt of Yanshanian movement on the northern edge of the North China Platform. The relevant natural conditions are the Yanshan Mountain and coastal hills, sandy beaches and low, densely forested hills.

Changshan National Geopark, Zhejiang. The major geological heritage is the Ordovician Darriwilian GSSP, reef limestone and karst landforms. The controlling geological setting is the stable carbonate neritic deposits on the Yangtze Platform, and the relevant natural condition is low karst hills.

Luochuan National Geopark, Shaanxi. The major geological heritage is the type section of loess deposits in China and loess landforms. The controlling geological setting is a loess deposition area in the western North China Platform, and the relevant natural conditions are loess gullies, plateaus, hills and ridges, and sparse arid vegetation.

Palaeontological heritage

Chengjiang National Geopark, Yunnan. The major geological heritage is the Early Cambrian (0.53 Ga) explosive biomultiplication and synchronous emergence of tons of biological groups and species. The controlling geological setting is a stable neritic environment, and the relevant natural conditions are the hills and rift lakes.

Bagongshan National Geopark, Anhui. The major geological heritage is the Huainan biota (0.7–0.8 Ga) and late Early Cambrian stratigraphic sections. The controlling geological setting is the southern edge of the North China Platform, close to the Yangtze Platform, and the relevant natural condition is the juncture of the north and south climatic zones of China.

Anxian National Geopark, Sichuan. The major geological heritage is the bioherms of Devonian siliceous sponges and karst landforms. The controlling geological setting is the western edge of the Yangtze Platform, and the relevant natural conditions are the Longmenshan moderate to low hills, and forests.

Zigong Dinosaur National Geopark, Sichuan. The major geological heritage is the burial site of many kinds of Middle Jurassic dinosaur fossils, with complete dinosaur skeletons and dinosaurian dungs. The controlling geological settings are the Yangtze Platform and Mesozoic inland lakes; the relevant natural condition is the red bed hills in central Sichuan.

Liujiaxia Dinosaur National Geopark, Gansu. The major geological heritage is the excavated dinosaurian tracksites, with the largest one over 1 m in diameter. The controlling geological setting is the Mesozoic inland lake in the western North China Platform; the relevant natural conditions are valleys in the upper reach of the Yellow River.

Yanqing Silicified Wood National Geopark, Beijing. The major geological heritage is the groups of silicified woods buried *in situ.* The controlling geological setting is the Mesozoic inland basin formed in the Yanshanian tectonic belt, and the relevant natural condition is moderate to low hills.

Jiayin Dinosaur National Geopark, Heilongjiang. The major geological heritage is the end-Cretaceous dinosaurian fossils (this is where the first dinosaurian skeleton was unearthed in China), and also angiosperm fossils. The controlling geological setting is the Wandashan massif, and the relevant natural condition is the natural landscape of northernmost China.

Shanwang National Geopark, Shandong. The major geological heritage is the diatomaceous shale sections yielding rich and well-preserved Miocene fossils of over 700 species belonging to more than a dozen taxa, including fish, reptile, amphibia, mammal, insects and plants, as well as abundant volcanic activity traces. The controlling geological setting is the volcanic maar lake in Miocene, and the relevant natural conditions are the linked volcanic cones, craters and moderate to low hills.

Structural geology heritage

Baotianman National Geopark, Henan. The major geological heritage is the traces of tectonic and metamorphic processes; the controlling geological setting is the central (Qingling) orogenic belt of continental China. The relevant natural conditions are biodiversity and dense vegetation at the juncture of the north and south climatic zones of China.

Longmenshan Mountain National Geopark, Sichuan. The major geological heritage is the long-range nappe structures (Longmenshan tectonic belt). The controlling geological setting is the converging area of the Qinghai–Tibet Platform and the western margin of the Yangtze Platform, and the relevant natural condition is the Zhongshan forest.

Geological–geomorphic heritage

These geoparks are based on different landforms.

Danxia landform
Danxia Mountain National Geopark, Guangdong. The major geological heritage is the typical and representative Danxia (meaning the rosy cloud in Chinese) landform (Figure 8.2). The controlling geological setting is the fault-depression basin on the South China Paraplatform, and the relevant natural conditions are hills and waters, and thick vegetation.

Longhushan National Geopark, Jiangxi. The major geological heritage is the Danxia landform, with peculiarly shaped rocks. The controlling geological setting is the fault-depression basin on the South China Paraplatform, and the relevant natural conditions are the hills and waters.

Chenzhou National Geopark, Hunan. The major geological heritage is the Danxia landform, with caves, gorges, natural bridges and cliffs. The controlling geological setting is the fault-depression basin on the South China Paraplatform, and the relevant natural conditions are low hills and waters.

Langshan Mountain National Geopark, Hunan. The major geological heritage is the Danxia landform with mesas, peak pillars, crevices and cliffs. The controlling

Figure 8.2 Danxia landforms, Danxia Mountain National Geopark, Guangdong.

geological setting is the fault-depression basin on the South China Paraplatform, and the relevant natural condition is the Zijiang River valley.

Ziyuan National Geopark, Guangxi. The major geological heritage is the Danxia landform, with mesas, peak columns, steep precipices and cliffs. The controlling geological setting is the fault-depression basin on the South China Paraplatform, and the relevant natural conditions are the upper reach of Zijiang River, waters and dense forest.

Dajinhu Lake National Geopark, Fujian. The major geological heritage is the lakeside Danxia landform, with peculiarly shaped rocks of red sandstone that give rise to reflections of red peak columns and steep cliffs in the lakes; the controlling geological setting is the fault-depression basin on the South China Paraplatform. The relevant natural conditions are the curiously shaped peaks and rocks scattered in and near the Dajinhu Lake, waters and dense forest.

Qiyunshan Mountain National Geopark, Anhui. The major geological heritage is the Danxia landform, with red cliffs, long walls, flat caves, mesas, valleys, lanes and dinosaurian fossils. The controlling geological setting is the fault-controlled Mesozoic volcano-sedimentary basin on the northern margin of the South China Paraplatform, and the relevant natural conditions are low hills covered with thick woods.

Yardang landform
Dunhuang Mountain National Geopark, Gansu. The major geological heritage is the wind-eroded landform, with curiously shaped landscapes derived from the physical erosion of loosely cemented mid-Oligocene fluvial-lacustrine deposition. There are strange winds at night. The controlling geological setting is the fluvial-lacustrine deposition in a Cenozoic fault depression basin in the northeast of the Tarim massif, and the relevant natural condition is the desert landscape with stretches of black desert lacquer.

Carbonate karst caves
Shihuadong Cave National Geopark, Beijing. The major geological heritage is the limestone karst caves of seven layers, with peculiarly shaped stalactites, stalagmites,

147

stalaco-stalagmites and rock flowers. There are underground streams in the two lowermost layers. The controlling geological setting is the repeated block-uplifting and erosion in the North China Platform during the neotectonic movements, and the relevant natural conditions are low hills and valleys, as well as the karst areas.

Xiong'ershan Mountain National Geopark, Shandong. The major geological heritage is an animal-shaped karst mountain, which is thrust high over the hills, with gorges, caves and stones. The landform is formed through the differential elevation and subsidence of carbonate rocks due to Cenozoic fault dissection on the North China Platform, and the relevant natural conditions are the low hills and typical karst landforms of North China.

Carbonate peak forest landform

Stone Forest National Geopark, Yunnan. The major geological heritage is the karst landform, with sword-like stone forests, 20–50 m high peak clusters, well-developed caves and waterfalls. The controlling geological settings are the repeated post-Permian differential elevations and subsidences on the southwestern edge of Yangtze Platform, as well as water erosion, and the relevant natural conditions are hills and the peak-forest plain.

Marble peak forest landform

Laiyuan Baishishan Mountain National Geopark, Hebei. The major geological heritage is the marble peak forest, peak columns, precipices, springs and source of Laishui River. The controlling geological setting is the Cenozoic differential block elevation and erosion, vertical faulting, well-developed joints, collapses and frost splitting. The relevant natural conditions are the moderate to low hills, and perennial springs.

Quartzose sandstone peak forest landform

Zhangjiajie National Geopark, Hunan. The major geological heritage is the quartzose sandstone forest with 3000 or more peak pillars, the highest reaching 400 m (Figure 8.3). In addition, nearby there are some carbonate karst caves. The controlling geological setting is the three sets of intersected faults cutting the horizontal quartzose sandstone beds on the South China Platform; collapses and scouring are present. The relevant natural conditions are the moderate hills, fluvial landscape and hills.

Granite peak forest landform

Huangshan Mountain National Geopark, Anhui. The major geological heritage is the granite peak forest landform with rock pillars, peculiar peaks and grotesque rocks, deep and secluded valleys and warm springs. The controlling geological setting is the Cenozoic faulting activities and differential elevation and subsidence, running water action and glaciation on the South China Paraplatform. The relevant natural conditions are the moderate hills.

Hexigten National Geopark, Inner Mongolia. The major geological heritage is the granite peak columns with well-developed horizontal joints, resembling human beings, animals or castles; these landforms have resulted from frost splitting, freeze-and-thaw action and wind erosion. In addition there are also some typical glacial vestiges in this geopark. The controlling geological setting is the

Figure 8.3 Quartzose sandstone peak forest, Zhangjiajie National Geopark, Hunan.

juncture of the Xingmeng geosyncline fault belt and the Yanshanian tectono-magmatic belt on the north edge of the North China Platform. The relevant natural conditions are the converging area of the Da Hing'an Range primeval forest, Hunshandake Desert and Horqin Desert.

Glacial geological heritage

Glacial geological vestiges include both fossil and modern glaciers.

Fossil glaciers
Lushan Mountain National Geopark, Jiangxi. The major geological heritage is the Quaternary glacial vestiges and their naming places, complete sections, old stratigraphic sections of southern China, and the fault-block mountain. The controlling geological setting is the old continental nucleus of the South China Paraplatform, and Cenozoic differential elevation and subsidence in the fault-block movement. The relevant natural conditions are the Lushan Mountain, Poyang Lake and Yangtze River.

Modern glaciers
Hailougou National Geopark, Sichuan. The major geological heritage is the 29-km long modern glacier on the east of the Gongga Mountains. The lowest ice tongue goes down to 2750 m above sea level, with many warm spring sites. The controlling geological setting is the juncture of the western edge of the Yangtze Platform and the folded belt of the Kangdian Hengduan Mountains, they were strongly uplifted in the Cenozoic era. The relevant natural condition is the co-existence of vast primeval forest, glacier and warm springs.

Volcanic geological heritage

Wudalianchi National Geopark, Heilongjiang. The major geological heritage is the volcanic landforms. Fourteen volcanoes erupted from the Tertiary to the Quaternary ages, and the latest eruption was in 1721. Typical morphological features include edifices, volcanic lakes and lava. The controlling geological setting is affected by Circum-Pacific tectonic activities and the East Asian Rift System. The relevant natural conditions are the plains, hills and well-developed vegetation.

Zhangzhou National Geopark, Fujian. The major geological heritage is the littoral volcanic rocks, basaltic columnar joints, volcanic vents and cones and marine erosion landform. The controlling geological setting is affected by Circum-Pacific tectonic activities and the East Asian Rift Series. The relevant natural conditions are the coastal hills, sand beaches and islands.

Tengchong Volcano National Geopark, Yunnan. The major geological heritage is the modern volcanic landforms, geothermal springs and various hot spring sinters; the controlling geological setting is the folded belt of Kangdian Hengduan Mountains and intensive neotectonism. The relevant natural conditions are the low hills, spring lakes and thick vegetation. The main humanistic characteristics are the ancient border city, customs and practices of ethnic minorities.

Huguangyan National Geopark, Guangdong. The major geological heritage is the volcanic landforms and the maar lake. The controlling geological setting is the Circum-Pacific tectonic activities, and the relevant natural conditions are hills, thick woods and lakes.

Fushan National Geopark, Anhui. The major geological heritage is the complete volcanic mechanism, volcanic cones, craters, lava flows and caves created by weathering of volcanic rocks. The controlling geological setting is a fault depression basin of the East Asian Rift Valley Series, and the relevant natural conditions are hills and thick woods.

Linghai National Geopark, Zhejiang. The major geological heritage is the Late Cretaceous volcanic rocks, volcanic landforms, columnar joints, and pterosaurian and bird fossils. The controlling geological setting is the Circum-Pacific tectono-volcanic rock belt, and the relevant natural condition is coastal hills.

Hydrogeological heritage

Hukou Waterfall National Geopark on the Yellow River. The Hukou Waterfall is the greatest waterfall on the mainstream of the Yellow River; the major geological heritage is the narrow and deep gorges, with retrogressive erosion. The controlling geological setting is a series of joints formed by the influence of the Indo-Sinian movement controlling the river erosion on the North China Platform. The relevant natural conditions are the Yellow River valley, lateral erosion and loess landforms.

Yuntaishan Mountain National Geopark, Henan. The major geological heritage is the long walls, red cliffs, narrow gorges, lane-like valleys, urn-like valleys and many waterfalls (the Yuntai Heaven Waterfall is as high as 304 m), created by the piedmont fault of the Taihang Mountains (Figure 8.4). The controlling geological setting is the differential elevation and subsidence of the piedmont fault of the

Figure 8.4 Spectacular confined gorge, Yuntaishan Mountain Geopark, Henan.

Taihang Mountains on the North China Platform. The relevant natural conditions are the moderate and low mountains, gorge landforms and dense forest.

Engineering geological heritage

Daduhe Valley National Geopark, Sichuan. The major geological heritage is the Daduhe river valley, the narrow gorges and lanc-like valleys of its tributaries, the Dawa Mountain and Quaternary glacier. There is also the Cheng-Kun Railways cutting through the valleys, with bridges linking to culverts and caves to tunnels. The controlling geological setting is the north–south trending Sichuan–Yunnan structural fault, with intense effects of neotectonism on the western edge of the Yangtze Platform. The relevant natural conditions are the moderate and low mountains, deep valleys and dense forest.

Geological disaster heritage

The heritage of geological disasters includes both earthquake-induced collapses and large-scale landslides.

Earthquake-induced collapses

Cuihuashan Mountain National Geopark, Shaanxi. The major geological heritage is the earthquake-induced mountain collapses and piles, and dam-block lakes. The controlling geological setting is the piedmont faulting on the north of Qinling Mountain, and the relevant natural conditions are the moderate mountains and talus of boulder gravels.

Large-scale landslides

Yi'ong National Geopark, Tibet. The major geological heritage is the large-scale mountain mass slides, moderate glaciers, high mountains and deep valleys, and vertical zonation of vegetation. The controlling geological setting is the uplifted belt of the Qinghai–Tibet Plateau, and the relevant natural conditions are the high mountains, deep valleys and modern glaciers.

China's Global Geoparks

On 6–7 July 2003, the Specialist Review Meeting for Recommending the First World Geoparks was held in Beijing. After the field investigations and inspections for primary qualified geoparks, eight of the National Geoparks were listed as candidates for Global Geopark status. This list was approved by the Leading Group of the National Geological Heritage Protection (Geoparks) Commission. The characteristics of major geological heritage and the global correlation significance of the eight Global Geoparks are as follows.

Mount Huangshan Geopark, Anhui. The major geological heritages of this geopark is the granite peak forest landform, with rock pillars, peaks and grotesque rocks, deep and secluded valleys and warm springs. Mount Huangshan of Anhui has been inscribed on the World Heritage List by UNESCO, not only for its natural landscape values but also for its abundant and colourful historic and cultural relics. It is one of the world-rare natural and cultural heritages.

Mount Lushan Geopark, Jiangxi. The major geological heritage is the Quaternary glacial vestiges and their naming places, complete sections and old stratigraphic sections of southern China, and the fault-block mountain. The Quaternary glacial vestiges in this geopark belong to the maritime piedmont glacial type, with some representative and global correlation significance. The establishment of Quaternary glacial sections in this geopark provides some guidance regarding Quaternary glacial study and glacial geology in China. The metamorphic core complex in Mount Lushan is of some typical and international correlating significance.

Mount Yuntaishan Geopark. This geopark is composed of typical structural and hydrological landforms, dominated by long walls and cliffs, narrow gorges, lane-like valleys, urn-like valleys and waterfalls, among them, the Yuntai Heaven

Waterfall (304 m). This geopark is characterized by the specific geological and geomorphic landscapes of gorge groups, criss-cross peaks, cliffs and walls, as well as peak clusters and peak forests. It can be compared favourably with the other major canyon national parks in the world.

Stone Forest Geopark, Yunnan. This is mainly composed of carbonate (karst) forest, dominated by the karst landforms and sword-like stone forest. This geopark is the sole representative area in the world that reveals a geological history in more than 200 m of stone forest karst heritage. Within the geopark the stone forest represents a long and complex evolutionary history, with various and complicated shapes. It is also called the museum of stone forest. The scenery of stone forest is natural and extremely beautiful. It plays an indispensable role in karst, Yi minority culture and history and tourism studies.

Mount Danxia Geopark, Guangdong. The major geological heritage in this geopark is the typical and representative Danxia (meaning the rosy cloud in Chinese) landform, dominated by the red walls and rosy cliffs composed by the red continental clastics. This geopark includes typical, abundant, various and beautiful Danxia landforms. These landform resources are the best for studying Danxia landforms, and so it is of great significance for scientific research and sustainable utilization.

Zhangjiajie Geopark, Hunan. The major geological heritage is the quartzose sandstone forest landform, with 3000 or more peak pillars, the highest reaching 400 m. It is quite different from the loess forest on loess plateau, other stone forests and Danxia landforms. The unique and magnificent quartzose sandstone forest is rare by world standards. In addition, the karst caves in the geopark are unusual, being large in scale and complete in types. The ecological environment and ecosystems are undisturbed and preserved in a natural condition in the geopark. This geopark integrates the peak forest, karst caves, lakes and waterfalls, and has a high aesthetic and scientific value. The Zhangjiajie was inscribed on the World Natural Heritage List in 1992.

Wudalianchi Volcano Geopark, Heilongjiang. The major geological heritage is the volcanic landforms, with fourteen volcanoes that erupted from Tertiary to Quaternary eras, the latest eruption being in 1721. There are also natural carbondioxide-bearing warm mineral springs, as well as the rare ore sludge and cool springs with medical effects. There are more than 1500 complete and well-preserved driblet cones and dishes. The geopark includes typical, complete and concentrated volcanic landforms, and has been likened to a natural volcano museum. It has great value for scientific study and correlation in the world.

Songshan Geopark, Henan. This geopark is dominated by stratigraphic, structural and other geological heritage. There are three clear angular unconformity boundaries of the Archaean/Proterozoic (2.5 Ga), the Proterozoic/Mid-Proterozoic (1.8 Ga) and Neoproterozoic/Palaeozoic (543 Ma), and the typical structural heritages. The three global tectonic orogenies are called the Songyang Orogeny, Zhongyue Orogeny and Shaolin Orogeny respectively, which are all named in this geopark. Besides the Archaean, Proterozoic, Palaeozoic, Mesozoic and Cenozoic metamorphic series, magmatite and sedimentary sequences are systematically and well outcropped. It is called 'the undivided family with five generations' in geology. The stratigraphy and structures in the geopark are of important significance in global correlation.

Conclusions

China's National Geoparks are natural parks that are dominated by special, rare, graceful and/or beautiful geological heritage. When integrated with local historic and cultural relics, they have great scientific value. The bases for the establishment of a geopark are the geological landscape, scientific involvement, cultural features and social development. Rather than a single geological heritage, the geopark is trying systematically and scientifically to integrate regional geological heritage with local ecosystems. It aims to protect the geological heritage by providing a place for scientific education, by geological popularization and by ecological tourism. The aim of a geopark is to unite its geological heritage protection with the development of the local economy.

China is vast in territory and complex in geological and geomorphic features. Many of the world's rarest and unique geological landscapes have been created during the Earth's history. So far 44 National Geoparks have been established in China, and many important areas of geological heritage are now protected. Thus geoparks can:

1. Provide the opportunity for studying key geological problems.
2. Provide sites for geological understanding and scientific popularization.
3. Improve the local economic development through scientific tourism, investigation, and environmental protection tourism.

In this way, local governments, economic entities and local communities can consciously take part in the work of geological heritage protection. As the implementation and construction of the UNESCO World Geopark advances, it may be expected that humanity will open a new page of geological heritage protection with it.

Part Three: Geotourism in Action

9

Geotourism: a perspective from the USA

Alexander E. Gates

Introduction

Geotourism is a new term for a relatively old idea, and as such there still remain conflicting definitions. On the one hand, the relatively broad definition 'Tourism that sustains or enhances the geographic character of the place being visited – its environment, culture, aesthetics, heritage and well-being of its residents' encompasses a large range of activities, and the 'geo' part of the definition refers to geography (Stueve *et al.*, 2002). On the other hand, the geologist's definition of geotourism is 'Tourism in geological landscapes', as coined by the Geological Curator's Group and the Geoconservation Commission of the Geological Society (London), where the 'geo' clearly refers to geology (Robinson, 1998). The *National Geographic Traveler* and the Travel Industry Association of America performed a survey of potential vacationers in 2003, and found that some 55 million Americans were willing to make an extra effort to partake in geotourism and were thus classified as geotourists, with various subcategories depending upon interest (Stueve *et al.*, 2002). Therefore, geotourism in any form is a very popular idea.

Although less than ten years old as a proper term, geotourism has been practised in the United States for more than a century. The first National Park was established by an Act of Congress in 1872 to preserve areas of natural wonder and beauty 'for the benefit and enjoyment of the people' (see Harris *et al.*, 1997). The National Park Service was created by Congress in 1916, and included the 40 parks and monuments that had already been set aside. All of these early preserved areas, and indeed a good proportion of the total National Parks, preserve features that were created through geological processes. The more famous parks, like Yellowstone in Wyoming (the first National Park), Grand Canyon in Arizona, Devil's Tower in Wyoming, and Crater Lake in Oregon (Figure 9.1), are preserved for their splendour but recognized as of geological origin by most visitors. Other parks and monuments are purely geological in origin, like Dinosaur National Monument in Colorado, Petrified Forest in Arizona and Volcanoes National Park in Hawaii (Figure 9.1). However, even many of the less famous and more regional parks and monuments also have geological origins. These features have been widely regarded as destinations for vacationers, but just for their beauty or curiosity rather than their geological significance.

Although geology was the premier science in the United States (and indeed the world) throughout the nineteenth century (Gates *et al.*, 2002), its popularity and

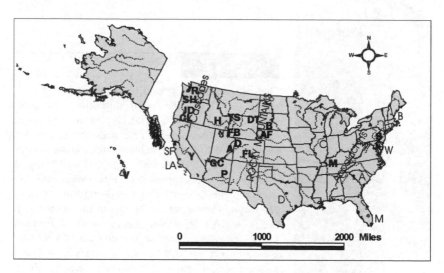

Figure 9.1 Map of the United States showing the locations of National Parks and local sites that are discussed in the text. (A) Arches National Monument; (AF) Agate Fossil Beds National Monument; (B) Badlands National Park; (CL) Crater Lake; (D) Dinosaur National Monument; (DT) Devil's Tower National Monument; (FB) Fossil Butte National Monument; (FL) Florissant Fossil Beds National Monument; (GC) Grand Canyon National Park; (H) Hagerman Fossil Beds National Monument; (JD) John Day Fossil Beds National Monument; (K) Katmai National Park; (M) Mammoth Caves National Park; (P) Petrified Forest National Monument; (S) Sterling Hill Mine; (SH) Mount Saint Helens National Park; (V) Volcanoes National Monument; (Y) Yosemite National Park; (YS) Yellowstone National Park. Cities (bold letters): A, Atlanta; B, Boston; C, Chicago; D, Dallas; LA, Los Angeles; M, Miami; W, Washington, DC; SF, San Francisco.

the interest in it varied significantly in the twentieth century. The last real peak of interest in the United States resulted from the energy crisis of the 1970s. Even popular news magazines rated geology as one of the, if not the, most sought-after professions. It was at this time that another step in geotourism was taken. In 1972, the first of the *Roadside Geology* series of books was published by Mountain Press. These books are written for specific states, and contain information regarding the background geology of the area in addition to a guide for places to see rock exposures, primarily along roadsides. To date there are some 40 states and regions covered by these manuals, and many are written by prominent geologists, making them of relatively high quality in terms of scientific content (e.g. Alt and Hyndman, 1978; Chronic and Williams, 1980; Sheldon, 1980; Caldwell, 1998; Dott and Attwig, 2002; Skehan, 2003). The main consumers of these books, however, are geologists and people with a great pre-existing interest in geology.

Another advance in geotourism during the late 1970s was the new introductory level college courses on the geology of the US National Parks, which were introduced and became popular on a large scale. The primary textbook for these courses, *Geology of National Parks* (Harris *et al.*, 1997) is now beginning its sixth edition, and is widely used throughout the United States. In explaining these geological features, the textbook relies on primary scientific literature rather than popular explanations – thus drawing the geological research community into geotourism. These courses served to show the strong control of geology, from blatant to subtle, on the formation of the natural landscape in 57 National Parks to date. They also made the connection of geology to these popular tourist attractions for many thousands of college students who may not have had a strong interest in geology but thought the course title sounded interesting. Like the roughly contemporaneous series of popular books by John McPhee on many regional geological phenomena in the United States from a scientific perspective (McPhee, 1981, 1983, 1986), these courses brought a general appreciation of geology to many people. They likely resulted in a general increase in geotourism, but they also left a wide gap between these general descriptions and actually going out and observing many of the features.

With the successful and widespread college courses, popular books and television documentaries, ever-increasing vacationers, new programmes and visitors' centres at National Parks, and the hype about geotourism that has arisen over the years, it would seem that the vast majority of people would be informed about geotourism and eager to participate. Yet, in a typical introductory geology college class in a relatively affluent and sophisticated area like northern New Jersey, of 200 to 250 students perhaps a handful, if any, would have visited one of these geology-oriented National Parks or even know much about them. The problem is that most of the really spectacular geotourism destinations in National Parks are distant from population centres, in areas that offer very little in terms of the cultural opportunities that would interest an otherwise urban sophisticate. People have to really want to see the natural splendour to be willing to forgo the pleasures of a vibrant nightlife or a fabricated theme park designed not only to entertain adults but also to occupy their children. Ultimately, for geotourism to achieve its potential impact, these urbanites and suburbanites will need to appreciate and desire visiting these spectacular features. However, it will require extensive education and marketing to have geotourism become a true priority. One of the big efforts of a project in Harriman State Park is to bring geotourism to the people of the largest population centre in the United States; the New York metropolitan area (Gates *et al.*, 2004).

Relation of geotourism to sustainability and policy issues

The setting aside of natural wonders and the creation of the National Park Service attests to the desire of Americans to preserve features for tourism regardless of the cost. However, the vast majority of these parks (if any at all) are not preserved for their geological significance but rather for their natural beauty or curiosity. Subsequently, geological significance may have been elucidated in displays in local museums and visitors' centres. Depending upon location, the geological significance takes on varying degrees of importance to the local population. For example, in Los Angeles and San Francisco, California, earthquake activity on the San Andreas Fault (Figure 9.1) reminds the residents of the importance of geological processes on a regular basis. Similarly, the majestic Mount Ranier hovering over Seattle, Washington (Figure 9.1), coupled with the memory of the catastrophic eruption of Mount Saint Helens in 1980, keeps residents keenly aware of the power of geological processes. In these and several other relatively populated areas, and the many minimally populated areas of the United States in the vicinity of the great National Parks, people are very interested in understanding the role of geology in their lives and consequently geotourism. In these areas, it is much more likely that this interest will have an impact on sustainability and policy issues than in most of the United States.

In many other areas of the United States, such as the heavily populated northeast, geotourism may be more popular in certain groups rather than the general population. In New Jersey, for example, geology is not a required subject or even offered in many high school curricula. Because New Jersey is on a tectonic passive margin, there are no volcanoes, few earthquakes and very few other geological phenomena that affect people in everyday life. The mining industry has long since closed down in the state, and the geological community has failed effectively to convey the connection of geology to environmental issues, of which there are many. The urban sprawl has covered the majority of interesting geological features with well-landscaped condominium complexes, housing developments and strip malls. People do not see geology on a daily basis, even in passing. Geotourism is not a major concern affecting sustainability and policy issues. Other factors may serve the role of protecting and preserving natural areas. New Jersey has recently begun legislation to prevent urban and suburban sprawl into the Highlands region, which covers the northwestern portion of the state and is under the highest pressure for development. This movement will ultimately help to preserve interesting geological features that can be used for geotourism, but only as an incidental benefit.

Local-scale preservation efforts are similarly unconcerned with geotourism. In two separate recent lawsuits that involved the destruction or preservation of natural areas in which the geology was introduced, neither considered it in the final outcome. In both cases (one the building of a power plant and the other the building of a golf course surrounded by luxury homes), significant natural areas in key locations would have been destroyed. Geology and geotourism were introduced in both cases and could have made an impact, but ultimately the areas were preserved because the construction would have destroyed the natural habitat of the northern rattlesnake, an endangered species.

Even though the United States began preserving its natural wonders long ago, in terms of geotourism, on a national scale, it has fallen well behind other efforts. The model of the UNESCO-sponsored Geopark system of Europe (Patzak, 2002) is truly the next step in geotourism for the United States. Several parks throughout Europe are being developed specifically for their geological resources. At present, there are parks in Greece, Germany, France, Spain and Italy, with several more planned in the near future. The development of these parks is clearly supported by local legislators for both sustainability and the economic boon of tourism in otherwise generally marginal to uneconomic areas. The United States has not yet followed this Geopark model in a meaningful way.

Current geotourism in the United States

Geologists worldwide love to attend field trips, and those in the United States are no exception. As a result, there is a plethora of published professional field guides available from organizations on the local to international level. The guides are first released in conjunction with field trips that are led by the scientists who wrote the guides, but professionals, students and teachers may later utilize these guides for educational or research purposes, or even just for enrichment or general interest. Some of the professional organizations have capitalized on this interest to offer the most sophisticated level of geotourism. The Geological Society of America, for example, offers their Geoventures as kind of a part-geotourism, part-serious series of field excursions to some of the most spectacular field exposures and field areas in the world. The general public, however, rarely participates in these offerings.

Geotourism that is designed more for the general public takes on numerous forms in the United States. Certainly, the best-organized and most utilized geotourism by far is for the National Parks. The sophistication and number of opportunities for geotourism vary by individual park. Many offer short, self-guided or ranger-led geology walks around the visitors' centres or onsite museums, which vary significantly in terms of the number and quality of stops. They also differ as to whether there is geology actually to be seen or just descriptions on a plaque. Park-scale guides also vary significantly by the park. In general, the National Park Service maintains their 'ParkNet' Internet site (www.nps.gov), which gives information on all of the National Parks (National Park Service). Within that site is the 'Nature Net' menu, which in turn links to a 'Nature and Science' menu. One link on that menu contains geology pages. The US Geological Survey also maintains Internet sites that contain even more information on the geology of many of the parks (www.usgs.gov). The two sites are well interlinked, so navigation between them to obtain the desired information is quick and convenient. The Digital Library for Earth System Education, a National Science Foundation-sponsored effort, is a repository for all geoscience education archival material, including these and other online field trip sites (www.dlese.org/dds/index.jsp). In addition to the government-sponsored websites, there are other sites typically sponsored by local organizations or universities that offer everything from pictures of recent outings to virtual flyovers and real and virtual fieldtrips (e.g. Scholle, 2002). These websites also vary significantly in terms of quality and relevance. Commercial books are also available for several of the National Parks and are typically far more detailed than the Internet sites, though they may also contain significant amounts of extraneous material. Some companies assemble maps, books and hiking guides into 'packages' to aid in self-guided tours of famous National Parks. Finally, there are commercial tours of geological features, including collecting locations that are available for a few of the parks at variable cost.

The National Park with probably the most opportunity for geotourism is the Grand Canyon (Figure 9.1). There are not less than five extensive geological guides to the Grand Canyon currently available through commercial bookstores (e.g. Collier, 1980; Price, 1999). There are also several videotapes available that discuss the geological history and processes that formed it. National Park Service rangers lead short tours that focus on the geology. There are several virtual hikes on the Internet, and even commercial tour guide outfits to lead visitors specifically on geotourist trips. The reason that the level of activity is so high is that the Grand Canyon is so visually breathtaking and it also offers other popular recreational activities. Many visitors come just to behold this awesome feature, and because it is clearly geological in nature they partake in the geotourist offerings as an afterthought.

Several other parks fall into this category of the geology being incidental to the magnificence of the main park features. In Yellowstone National Park, most visitors come to see the geysers – specifically, Old Faithful (Figure 9.1). Because the geysers and hot springs in the park are geologically controlled, visitors are also willingly exposed to geotourism. Like the Grand Canyon, there are ranger-led tours, concessioner-led tours and books (e.g. Keefer, 1971; Good and Pierce, 1996). There is also an outstanding virtual tour of Mammoth Hot Springs terraces from the park website that can be printed and used as a field guide for a self-guided tour. The Yosemite National Park (Figure 9.1) website offers several similar virtual geological hikes with specific stops along trails and excellent images that can also be easily printed and used as field guides. The geological descriptions of stops are generally relatively elementary, using a 'one size fits all' approach, rendering them of limited usage for many visitors. Although some parks mark the locations of stops along trails, many do not. Instead, they present large views of features that are relatively obvious along trails by their size. Few if any of the images shown in these virtual self-guided tours are annotated, so viewers must work to integrate the text with the features on the images. The effectiveness of these tours depends upon the motivation of the visitor. In general, the geological field activities are just small parts of the menu of recreational offerings of these parks, and typically they are not greatly emphasized. Clearly, the featured attraction to most of this category of parks and monuments is not the opportunity for geotourism; this is more an added bonus to help sell the park as a vacation destination.

Other large National Parks are specifically centred on geological phenomena, and accordingly they become the central theme in any visit. Volcanoes National Park in Hawaii is designed purely for geotourism (Figure 9.1). Tours, both from the Park Service and through commercial outfits, centre largely on the eruptions of Kilauea and the features produced, and range in sophistication from short hikes to helicopter tours. Virtual tours are well designed, including self-guided hikes along trails with hot zones on the stops. These hot zones open into outstanding images of the features, though they are rarely annotated and explanations are generic and elementary. With the emphasis on geological research of the active volcanoes and spectacular features, geotourism is a major industry in Hawaii – though clearly, there are other activities for vacationers.

The Casacade Mountains of northern California, Oregon and Washington (Figure 9.1) though a much broader area, also attract significant numbers of geotourists using this same volcano theme. The more popular of these areas are Crater Lake, California, and Mount Saint Helens and Mount Rainier, Washington (Figure 9.1), though others are also quite popular. There are numerous guidebooks for these areas as well as commercial and several park-sponsored tours, most of which emphasize the 1980 eruptions of Mount Saint Helens. There is a detailed virtual tour of Mount Rainier (armchair geology) and several of Mount Saint Helens, but most describe the geology of large views rather than individual rock exposures, and they are not annotated. The quality of explanation of the events and processes in these (and other) active volcanic areas is generally excellent. In several cases, professional literature appears in explanations and websites. Even state governments provide information and sponsored tours and literature for self-guided geotourism. Other volcano parks, like Katmai in Alaska (Figure 9.1), receive significant numbers of geotourists, but the less recent the activity in the area, the more other recreational attractions are featured (Katmai-Novarupta last erupted in 1912 and produced the Valley of 10000 Smokes). Unless the geological features are really spectacular, geotourism quickly moves to a position of secondary interest for the majority of park visitors.

There are several parks that exist purely for their geological significance. This geology may be visually impressive as well, as in the case of the Petrified Forest in Arizona, Arches National Monument in Utah, Devil's Tower in Wyoming and Mammoth Caverns in Kentucky (Figure 9.1), among many others. Even though visitors may be aware of the geology, it is not the primary reason for the visit in many cases. On the other hand, Dinosaur National Monument, Colorado and Utah, exists purely for the more than 1500 spectacular fossil dinosaur bones that can be observed in the Douglass Quarry (Figure 9.1). Virtually all visitors come to this park for geotourism. Because this is a relatively long trip just for geology, park promotional media emphasize panoramic views, nature trails, Native American petroglyphs, and canoeing/rafting trips with the dinosaur quarry as just one of these activities. There are several other National Parks in this purely geotourism category, like Fossil Butte National Monument in Wyoming, Agate Fossil Beds National Monument in Nebraska, Hagerman Fossil Beds National Monument in Idaho, John Day Fossil Beds in Oregon and Florissant Fossil Beds National Monument in Colorado, among a few others (Figure 9.1). Although also quite spectacular, most of these tend to be far less developed, accessible and advertised than Dinosaur National Monument, commonly comprising a visitor's centre with a few geology trails and a far more extensive hiking trail network. Nonetheless, people visiting these parks are keenly interested in geotourism and come in large enough numbers to keep the parks open, if not thriving.

The ultimate geotourism experience is to participate in an active geological research programme (Hall-Beyer, 1997). There are several organizations, like the Earthwatch Institute and the National Geographic Society, that sponsor research to specifically include member participation and/or to be marketed thereafter. Some of them include geological research, though it is typically not the most popular programme. To involve more visitors at least peripherally in active research, in collaboration with the South Dakota School of Mines, staff at the Badlands National Park, South Dakota (Figure 9.1) have developed the 'Pig Dig Wayside Exhibit' (Benton, 2003). The exhibit involves the active excavation of the ancient pig-like mammal Archaeotherium (thus the name 'pig dig'), in addition to several other early mammals, by professional geologists and assistants. The park has assembled several visitor facilities around the active site, which receives 5000 to 10 000 visitors annually. The excitement of experiencing the discovery process in science cannot be overemphasized in the geotourism experience.

The quantity and quality of geotourism opportunities on the local level vary tremendously. At the basic level, most major cities have self-guided tours of the building stones that are readily observed on prominent buildings. Whether any-one besides geologists and possibly historians and builders use these books is questionable. In the larger cities, natural history museums commonly offer geo-logical tours of the region to their members for a fee. These same museums may also offer educational enhancement programmes to high school students, which can include geology. Many famous geologists attribute their beginnings in geol-ogy to such programmes (Gates, 2002). The other major outlet for geotourism in many urban to suburban areas is through the huge number of local societies. There are gem and mineral, geological, palaeontological and environmental soci-eties and clubs, among others, from the state to city to county scale, that number in the thousands in the eastern United States alone. These societies have the com-bined advantage of serving as an outlet for science (talks and publications), geo-tourism and recreation through fieldtrips as well as socialization with people with similar interests. With typical memberships ranging to several hundred people, the societies, in total, represent a significant group.

Local opportunities for geotourism through parks and commercial ventures vary from non-existent to small but impressive, depending upon the resources of the area (Figure 9.1). In New Jersey, for example, the old Franklin zinc mine (Sterling Hill Mine) was converted to a successful mine museum to utilize its repu-tation as the fluorescent mineral capital of the world. To the east in Connecticut, dinosaur footprints can be viewed in a small park within the Mesozoic Hartford basin. To the west in Pennsylvania and laterally throughout the Appalachians, commercial caves are common in the areas underlain by limestone. Still farther west in Pennsylvania, mine tours of abandoned coalmines are available. Other mine tours, ranging from gold mines in North Carolina to pegmatite mines in Virginia, vary according to the geology and the extent of the local population's willingness to support such ventures. Local public parks may also contain geological features that are used to attract tourists. These are primarily solitary features, like a single fold along a Maryland highway, and of limited usage.

On the west coast, the opportunities are far more extensive because the geol-ogy is better exposed and far more relevant to everyday life. In addition to the mines and caves common to the east coast, the west coast has additional attrac-tions. There are earthquake displays, museums and explanations (Collier, 1999) throughout California, reflecting the concern about seismic activity. The La Brea tar pits in the greater Los Angeles area are a local museum. Many other well-exposed geological features, from unique rock units and structures to the ter-raced Pacific coastline, are commonly used for local activities in geotourism. In Oregon and Washington the emphasis shifts to the volcanoes, but wider geo-tourism interests are equally popular. In Seattle, Washington, there is at least one

Case study 9.1: Harriman State Park, New York

The Harriman State Park geotourism project is attempting to accomplish two main goals:

1. To develop a national model for the packaging and marketing of geoscience educational and recreational resources of public parks that preserve nature within large urban/suburban areas
2. To convert the products of an active scientific research programme into concepts and products that can be utilized and appreciated by the general public.

Both of these goals are designed to increase the awareness and appreciation of the local population regarding geology in these huge population centres, where exposure to it is minimal. If these city people can partake in geotourism on an enjoyable daily basis rather than an expensive vacation that precludes them from participating in other recreational activities, they may be more amenable to it. Seeing scientists participating in active research projects while at the park and seeing new ideas constantly being added to the body of knowledge is much more exciting than reading old information that no one has bothered with for many decades. This energy and excitement ideally would increase participation in geotourism.

commercial geological tour concessioner that leads trips to a variety of local destinations.

In the Gulf Coast region, the great popularity of geology is expressed in many oil and gas displays in museums and visitors' centres, but there is little true geology to see on the ground east of West Texas. Such displays continue into the Midwest oil and gas province through Ohio, Illinois, Indiana and Pennsylvania, and even west into California depending upon the local population. Local commercial caves and mines also exist in the upper Midwest, depending upon population density, though the interest in geotourism is similar to that in the east. There is a reasonable number of geotourism opportunities across the middle north of the country, largely reflecting the extensive mining industry in the area and somewhat reflecting glaciation. In general, as the population thins in the west, so do the non-National Park-run opportunities for geotourism.

Case study 9.1 describes the Harriman State Park geotourism project.

The project

The billion-year-old crystalline rocks within the Harriman–Bear Mountain–Sterling Forest State Park of the Palisades Interstate Park in the western Hudson Highlands of New York (Gates *et al.*, 2001; Gates and Grant, 2002) are being researched in an ongoing scientific project (Figure 9.2). Although, at first glance, many of the rocks appear to be dull and grey, they are actually quite exciting in that they reflect part of the Rodinian supercontinental cycle in which all of the

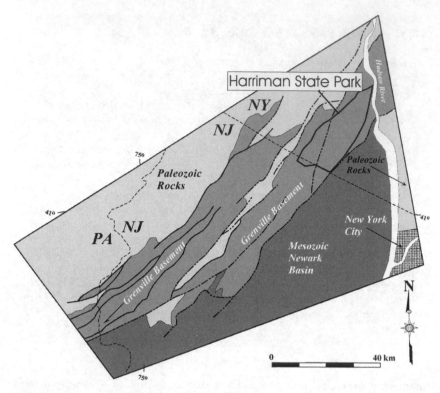

Figure 9.2 Geologic map of the Highlands region showing the location of Harriman State Park (including Bear Mountain and Sterling Forest State Parks) and New York City (after Gates *et al.*, 2001).

continents of the Earth were joined in a single supercontinent about a billion years ago. These rocks are the roots of perhaps the largest and most extensive mountain system ever on Earth. The scientific resources of this geology that are being uncovered on a daily basis by a team of active researchers are being immediately packaged and delivered to the public in both informal and formal science educational products. Although similar approaches have been attempted in several prominent National Parks on a smaller scale, these parks are distant from population centres and generally cannot be accessed on a regular basis by most people. This project is designing a model to package and market successfully the relatively non-spectacular (in comparison to those of the US National Parks) geoscience resources of a public park in an urban–suburban setting. To accomplish this on a large scale, an entertaining videotape on the geology of the park was produced and widely distributed to inform the public and drum up interest and excitement (Figure 9.3). Interested people then are encouraged to visit a website to take a virtual geological field trip of the park (Figure 9.4). Ultimately, they are further encouraged to visit these rock exposures in a pleasurable recreational setting for the full scientific experience. Coverage by the local media has enhanced this process significantly.

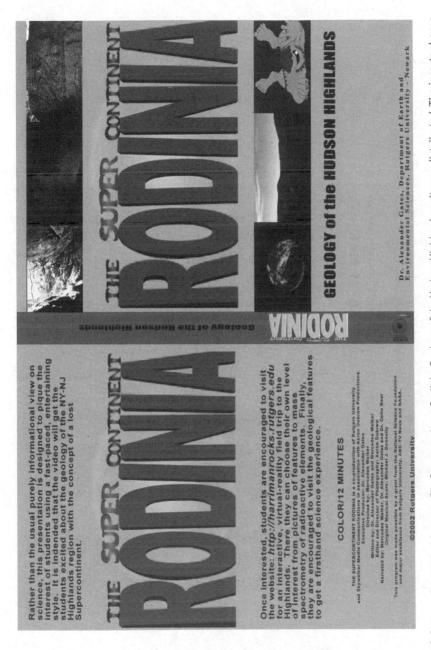

Figure 9.3 Cover for VHS videotape *The Supercontinent Rodinia: Geology of the Hudson Highlands* as it was distributed. The inserts show a selection of still images from the video.

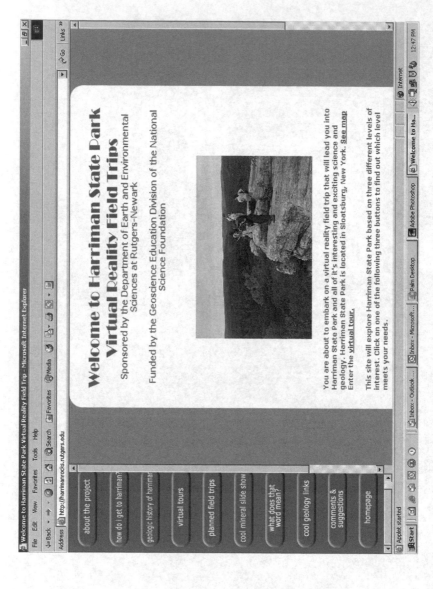

Figure 9.4 Home page for the website for the geology of Harriman State Park, http://harrimanrocks.rutgers.edu (Gates and Grant, 2002).

The field area

The Harriman–Bear Mountain–Sterling Forest State Park complex is a 72 000-acre contiguous wilderness recreation area that comprises the largest part of the Palisades Interstate (New York–New Jersey) Park system. It is located about 50 km northwest of New York City in the Hudson Highlands, west of the Hudson River in southeastern New York State (Figure 9.2). The Palisades Interstate Park system began in 1900 with the creation of the Palisades Interstate Park Commission. The mission was to protect and preserve the New York–New Jersey Palisades cliff landscape. Significant park expansion resulted from donations by prominent local families, including Harriman, Rockefeller and Perkins. Previously, it had been one of the most extensive iron-mining districts in the United States for some 150 years (Hotz, 1952) – thus it had its beginnings in geology.

The derived iron from the more than 300 mines figured prominently in early American history, from the making of the chain across the Hudson to prevent a British incursion during the Revolution to forming the majority of the old rail system in the early republic. However, the discovery of large deposits in Minnesota in the late 1800s rendered the area uneconomic, and operations slowly ceased by about 1910. The entire region was an industrial environmental disaster at the time it was donated. Upon obtaining the land, New York State went to great lengths to restore it. In addition to immense quantities of waste rock from the mining operations, because there is no ready source of fuel in the area most of the trees had been harvested and charcoaled for the smelters, so it was barren. Waters from mine run-off were highly polluted, and the air hung heavy with smog from the smelters. Animals and fish were few, if any. In the 1870s, the sighting of a single deer in the area (now numbering in the tens of thousands) literally made front-page news in local newspapers. Virtually all of the wildlife had to be repopulated, and much of the cleaning and grooming of the park was accomplished through federal work projects during the Great Depression in the 1930s. It is ironic that this once industrial wasteland is now valued for its natural beauty and is regarded by most visitors as a primeval forest.

The Sterling Forest lands (20 000 acres) were added to the park in phases, beginning in 1998, at a cost of some $87 million from federal, state and local sources, mainly for watershed protection in this environmentally sensitive area. The events of this acquisition gave the area a recent high public profile as it regularly appeared in the media. This attention has contributed to the interest in geotourism in the area.

The Palisades Interstate Park system receives over nine million visitors annually for recreational purposes. Within perhaps a 50-mile (80-km) radius of the Park the New York metropolitan area has more than 20 million residents, giving it the greatest population to draw from in the United States. Included in the visitors are significant numbers of people from racial and ethnic groups, who are generally under-represented in the sciences. Addressing this group with the potential of geotourism could serve to mitigate this problem of under-representation. The Park maintains a Trailside Museum that concentrates on natural and historic resources (including a geology museum) and receives about 250 000 visitors per year. It maintains four satellite museums in the camping areas specifically for camping groups composed largely of minority and underprivileged children from urban settings. Therefore, there is a local vehicle for dissemination of the geo-logical features.

Scientific research programme

The basic research in this area is driven by a geological field mapping that has been supported by the New York State Geological Survey and the US Geological Survey. Topical studies have emanated from the mapping, and include investigation of fault movement and processes and the plate tectonic interactions during the two separate deformational events, and the origin and geochemistry of metavol-canic rocks, of granite plutons and of several magnetite (iron ore) deposits. Determining the ages of these various geological events was accomplished by using Ar/Ar thermochronology (laser and conventional) and U/Pb geochron-ology using the SHRIMP (Super High Resolution Ion Microprobe) at the Geological Survey of Canada in Ottawa (Gates et al., 2001).

This new research confirmed that the geological setting was one of a volcanic island arc that probably resembled modern Japan during the formation of most of the rocks. There were two distinct plate tectonic events during this time of the building of the Rodinian supercontinent (known as the Grenvillian orogeny), rather than the single event that was previously proposed (Gates et al., 2001). The earlier event appears to have been a Himalayan-type (head-on) continent-to-continent collision of two large landmasses. This event formed likely the largest, most extensive mountain system ever on Earth. Evidence for it is found along the entire east coast of North America and westward as far as Texas, in South America and in Scandinavia – among other places. The mountains arose from a phenome-nally thickened crust that formed through large-scale recumbent fold nappes that were emplaced east to west across the area, and which doubled the crust over on itself like a rug pushed until it folds over on itself. The thickened crust was heated and pressurized beneath the mountains, and the rocks were transformed into banded gneiss and locally melted. The present level of observation was once 25–30 km deep in the crust. The nappe folds are readily observable in rock expo-sures, as are the gneisses and partly melted rocks (called migmatites). Some layer-ing in the metavolcanic rocks appears to be original, but it is mainly geochemical studies that reveal its history. There are some large, impressive minerals (e.g. mag-netite, pyroxene, hornblende, cordierite, garnet, etc.) observable in the metamor-phic rocks.

After the collision ended and the mountains reached their peak height, there was a period of bimodal plutonism (granite and diorite) in which magma invaded the crust in large sheet-like bodies (Gates et al., 2001). The granite is in sheets that form cliffs in the area. Both the granite and diorite plutons contain chunks of the gneiss that were broken and pulled into the magma as it intruded. These chunks (xenoliths) are excellent examples and are readily observable in rock exposures.

The second plate-tectonic event resulted in the formation of a large-scale strike-slip fault (shifts land laterally rather than vertically) that rivals the San Andreas fault of California (another strike-slip fault) (Figure 9.1; Gates et al., 2001). The faulting formed a 35+ km-wide belt of anastomosing ductile shear zones, which are wide areas of very deformed rock (mylonite) that has been stretched into the fault zones at conditions of great depth. In contrast, the more familiar shallow faults crack the rocks and produce earthquakes. The rocks are ribbon-banded mylonite zones that are razor sharp and arrow straight for tens to hundreds of kilometres. In addition to the mylonite rock, adjacent to the zones there are arch-like folds, stretched out cigar-shaped rock bodies called boudins, and flattened bulls-eye pattern folds called sheath folds, all of which can be seen in rock exposures. This strike-slip system appears to have resulted from escape tectonism, and had fault movement in the order of hundreds to perhaps a thousand kilometres. Escape tectonism results when a colliding continent impinges upon another continent, forcing lateral movement of landmasses away from the collision zone. Such is the case in the Himalayas, where large pieces of southeast Asia are being forced eastward away from the collision zone. Late in this second event iron-rich fluids were mobilized from deep in the Earth and flowed into the fault zones, where they deposited magnetite (iron ore) in the dilational fractures (Gates et al., 2001). These deposits were mined, and are therefore not as easily observable as they may have been 250 years ago before mining began, but there are plenty of fresh rock samples to observe around the mines.

Results from the Ar/Ar thermochronology (which determines the age at which rocks cool to certain temperatures) indicate slow uplift and cooling after about 925 Ma, although some of the strike-slip faults were active as late as 875 Ma (Gates and Krol, 1998). The SHRIMP analyses quantities of radioactive uranium and its decay to lead within the mineral zircon, which contains significant quantities of both elements. This analysis yields the ages of formation of rocks, and indicates a typical 1.2–1.3 billion year-old age for metavolcanic rocks and accompanying metasedimentary rocks (Gates et al., 2001). The peak of the mountain-building event (Grenville orogeny) occurred at about 1010–1050 million years ago. The intrusion of magma to form the bimodal plutons occurred almost immediately thereafter, at about 1004 million years ago. A new find is that there are distinct cores in the zircon grains from metasedimentary rocks that yield ages of 2.05 billion years old. These are the oldest ages of any rocks thus found in the central Appalachians, and are more consistent with rocks from the TransAmazonian orogen of South America than any in the area of the Hudson Highlands. This evidence shows that South America was likely attached to North America in this area, and that the Hudson Highlands could have been part of South America originally but were left behind when the supercontinent Rodinia broke apart about 550 million years ago (Gates et al., 2001). All of these new pieces of data and the theories that resulted from them were conceived in the recent past at the same time as the educational information was being prepared. Therefore, the findings were released to the public immediately after they appeared in the scientific literature.

A second area of scientific research in the Park involves the lingering environmental effects of the iron-mining industry. An ongoing study of acid mine drainage has identified significantly acidic water in most areas of extensive mine tailings, with pH as low as 2.6 (7 is neutral and lower numbers are progressively acidic). Considering that the pH of mine run-off in the coalfields of Pennsylvania, where acid mine drainage is a major problem, is rarely below 3, these findings are significant. The cause of acidity is the weathering of sulphur-rich minerals to produce dilute sulphuric acid. Around some mines, the sulphur odour can be smelled up to one kilometre away, and the mine areas are barren of vegetation though they have been inactive for nearly 100 years. Not only do these acidic waters kill all animals and most plants; they can also strip heavy metals (lead, mercury, arsenic, chromium, etc.) from the minerals exposed on the surface of the tailings. Normally, surface rocks are so weathered that heavy metals have long since been removed. However, freshly mined rocks can contain high concentrations of heavy metals on easily weathered surfaces. The old mine shafts are readily observable throughout the Park, as are the extensive tailings piles around them.

The run-off waters that infiltrated the tailings may also have transported these and the other industrial mine-related pollutants into the many lakes of the area, where they may still be stored in the sediments. Another research study is investigating the existence and distribution of these stored pollutants in lake sediments near mines. Finally, an area adjacent to the Park and in the same geological setting contains the only operating uranium mine ever east of the Mississippi River. Exxon Inc. drilled another uranium prospect in the 1970s, during the energy crisis. Considering that the Hudson Highlands are part of the Reading Prong, famous for occurrences of record levels of indoor radon, radioactive elements and their progeny are another environmental concern in the area.

The videotape: *The Supercontinent Rodinia*

A series of videotapes are planned to illustrate different geological aspects of the Park. The first is complete, and is entitled *The Supercontinent Rodinia: Geology of the Hudson Highlands* (Figure 9.3; Gates *et al.*, 2002). The videotape was produced using footage shot in the Park for this project, along with supplementary footage donated to the project by ABC-TV NewsOne and animations produced by senior art students from Rutgers University-Newark. The videotape was produced at two lengths, approximately 13 minutes for group or school usage and an edited-down 9-minute version for busy museums and visitors' centres. The videotape does not attempt to explain all of the science of the Park, but instead concentrates on a single topic – plate tectonics and the building of the Rodinian supercontinent. The reason this topic was chosen is that these events happened first and this aspect of the field project has received the most public interest to date, appearing in newspapers, radio and local magazines. The footage shot in the Park includes many of the most visually appealing geological features previously described, with a research geologist dressed in an Indiana Jones outfit explaining them as well as their origin in easy-to-understand language.

Just having explanations of rocks by a geologist would only attract the attention of already interested people. The point of the project is to address people with no prior interest. Therefore, rather than producing the staid and serious presentation that is typical of science videos, a fast-paced, entertaining video was produced. The video includes an animated Neanderthal man named 'Rocky Tectonic', who speaks with a British accent, explains features and processes, and interacts with the geologist. The donated video clips are from modern analogues to the interpreted processes on a worldwide basis, and are used to illustrate what the area may have looked like during each point in the geological history. Static graphics and animations explain the geological processes and plate tectonic reconstructions. The geological features that are emphasized in the videotape can be readily observed in the Park, and are used in the interpretation of geological history.

The point of the video is to get people interested in and enthused about this romantic 'lost world' story, as it has been designated. The fast-paced action with a carefully chosen popular musical score and interesting characters is designed to get people interested enough in the topic to visit the accompanying website to learn more about the geology. The web address is emphasized at the end of the presentation.

The website

The use of the Internet has proven to be very effective for introductory geoscience education (Sullivan and Dilek, 1997). To take advantage of this powerful educational tool, a website was developed to provide browsers with a virtual reality visit to the rocks in Harriman State Park. The website is available at http://harrimanrocks. rutgers.edu/ (Gates and Grant, 2002; Figure 9.4). The menu offers visitors several options, including a description of the project, a geological history of the Hudson Highlands, directions to the Park, and slide shows of common minerals. Teachers and group leaders can apply for a visitor's permit online. The main function of the site, however, is to offer visitors a virtual field trip of the geology of the Park. There is an animation of a geological map overlay that can be displayed on a detailed topographic hiking trail map of the area, which is produced by and available from the NY/NJ Trail Conference. The geological map shows the distribution of the various rock units in the area. There is a series of locations marked with numbers all over the map that are hot zones. These hot zones open an annotated image of the geological feature as it looks in the field. The annotations invite the browser to learn more about the feature. They will open windows to progressively more complex concepts of the science in layers. Visitors are encouraged to investigate the site to their level of interest and/or background, but they are also challenged to go deeper. This stepwise increase in complexity allows visitors to maintain their interest without becoming overwhelmed with details of the science. Therefore, the site can be used by novices and professionals with equal utility.

After viewing the image of the rock exposure, the first level commonly opens to a microscopic scale photograph of the rock in the feature. Minerals are identified and highlighted in the text. These links open images of those minerals from ideal samples in the New York State Museum. Otherwise, highlighted words open to definitions in an online geological glossary, which can also be independently accessed. Depending upon the feature, at the next level they might see mineral or rock chemistry and explanations of how the analyses are used to determine chemical reactions in the rock. A link from there shows how mineral chemistry is obtained using an electron microprobe. Other locations address the bulk chemistry of the rock and how the plate tectonic setting of them is determined using discrimination diagrams based upon immobile elements in successive levels. Still other locations are important for the results of the age determinations using analyses of isotope geochemistry. Several were analysed using a SHRIMP. High-energy, microscopic cathodoluminescence images of these mineral grains that were analysed using SHRIMP are shown, as are the ages resulting from this analysis in successive window levels. Structural analyses, among others, are similarly presented in the levels of complexity. As detailed topical studies continue to be produced, they too will be added to the site.

There are several additional links on a bar above the images at each level. They explain basic techniques used in the analysis of such field samples. From there, interested persons can see how thin sections of rocks (mounted on a microscope slide and thin enough to see through) are made and how a petrographic (geological optical) microscope works. Another link shows how rock ages are determined. Use of the SHRIMP is also shown.

In addition to the map-based information, several field trips are suggested. These field trips are topically based, and are directly linked to the locations on the map so the same details and levels of science are available. The trips are around recreation areas, along scenic trails, and in aerially restricted areas in the Park. Topical trips are based on mines, igneous rocks and bodies, metamorphic rocks, structural geology and surface features, among others. Several of the topical trips are designed to address the K-12 science standards for New York, New Jersey and nationally (American Association for the Advancement of Science, 1993; National Academy of Science, 1996). Therefore the trips may be used by local college and high school Earth Science teachers to enhance their classes.

Marketing and dissemination

One of the major aspects of this model is the effective dissemination of the ideas and materials. In order for the project to be a success, there must be broad public exposure to cultivate interest and support. There are many ways this can be accomplished, but finances impose heavy constraints. Marketing of Harriman State Park as a destination for geotourism mostly utilized existing institutions of formal and informal science education. The most effective and popular mode of disseminating information on the geology of the Park is through field trips led by scientists. Trips have been requested by a staggering number of both professional and casual groups, and continue to be requested today. Typical groups consist of about 45 people, most of whom gain a good understanding of the science through this experience. However, only about 200–250 people per year can be served by this method.

To disseminate information to a larger audience requires other modes. Public lectures are also commonly requested, but still address only 100–300 people at a time. Mass marketing in informal science education settings is being handled through displays at museums and visitors' centres. The Newark Museum recently opened an outstanding new 'Dynamic Earth' exhibit in the new Victoria Hall of Science. This exhibit contains a condensed scene from the Highlands region, and emphasizes the interrelation of geology and evolution. The short version of the videotape is a permanent part of the exhibit. The exhibit has already attracted over 1700 visitors per day during times of peak usage, and it is just over a year old. The short version is also a permanent exhibit in the new Lautenberg Visitors' Ventre in Sterling Forest State Park. The recent opening of this centre was conducted by the Governor of New York State and US Senator Lautenberg, among other dignitaries, which attracted significant media attention.

To market the programme to institutions of formal science education, some 3000 copies of the video were produced and distributed to local high schools and colleges in New Jersey and southern New York. They have been and are being shown to high school classes throughout the region on a daily basis.

Exposure of the video to the public through mass media is also desirable. This project received enhanced public attention through a front-page newspaper article in the Metro Section of the *New York Times* (Collins, 2002). The article came out several months before the programme was released, and thus prepared many interested people for its commencement. When the videotape was disseminated and the website came online they were anticipated by that segment of the public attuned to science. The Rodinia aspect of the research has gained wide interest by virtue of a 'lost continent' mystique. Even before the geotourism aspect of the project began, there was interest in the research findings. A front-page story appeared in the *New York Times* and similar stories appeared in local newspapers and even as far away as Vienna, Austria. Interviews and features were aired on the most subscribed-to news radio station in New York City as well. This media coverage greatly enhanced the effectiveness of dissemination and marketing efforts.

The next step

The next phase of the Harriman State Park project is to address the environmental aspects. The recovery of this industrial area to one of pristine forest, at least in appearance, has been well received by the public. Although geotourism may be a new concept in the area, protecting the environment is not. Considering that most of the reservoirs for drinking water in New Jersey are in the Highlands, there are many environmental groups who are very interested in having science to support their claims and, in general, the local population is eager to learn.

In addition to acid mine drainage and stored pollutants in sediments, there is a number of other topics of environmental concern. Foremost is the study of water resources and water flow. Because water flows downhill, the environmental health of the Highlands is not only of great concern to the people that live there or get their drinking water from reservoirs located there, it is also of concern to the people of the surrounding lowlands. Water not only flows from the Highlands to the surrounding lowlands down gradients in streams, it also flows down in the groundwater system – and in both cases can be driven quite a distance into the lowland systems. This concern about water quality and quantity can be translated into a general interest in learning about the science of water and water transport. Aquifers are rock units or sediments that readily transport and store groundwater. Clearly, the water must be clean and potable for aquifers to be of value. The ideal aquifer can be thought of as similar to beach sand. As water is poured into beach sand, it must wind around the individual grains. It makes maximum contact with grain surfaces, thus allowing chemical reactions between the grain surface and water, which remove pollutants. The narrow necks between grains trap bacteria in a similar way to a water filter, and further clean the water.

Because the Highlands form a crystalline terrain, they contain no porosity and permeability like beach sand because the minerals are large and tightly interlocked as a result of metamorphism. Water can only travel through cracks in the rocks called joints (regular cracks) and fractures (irregular). Joints are dominant, and tend to be straight and open. Water flows through them quickly and with minimal contact with the walls of the joint. Thus there is minimal filtering of bacteria and minimal water–rock chemical reactions as the water passes through.

This situation means that the water of the Highlands is highly environmentally sensitive, and from the old mining industry and relatively minimal development is already rated as fair by the US Environmental Protection Agency. Fractured-rock aquifers like this are all subject to the same environmental problems.

The people of the Highlands are very concerned about the water situation, often requesting experts to attend town meetings to explain the processes. This interest allows other concepts to be introduced, such as watershed analysis, watershed management and even continental glaciation as the glacial deposits atop the crystalline rock in aerially restricted locations form a unique double aquifer system. By combining the topics related to water with other environmental concerns like those related to the old mining operations (acid mine drainage, mine collapse, polluted sediments, etc.) and topics like anomalous environmental radon for which the Reading Prong (Highlands) is world renowned, a respectable environmental programme has been assembled. This programme has been presented to several groups, including high school teachers, to be used in lesson plans, and is applauded by environmental groups. It will also constitute a large part of a soon-to-be-aired public television documentary on the Highlands. This great interest adds yet another opportunity for geotourism in the Park.

The problems

Even with all of this publicity and interest, this project has a long way to go before geotourism in the Highlands can really be considered a success. The first problem is one of funding. There are no federal funding agencies that truly address such geotourism-type projects. Proposals to standard agencies such as the National Science Foundation and Environmental Protection Agency are out of the mainstream and appear almost whimsical. Obtaining large grants to complete the entire programme in a quality manner has been nearly impossible to this point. Therefore numerous small grants from a variety of sources must be cobbled together to complete the segments of the project, many of which must remain partially complete for long periods of time as a result. The missing, unfinished and poorly finished segments greatly detract from the overall quality of the programme, and in turn undermine its effectiveness. Until funding agencies regard geotourism as a viable method for increasing interest in science in the United States, the concept will never be truly effective.

The second major obstacle comes from the environmental and naturalist groups. Although they roundly applaud the concept of geotourism for bringing attention to environmental issues, they strongly oppose the steps needed to truly bring geotourism to the public. Many parks, including Harriman State Park, provide geology walks that give overviews of the geology of the area. These walks, however, are short, and either utilize the geology of the chosen convenient location, truck in a representative piece of geology from elsewhere in the Park, or ask visitors to use their imagination. This method is more like a poor museum in an outdoor setting, and is hardly effective for attracting interest. Asking visitors to buy a self-guided tour book or print guide from a website and then carry it around in the field eliminates all but the most interested of geotourists. Even mentioning marking and signage at the field locations, no matter how subtle or tasteful, brings protests from naturalists and environmentalists alike in many areas. They feel that such signs would spoil the natural beauty of the area. How adamant and powerful these groups are varies by community, but to date this problem has been impenetrable in Harriman State Park. On the other hand, the lack of clear demarcation of potentially interesting features to geotourists in the field severely limits the effectiveness of geotourism in Harriman State Park and indeed much of the United States.

Figure 9.5 Fold structure, Harriman State Park, USA.

Figure 9.6 Group examining rock outcrops in Harriman State Park, USA.

References

Alt, D. and Hyndman, D. W. (1978). *Roadside Geology of Oregon*. Mountain Press Publishing Co.

American Association for the Advancement of Science (1993). *Benchmarks for Science Literacy*. Oxford University Press.

Benton, R. (2003). The big pig dig: integrating paleontological research and visitor education at Badlands National Park, South Dakota. *Journal of Geoscience Education*, 51, 313–316.

Caldwell, D. W. (1998). *Roadside Geology of Maine*. Mountain Press Publishing Co.

Chronic, H. and Williams, F. (1980). *Roadside Geology of Colorado*. Mountain Press Publishing Co.

Collier, M. (1980). *An Introduction to Grand Canyon Geology, Phoenix, Arizona*. Grand Canyon Natural History Association.

Collier, M. (1999). *A Land In Motion – California's San Andreas Fault*. Golden Gate National Parks Association.

Collins, G. (2002). Making the Rocks Speak. *New York Times* (Metro Section), 25 July, 1.

Dott, R. H. Jr and Attwig, J. W. (2002). *Roadside Geology of Wisconsin*. Mountain Press Publishing Co.

Gates, A. E. (2002). *A–Z Biographies of Earth Scientists*. Facts On File, Inc.

Gates, A. E. and Grant, E. S. (2002). *Harriman State Park: A Virtual Field Trip* (available at http://harrimanrocks.rutgers.edu.).

Gates, A. E. and Krol, M. A. (1998). Kinematics and thermochronology of late Grenville escape tectonics from the central Appalachians. *Geological Society of America Abstracts with Programs*, Vol. 30.

Gates, A. E., Valentino, D. W., Chiarenzelli, J. *et al.* (2001). The assembly of the Supercontinent Rodinia in the western Hudson Highlands. *New York State Geological Association Field Trip Guidebook*, 73, 174–204.

Gates, A. E., Walker, M. and Dubrow, A. (2002). *The Supercontinent Rodinia: Evidence in the Hudson Highlands*. Rutgers University Television and Mass Media Production (Sponsored by the NSF and ABC-TV), 9 and 12 minutes (two versions).

Gates, A. E., Walker, M., Grant, E. and Dubrow, A. (2004). Multimedia model for the utilization of geoscience educational resources in public parks near urban centers. *Journal of Geoscience Education*, 52, 149–153.

Good, J. M. and Pierce, K. L. (1996). *Interpreting the Landscape: Recent and Ongoing Geology of Grand Teton and Yellowstone National Parks*. Grand Teton Natural History Association.

Hall-Beyer, M. C. (1997). Field geology for the National Park visitor – luring a general audience into research. *Journal of Geoscience Education*, 45, 456–459.

Harris, A. G., Tuttle, E. and Tuttle, S. D. (1997). *Geology of National Parks*, 5th edn. Kendall/Hunt Publishing Co.

Hotz, P. E. (1952). Magnetite deposits of the Sterling Lake, New York–Ringwood, New Jersey area. *US Geological Survey Bulletin*, 982-F, 153–244.

Keefer, W. R. (1971). The geologic story of Yellowstone National Park. *US Geological Survey Bulletin*, 1347, 92.

McPhee, J. (1981). *Basin and Range*. Farrar, Straus and Giroux.

McPhee, J. (1983). *In Suspect Terrain*. Farrar, Straus and Giroux.

McPhee, J. (1986). *Rising from the Plains*. Farrar, Straus and Giroux.

National Academy of Science (1996). *National Science Education Standards*. National Academy Press.

Patzak, M. (2002). *Tourism and Geodiversity: The Case of Geoparks*. UNESCO (available at egis.cefe.cnrs-mop.fr/Tourism%20Frontpages/patzak%20article. htm).

Price, L. G. (1999). *An Introduction to Grand Canyon Geology*. Grand Canyon Association.

Robinson, E. (1998). Tourism in geological landscapes. *Geology Today*, 14, 151–153.

Scholle, P. (2002). *An Introduction and Virtual Geologic Field Trip to the Permian Reef Complex, Guadalupe and Delaware Mountains, New Mexico-West Texas* (available at http://geoinfo.nmt.edu/staff/scholle/guadalupc.html).

Sheldon, R. (1980). *Roadside Geology of Texas*. Mountain Press Publishing Co.

Skehan, J. W. (2003). *Roadside Geology of Colorado*. Mountain Press Publishing Co.

Stueve, A. M., Cook, S. D. and Drew, D. (2002). *The Geotourism Study: Phase I Executive Study*. Travel Industry Association of America.

Sullivan, M. A. and Dilek, Y. (1997). Enhancing scientific literacy through the use of information technology in geoscience classes. *Journal of Geoscience Education*, 45, 308–313.

10

Geotourism in Ireland and Britain

Patrick Mc Keever, Jonathan Larwood and Alan McKirdy

Introduction

When people from outside Ireland and Britain think of this group of islands off northwest Europe, images are conjured up of a diversity of natural and cultural heritage that far outstrips their physical landmass. From Norman and Tudor castles to Neolithic forts, stone circles and burial chambers, Ireland and Britain contain a wealth of sites that represent most stages in the development of European civilizations. No less diverse is the natural foundation of these islands. Here, at the edge of northwest Europe, is the place where many of the founding principles of geological science were first formulated and demonstrated. A glance at a geological map of Ireland and Britain clearly shows the great diversity in geology, ranging from some of the oldest rocks in the world, in northwest Scotland, to the more recent deposits of Neogene times in southeast England. Indeed, many of the periods of geological time derive their names from associations with Ireland and Britain – for example, Cambrian (from the Latin name for Wales), Ordovician and Silurian (from ancient Welsh tribes) and Devonian (after Devon, in England). This diverse geology has been cut into and moulded by the force of ice during the Pleistocene Ice Ages, and has given rise to a spectacular range of landscapes.

It is these landscapes that draw visitors to Ireland and Britain from all over the world and which, for many parts of these islands, support a thriving tourist industry. Yet how many of these visitors are aware of the fascinating stories behind the formation of these landscapes? Furthermore, how many of these visitors, or indeed our own general public, are able to access information, at an appropriate level of interpretation, that helps reveal these great stories from geological time? Geological tourism in Ireland and Britain has a long established pedigree. However, until recently it operated as a bit of a 'closed shop' in which only geologists (both professional and amateur) were able to partake, largely because publications and presentations were couched in scientific terms. In more recent years, a concerted effort has been made to bring the great and diverse geological heritage of Ireland and Britain to the wider, non-geological, public.

This chapter provides an up-to-date account of these efforts, and discusses their merits and successes or failures as well as possible trends for the future. While the chapter discusses, in turn, recent efforts in England, Ireland and Scotland, it should be remembered that while these regions have followed different developmental paths with regard to geological tourism, there is a strong and constant exchange of ideas and experience among personnel and organizations within them.

Achieving sustainable geotourism in England

England's diverse geology is expressed in the varied character of the English countryside. From the uplands of the Lake District to the rolling hills of the Cotswolds, from the chalk of the Downs, Chilterns and Wolds to the red Triassic sandstones of the south Devon coast, the underlying geology and geological history directly influence the nature of our landscape and natural environment, and the character of our towns and cities (Figure 10.1). Whether it is implicit or explicit, England's attraction to the tourist is as much about its geology as it is about its history and culture – in fact the two are inextricably linked.

In recent years there has been a growth in geotourism throughout England and the realization that geodiversity, as part of our environment, is an essential element of environmental tourism. At a local level geology is widely used in town trails and guided tours, and there are numerous examples of geological sites managed with the visitor in mind. In Yorkshire the Dinosaur Coast Project (www.dinocoast.org.uk) has marketed geology directly to the tourist, and the recently inscribed Dorset and East Devon Coast World Heritage Site demonstrates the importance of geology in one of the most visited regions of the country. In 2003 England's first two European Geoparks were established, the North Pennines Area of Outstanding Natural Beauty, and the Abberley and Malvern Hills (Figure 10.1). Arguably, without the advanced state of conservation in England none of this would have been feasible, but how does geological conservation relate to geotourism?

The primary justification for geological conservation is 'the need to maintain our geodiversity for both present and future generations to experience, learn

Figure 10.1 A map of Britain and Ireland showing the location of sites of geological interest referred to in this chapter.

from and enjoy'. This is mirrored by geotourism, which in simple terms is 'travelling in order to experience, learn from and enjoy our geodiversity'. Geotourism is therefore in part a consequence of successful geological conservation, as this ensures the presence of a resource to 'experience, learn from and enjoy'.

Whilst the conservation audience is quite narrow, the geotourism audience is potentially very wide. For geology and geological conservation, geotourism offers the greatest opportunity to reach the wider audience; the special-interest tourist motivated by enjoyment of and interest in the environment, and the wider public impressed by the scale and beauty of the landscape. It is important, however, to get the balance right and to ensure that growth in tourism does not destroy the geological resource upon which it is based.

Achieving the right balance

It is essential that geotourism is sustainable. Increasingly, many organizations and businesses share a common goal of sustainable development, adopting an approach that combines environmental, economic and social benefits. As for any industry, so sustainable development is very relevant to tourism. Economic growth, achieved through tourism, needs to be integrated with policies and practice that ensure that the environment remains undamaged and, wherever possible, enhanced. Much of tourism is dependent on unsustainable activity, and there are key issues that need to be balanced for geotourism to ensure it remains sustainable.

Site impact – ensuring the impact of geotourism is balanced against the available resource

Many geological sites are robust and can withstand large visitor numbers, and most recreational activities will not damage the geological interest of an area. However, where sites are sensitive, restricted or delicate, care must be taken to manage visitor access and site use. For example, fossil collecting (an activity enjoyed by many tourists) should be tailored to the available resource. It will have little impact where sites are extensive and frequently renewed – for example in the case of most eroding coasts – as long as it is carried out in a responsible, sustainable manner. Conversely, where fossil resources are restricted and not readily renewed, fossil collecting needs to be more closely managed to ensure long-term sustainability (Larwood and King, 2001). Where careful site management is crucial, it is important that visitors are informed and advised about how to act.

Environmental impact – ensuring that geotourism is set in the context of the wider environment

Most geological sites support a range of habitats and species, many of which are more sensitive than the surrounding geology. There is an intimate link between geodiversity and biodiversity (English Nature, 2004), and in establishing and encouraging geotourism it is important that geotourism is managed in the context of the whole environment. For example, limestone in its many forms can support equally diverse, and often rare, fauna and flora. It is important that visitors are managed to avoid disturbance (for example, during nesting) or erosion whilst maintaining access to the geology.

Development impact – ensuring that geotourism minimizes the impact of associated development

One of the biggest threats to our environment is increased and inappropriate development. Tourism can bring greater development demand and can overload existing facilities and transport infrastructure. Wherever possible, the spread of development should be restricted and options of access through public transport taken. It is important that local planning policy clearly reflects the importance of geodiversity, with appropriate policy statements and guidance ensuring that adverse development impacts on geology are minimized.

Community impact – ensuring the local community benefits from geotourism

Tourism is focused on bringing visitors into areas. This can have a negative impact on the local community, with periods of overcrowding and excessive visitor pressure. The benefits of geotourism for the local community, however, can be significant. Geotourism can extend the tourist season, as it is not entirely weather-dependent, and can bring real economic benefits to a tourist destination area. Local businesses can be engaged in the process and actively encouraged to be advocates for their local geodiversity. Many of the events and activities for the geotourist can be equally enjoyed by the local community. Geotourism will also offer the opportunity to raise the awareness of the local community to the importance of the geological resource in the area in which they live. In the long term, it is the local community that is the key to sustaining the geological resource.

There are clear barriers to sustainable geotourism, including inappropriate planning policy; lack of understanding, training and incentive; and short-term thinking. For geodiversity this is further compounded, as geotourism is a new concept for the tourism industry which itself needs to understand what geotourism can bring. To overcome these barriers there are clear drivers, including the support that local communities can bring, the potential for economic return, and the reinforcement of the local distinctiveness that geodiversity and geotourism can achieve. The following two case studies demonstrate the benefits that geotourism can bring in different areas – Case study 10.1 describes the Wren's Nest National Nature Reserve, in the heart of the industrial West Midlands, and Case study 10.2 concentrates on the Dorset and East Devon Coast World Heritage Site, one of the most visited and spectacular coastlines in the United Kingdom.

Case study 10.1: The Wren's Nest National Nature Reserve, Dudley, West Midlands

The area around Dudley in the West Midlands is the heart of the 'Black Country', so called because it was here that saw the birth and growth of the nineteenth century industrial revolution. Geology was central to this, with local Silurian limestone, carboniferous coal measures and transported iron ore providing the raw materials for the developing industry. The area is internationally famous for its geology, being the subject of the nineteenth century studies of Sir Roderick Impey Murchison and containing some of the richest Wenlock fossil localities in the world, of which the most well known is the Wren's Nest National Nature Reserve (NNR) (Figure 10.1). It is the link between geology and heritage that is crucial to geotourism in the area.

Site impact

The Wren's Nest exposes the Wenlock limestone and associated reefs in a network of disused quarries and caverns in the heart of Dudley. The Wren's Nest NNR is openly accessible, with trained, full-time site wardens. Fossil collecting is carefully managed and an established trail guides visitors around the site, restricting access to more sensitive and dangerous areas. The Wren's Nest exemplifies an approach to visitor management that is aimed at allowing open but managed

Figure 10.2 Ripple beds and visiting school party at the Wren's Nest National Nature Reserve, Dudley, West Midlands, England. The ripple beds form a spectacular view in the Reserve, which is regularly visited by school groups – here discovering the biodiversity of a Silurian reef (photography courtesy of Peter Wakely, English Nature).

access. The site is regularly visited by geologists and educational groups, and is increasingly promoted as a tourism asset to the region (Figure 10.2).

Environmental impact

The Wren's Nest, as with many of the now disused industrial sites in the region, is an important wildlife haven. The NNR is managed for both geodiversity and biodiversity. Since falling into disuse in the 1920s and subsequent management as a National Nature Reserve since 1956, the fauna and flora of the site have progressively diversified. Habitat management is undertaken alongside geological management. The former quarries of the Wren's Nest provide a habitat which otherwise would not exist in this urban area, and the Wren's Nest Caverns provide a roost and hibernaculum for one of the region's most important bat populations.

Development impact

The Wren's Nest NNR has little direct development impact. The site is linked by local bus routes, and in planning for the future development of the site the transport links between the Wren's Nest and the nearby museum should be improved. Uniquely, visitors can travel on the canal network that takes visitors into the limestone caverns of the Wren's Nest Hill – caverns which are open to the Wren's Nest NNR. Limestone was once quarried from the Wren's Nest and removed via the canal to local iron and steel works. The value placed on geology locally is clearly reflected in local planning policy and guidance, which not only has a presumption against damage to geological sites but also actively seeks opportunities for establishing new geological sites associated with new development.

Community impact

The Wren's Nest exemplifies how the link with geology can be used to draw tourists to an area and raise the community's valuing of the geological resource. Locally, the message is very clear – that geology is closely linked to industrial growth of the region and is an important part of the local heritage of the region. Today, geology, as part of this heritage, and in its own right, is a primary draw for visitors to the area. This brings much-needed economic growth in an area that has suffered from the collapse of local industry.

Case study 10.2: The Dorset and East Devon Coast World Heritage Site

The Dorset and East Devon Coast World Heritage Site (www.swglf.org.uk/jurassic) was inscribed in December 2001. This linear site stretches 150 km from Exmouth in Devon to Studland in Dorset (Figure 10.1). It encompasses a complete Mesozoic sequence, as well as classic coastal geomorphology and coastal land slips. This is the only natural World Heritage Site on the UK mainland and is one of the most visited areas in the country, with several million tourist visitors each year.

Site impact

The World Heritage Site is extremely complex, and is made up of thirteen separate sites of special scientific interest. Large visitor numbers can mean high visitor impact, particularly as fossil collecting is an activity that many of the visitors to the area are keen to enjoy. As part of the management of the World Heritage Site, clear guidance is given on fossil collecting – particularly in the area around Charmouth and Lyme Regis, where collecting is at its greatest. A fossil-collecting code of conduct and recording scheme has been established to encourage a wider understanding of the value of the resource and encourage best practice. Since the establishment of the World Heritage Site the on-site information has progressively increased, informing visitors about the geology, why it is important, and how to look after it. Each year there is also a programme of events and guided walks across the whole site.

Environmental impact
The World Heritage Site supports a range of nationally and internationally important habitats and species, including cliff, foreshore and marine habitats. Its management plan integrates the management of the geology and geomorphology as well as its associated habitats and species. Maintaining the natural processes and dynamics of the coastline is essential to both geodiversity and biodiversity. As is true for geology, some areas will be more sensitive, with delicate habitats and species requiring careful visitor management.

Development impact
This coastline is under extreme development pressure. The Site has started to provide the impetus to achieving more innovative local solutions to the already high visitor pressure. In the last two years a World Heritage Site bus has been established which links each end of the linear site. The bus carries information about the geology of the Site, where to visit and what to see. It takes tourists to the different access points within the site, allowing walkers to be dropped off and picked up, and reducing the necessity for personal transport when visiting the area. The bus service has also provided a link route for the local community – a service that did not previously exist.

Community impact
Tourism is already well established in Dorset and Devon; however, the World Heritage Site has firmly established its geotourism role. Geotourism is viewed as providing the opportunity to extend the tourist season, which is traditionally restricted to the summer months and public holidays. Also important has been the engagement of the local tourist industry in understanding the importance of the World Heritage Site and issues regarding its management. Two initiatives currently address this directly. First, a series of presentations is being provided to local tourist businesses, particularly hoteliers. The presentations are aimed at providing an insight into why the World Heritage Site is important and what can be seen within the area, as well as making the link between coastal geology and the geology of the surrounding counties. People who have taken part in the presentations are awarded an accreditation recognizing that they will be able to provide consistent information to visitors about the World Heritage Site. Secondly, boat owners and the fishing community have for some time been running boat trips to view the coastline. To assist with this, and to ensure a consistent approach, an audio presentation and associated literature are currently being developed to be used directly by the boat-trip organizers.

Finally, in part to start to establish visitor payback, a World Heritage Trust has been established. The Trust's income will help support work within the World Heritage Site, focusing on conservation and education. The first of a series of guides has been published, with a proportion of the sales being returned to the Trust. The Trust will also manage the use of the World Heritage logo.

Conclusions on geotourism in England

Geotourism and geological conservation in England have a clear mutual benefit. Geotourism can bring support for geological conservation, and conservation can ensure a resource for the geotourist. It is essential that a long-term view is taken, and it must be achieved within a sustainable development framework in which the needs of the environment are met alongside those of the local community and geotourist. Geotourism offers opportunities for economic growth. Given the desire for sustainable geotourism, a strong case should be made to return a proportion of this wealth to the conservation of geodiversity.

Geological tourism in Ireland

Tourism in Ireland is second only to agriculture in its importance to the Irish economy. For years Ireland has successfully marketed itself as a green, unspoilt and value-for-money visitor destination, where the advance of time has made slower progress than the rest of Europe. This, coupled with the rich natural and cultural heritage of the island, has proven to be a winning formula for the Irish tourism industry. Indeed, extensive research has isolated three properties that conceptualize Ireland as a brand to prospective tourists – the people, the culture (both living and historical) and the outstanding natural environment.

In 2003, Tourism Ireland Limited (the agency charged with marketing the island overseas) estimated that over 7.3 million people visited Ireland, generating revenue of €5.1 billion – an estimated growth of 4.5 per cent on the previous year's figures. Tourism Ireland is aiming to increase this figure to 8.6 million people by 2006. The strategy that Tourism Ireland is using to achieve this goal includes focusing on tourist holiday needs, which for most market segments includes culture/ sightseeing and outdoor activities. This is where geological tourism has the potential to make a real impact. Many of the most visited sites in Ireland are either explicitly geological in nature (such as the Giant's Causeway in Antrim, or the Burren and Cliffs of Moher in Clare) or implicitly geological (such as the mountains of Cork, Kerry, Connemara, Donegal and Down). However, prior to the mid-1990s Ireland, in common with Britain, had made no real concerted effort in developing geological tourism. Historically, areas such as the Antrim Coast in the northeast, Donegal in the northwest and Connemara in the west were popular destinations for geological field parties (Figure 10.1). However, the political unrest in Northern Ireland effectively removed that part of the island from the itinerary of even these groups. It was that very same unrest that has proved to be the catalyst for some major advances in Irish geological tourism in recent years.

The early years

During the 1980s, under the auspices of the Irish Geological Association, events such as Irish Geology Week were established where members of the Irish geological community volunteered to lead geological walks or give talks to the general public with the aim of widening awareness about Ireland's rich geological heritage. By 1993, the Geological Survey of Ireland (GSI) committed to formalizing these largely *ad hoc* 'geotourism' actions as a corporate 'public outreach' activity – a commitment that continues to this day. It subsequently sought and obtained funding to develop three pilot thematic products under the auspices of the EU LIFE Programme-funded 'Scenic Landscapes' Project, managed by the *Bord Fáilte*/Irish Tourist Board. Three leaflets were produced, each designed to make geology accessible to the general public by creating links with established facets of natural and cultural heritage – built heritage, mining history and landscapes. These leaflets marked the first serious modern attempt at geological tourism in Ireland (Tietzsch-Tyler, 1995, 1996a, 1996b).

By 1994 the political situation in Northern Ireland was becoming more stable, and countries with strong links to Ireland (such as Britain, the USA and Australia) were donating large amounts of money to help stimulate, stabilize and grow the Northern Irish economy. Some of this funding was also available for government departments from both the north and the south to work more closely together and to develop joint projects. As such, in 1995 the Geological Survey of Northern Ireland (GSNI) and GSI secured funding from the International Fund for Ireland to operate a joint project based in Counties Cavan (in the Republic) and Fermanagh (in the North). While one strand of the project looked at the mineral potential of both counties, the other strand looked at developing the geotourism potential of the area. Working in close cooperation with the local authorities and tourism organizations, by 1997 GSI and GSNI had produced three products aimed not at the geological community (either professional or amateur) but at the general public and tourists. Two of these products took the form of touring leaflets for cyclists and motorists (Mc Keever, 1997a, 1997b). The third product was a laminated set of fifteen cards, ten of which highlighted circular walking routes in the area, while the remaining five highlighted the geological, natural and cultural heritage of the area as well as providing some general tourist information (Mc Keever, 1997c). These products were well received both locally and in wider tourism circles in Ireland, and encouraged the GSI and GSNI to seek funding to develop a similar suite of products over a much wider area (see Case studies 10.3 and 10.4).

Case study 10.3: 'Landscapes From Stone', Ireland

In 1998, the GSNI and GSI secured major funding from a new EU initiative, the Special Support Programme for Peace and Reconciliation (SSPPR), to develop geological tourism products across the northern twelve counties of Ireland. In addition, the two Surveys secured funding from the EU INTERREG IIC Programme for a major international marketing exercise aimed not only at promoting the tourism potential of the region's geological heritage, but more specifically at re-stimulating the geological field trips that were once so common in the north of Ireland. Working in ever-closer partnership with the mainstream Irish tourism industry, at local, regional and national levels, the GSNI and GSI decided to brand these projects under the name 'Landscapes From Stone'. Furthermore, and as with the previous Cavan–Fermanagh-based project, all literature produced under this brand was to be geologically jargon-free as far as practicable, and to use the same holistic approach to describing the region's geological, natural and cultural heritages.

By 2002, and following the award of a second tranche of EU SSPPR funding, seven walk sets (each containing ten walking routes) had been published as the Landscapes From Stone 'Walk' series (e.g. McKeever, 2000). Additionally, eleven folded A5-sized touring guides had been published as the 'Explore' series (e.g. McKeever, 2001). Finally, these products were complemented by a book (*A Story Through Time*) and a map (*Landscapes From Stone*) which aimed to provide a non-technical account of the region's geological story (McKeever *et al.*, 1998; McKeever, 1999). The products were then marketed to the public through a coherent sales drive, and stock was placed not only in the major bookshops but also in tourist information centres. To date, over 6000 'Explore' guides, over 5000 'Walk' sets and over 3000 copies of *A Story Through Time* have been sold. Many of these products are presently being reprinted. Furthermore, some guidebooks to Ireland, such as the Lonely Planet walking guide to Ireland, now list them as recommended reading for the general visitor to Ireland (Bardwell *et al.*, 2003).

Alongside the publication of literature, the GSNI and GSI embarked on an ambitious marketing drive to encourage geological field parties back to the region. By using standard tourism marketing techniques such as having stands at trade fairs (e.g. major geological conferences) and organizing familiarization trips (e.g. trips to the region for those individuals from universities that organize field trips), the Surveys planned to re-invigorate this market. They worked closely with tour operators in the region as well as accommodation providers, with the aim of providing universities with a high-quality, value-for-money package. This strand of the project was also a success, and not only are universities from the UK, mainland Europe and North America now visiting the region, but also an added side-benefit has been the return of amateur geological society field trips from Great Britain.

While all of the products referred to above were funded by the EU SSPPR fund, the Surveys also produced several other products under the 'Landscapes From Stone' brand. The GSI has published walk sets for the Wicklow Way, the East Clare Way and the coast of County Waterford under this brand, while the GSNI has used the brand on two of their 1 : 50 000 geological maps (McArdle, 1997; Maher, 1998; Morris, 1999; GSNI, 2000, 2002). These maps, covering the Causeway Coast and Ballycastle areas, not only provide the map reader with the standard information found on a geological map, but also attempt to make the transition into making geological maps accessible to the general public. They include a non-technical account of the geological history of each map area (in French and German as well as English), accompanied by visual reconstructions from episodes in each area's geological past. They also include photographs of geological features in both areas, as well as excursion guides for tourist and geologists alike. Sales of both maps have far outstripped sales of conventional 1 : 50 000 series geological maps, and the GSNI has now adopted this format as the standard for most of its new maps.

Finally, by the end of 2002 Ireland had hosted two major international conferences with the general theme of landscape heritage and geological tourism. In 1998 the Ulster Museum in Belfast hosted an international conference entitled 'Tourism in Geological Landscapes'. This was followed in 2002 by a conference in Dublin, hosted by the Royal Irish Academy, entitled 'Natural and Cultural Landscapes: The Geological Foundation' (Parkes, 2004). Both of these meetings provided valuable platforms for the geological community in Ireland and further afield to take stock of progress made to date regarding the development of geological tourism, as well as providing a medium through which ideas and experience could be shared and exchanged.

Case study 10.4: European Geoparks Network

In late summer 2000, a community group in County Waterford contacted the GSI after receiving notification, through the EU LEADER programme, of a meeting to be held in Spain in November that year entitled 'European Geoparks Network'. The GSI had been working with the Waterford group to help them develop the tourism potential of their geological heritage, and the group had just recently branded their area as 'The Copper Coast' (Figure 10.1). The GSI quickly contacted the GSNI about the geoparks initiative, and contact was made with the Marble Arch Caves (Figure 10.3) and Cuilcagh Mountain Park (MAC/CMP) in County Fermanagh – an area in which both Surveys had, by now, a long record of working with the local authority there in developing geological tourism (Figure 10.1). Representatives of all four organizations attended the meeting in Spain, and soon afterwards took the decision to apply for membership of the fledgling European Geoparks Network (EGN). At that time the network consisted of only four areas (one in each of France, Germany, Greece and Spain). They had for many years been developing geological tourism in their territories with the aim of building sustainable economic development – the same aim that led the GSNI and GSI to start working in the field of geotourism. It therefore made sense to work with partners from elsewhere in Europe so that, in partnership, it would be possible to build a strong, high-quality geotourism product in Europe for the benefit of all our local communities.

By autumn 2001, the EGN had expanded to twelve members and had signed a formal agreement with UNESCO that saw that organization give its full endorsement to the EGN. This was an important step towards ensuring a high-quality standard for geopark activities and products. By late 2004, the EGN had expanded to 21 members across 8 nations and was making important strides in achieving its aims of using geotourism to bring sustainable economic benefit to geopark communities. Partnerships formed through the network have allowed geoparks to apply for major European funding.

The Copper Coast and MAC/CMP, in association with the GSNI and GSI and together with the Vulkaneifel and Bergstraße-Odenwald European Geoparks in Germany, have recently embarked on a project with a total budget in excess of €5 million. Funded by the EU INTERREG IIIB (Northwest Europe) Programme, this project will allow all three geoparks to greatly improve the tourism infrastructure in their areas as well as allowing them to develop new and innovative products for the tourist aimed at enhancing the visitor experience. The two Irish geoparks are also partners in another EGN project. Funded by the EU INTERREG IIIC (North South East West) Programme, and with a total budget approaching €1 million, this project will allow the network to greatly improve existing common products as well as to develop new ones.

Early 2004 also saw a further strengthening of the link with UNESCO, which created a new Global Network of Geoparks. Together with eight geoparks in the People's Republic of China, all seventeen members of the EGN were admitted into the new network and three individuals from the EGN were invited by UNESCO to become international advisors to that organization on geoparks.

Figure 10.3 Marble Arch Caves, County Fermanagh, Ireland.

The future

In addition to the new projects mentioned above, the MAC/CMP European Geopark is part of a consortium, again with the GSNI and GSI, that is working to develop a high-quality tourism product for the Bréifne area of northwest Ireland. With funding from partners and the EU PEACE II fund of €2.4 million, this project aims to develop the combined natural and cultural heritage of the area into one holistic sustainable tourism product. Here again, geology has been recognized by the local authorities and tourism organizations as a theme with as valid a contribution to make to the tourism industry as any other aspect of heritage. Other regions and communities across Ireland are now also realizing that their geological heritage is a valuable tourism product worth exploiting in the sustainable manner of previous projects. Many geological groups and organizations in addition to the Geological Surveys are intimately involved in this work, and new projects are appearing all the time. Geology is increasingly being regarded in Ireland as a vital part of the heritage – something that should be valued and enjoyed, and not something that belongs to a small, elite group of individuals. Thus, at this juncture in time, geological tourism in Ireland has arrived.

Geotourism in Scotland

Scotland has a great deal to offer the visitor. The landscapes, particularly those of the Scottish Highlands, are world-renowned. VisitScotland, the government agency that promotes the Scottish tourism brand at home and abroad, has established that the majority of visitors come to Scotland not for the weather, but to visit the wilder, more scenic areas of the country. Most are also aware of the historical heritage that the country has to offer, in terms of castles and other sites of historical importance. Thus it is a mix of natural and historic heritage that is the irresistible draw for many visitors from abroad and also other parts of Britain. Tourism is now one of Scotland's biggest industries, earning the country some £2.5 billion every year and supporting 180 000 jobs. Some of those jobs are in the remotest parts of the country, and are an essential adjunct to farming, fishing, crofting and other indigenous occupations where jobs in manufacturing and other forms of service industry are thin on the ground. Ecotourism is already well established, with marine wildlife tourism particularly well developed. Nationally, wildlife tourism earns the country £57 m directly and supports an estimated 2000 jobs.

By comparison, geotourism is in its infancy. Although there are many important sites in Scotland seminal in the development of the science of geology, organized tours of geological sites are only offered by a very few specialist providers. However, visits are paid by the cognoscenti of the geological world, who already know about the existence of the sites described by James Hutton, the founder of modern geology. These include the world-famous exposures of the Moine Thrust at Knockan Crag and the many other geological riches that Scotland has to offer. However, overall, the numbers involved are very small. The potential for further development is considerable. The idea has already been put forward that this development should take place by way of identifying a series of geological 'hubs' or concentrations of geological interest across the country (McKirdy et al., 2001). Edinburgh, Skye and Arran are examples of three popular tourist destinations that already offer a high-quality environment and tourist support infrastructure. Within these areas lies a myriad of historical and representative geological and landform sites that could be 'packaged' to sell as a coherent visitor experience. To date Scotland has not exploited these opportunities, so the potential remains largely unrealized.

Case studies 10.5–10.7 describe some of the efforts to increase geotourism in Scotland.

Case study 10.5: 'Our Dynamic Earth', Edinburgh

Perhaps the most ambitious project undertaken to date in Scotland that connects with the geotourism theme is the Millennium project Our Dynamic Earth, constructed under Salisbury Crags in the heart of Edinburgh. This futuristic building was opened by Her Majesty The Queen on 2 July 1999. A number of science centres were built across Scotland with the express purpose of taking science to the public, but Our Dynamic Earth was the only one that explored any aspect of the Earth sciences in any detail. It is a tourist destination of some significance, attracting over half a million visitors in its first full year.

Since its opening, it has presented a holistic view of Planet Earth – its formation and early development, the stewardship of our finite planetary resources, and generally the way in which the human species has interacted with the natural environment. It differs in its presentational style from a museum or other static displays by relating these stories in an interactive and involving way. In the words of its first scientific director, Dr Stuart Monro:

> the story is communicated as an immersive experience, taking people on
> a trip through the Universe, to the edge of a volcano, across glaciers,
> and into the oceans, polar areas and the tropical rainforest. It is a story
> that is gradually built up, first exploring the physical formation of the
> planet and its landscapes, then of its life and diverse environments.
>
> (Monro and Davidson, 2001)

To sustain its position in the competitive Edinburgh tourism marketplace where many established distractions, such as Edinburgh Castle, the Zoo, Botanic Gardens and the vibrant city centre attractions and shopping outlets are already well established, Our Dynamic Earth needs to get paying guests through the door. It is a well-known phenomenon in the visitor attraction field that sustaining such a facility long-term requires innovation and aggressive marketing to ensure those who have not yet visited are tempted to come; and that those who have paid just one visit are encouraged to return by a new display or other enticement. Our Dynamic Earth is just about to enter a critical phase that will determine whether or not it will remain a player in the global geotourism marketplace.

Case study 10.6: Scottish Natural Heritage

Since it was founded in 1992, Scottish Natural Heritage (SNH), the official government agency with responsibility for the stewardship of the natural heritage, has worked hard to take geology and landscapes to a wider audience. Although the key conservation sites, preserved as sites of special scientific interest, are identified on strict scientific criteria (Ellis *et al.*, 1997), much of their output of publications, broadcasts and interpretative work on

Figure 10.4 Knockan Crag, in the remote Northwest Highlands of Scotland, is the setting for one of Scottish Natural Heritage's most ambitious interpretive projects. Our boast is to 'come to Knockan and discover the planet' – hence the construction of a globe in stone. This is one of the many art installations on the trail that help to tell the geological story for the benefit of all visitors to the place.

the Earth sciences is aimed at an audience that would not know a belemnite from a quartz mica schist! There is a compelling logic in adopting this rather pragmatic approach, as those in this happy state of ignorance about rocks and fossils outnumber the geologically literate by at least 999 to 1. By raising that wider awareness about the interesting facts of Scottish geology, the intention was to engender a more extensive appreciation for the effective conservation of such sites. To the non-expert eye one rock section very much resembles another, and why some should be more scientifically valuable than others is an esoteric argument that is not widely appreciated. As a by-product of this awareness-raising process, it became clear that a niche tourist market existed – although it must be said that this was not the original intention of the awareness-raising campaign. However, the staff in SNH were soon alerted to these wider economic possibilities as the campaign gathered momentum.

Work at Knockan Crag in the northwest Highlands of Scotland and the type area for the Moine Thrust, is perhaps the showcase project to date (Figures 10.1 and 10.4). The site was first interpreted around 30 years ago, but the main audience was those who already knew about the site but were visiting for the first time. The trail leaflet and interpretive material were uninspiring and relentlessly academic. It did nothing to draw in the casual visitor. As part of a campaign which brigaded a number of projects under the heading of 'Reading the Landscape', SNH set to work to create an interpretive experience rather more tailored to the casual visitor and general tourist to the area. Financial support was attracted from a large number of funding partners, including the local enterprise companies, the Heritage Lottery Fund and the Geologists' Association. One of the key arguments deployed in favour of the project was the beneficial effect that the development would have on the local economy.

It would appear that persuading visitors to linger in the vicinity of Knockan Crag for a few hours longer would considerably increase the likelihood that those tourists would stay for another night in the locale, rather than moving on to their next destination. The project has not been operating over a sufficient number of years to substantiate whether or not this idea has worked in practice, but anecdotal evidence suggests that the effect on the local economy has been considerable. Knockan Crag now forms part of the newly established (November 2004) Northwest Highlands European Geopark – Scotland's first geopark. A recently refurbished visitor centre at nearby Beinn Eighe National Nature Reserve also has a strong Earth science content, and the same arguments apply in terms of the benefits to the local economy.

SNH's efforts to describe these important historical sites in plain language have not been met with universal praise and acclaim. Although exit surveys have shown that the majority greatly appreciate the service provided, some academics have poured scorn on these attempts to make the science accessible. 'Dumbing down' is one of the more polite observations made by some on SNH's efforts at Knockan. There is also a concern about spoiling the purity of the experience for any visiting scientists. Interpretation is inevitably intrusive to some degree, although every effort has been made to ensure these interventions are appropriate in every case.

The second flagship project in the 'Reading the Landscape' programme is the 'Landscape Fashioned by Geology' series of publications produced jointly with the British Geological Survey. The purpose of the series is to celebrate the geological diversity and complexity of particular areas of Scotland, with the commentary provided in plain language, accessible to all who live in or visit the area. The books are also well illustrated with photographs and diagrams, so the lay reader is better able to appreciate the subject matter (e.g. *Rum and the Small Isles*, by Goodenough and Bradwell, 2004). It sounds a straightforward concept, but how many books have we seen that aspire to engage the lay audience but in reality talk above their heads? This project is a contribution to geotourism, because most people who visit an area that is new to them look to find a guide to what they might expect to see whilst in the area, and also to have a memento of their visit. This series fulfils both functions.

Case study 10.7: 'Geowalks', Edinburgh

Geotourism is not entirely underwritten by agencies of government and big-budget Millennium projects. Independent operators also have an important place in the market. 'Geowalks' (www.geowalks.demon.co.uk) has been operating out of Edinburgh for over five years. Thousands of visitors and locals have joined Angus Miller, the company's proprietor and rock enthusiast, for his perambulations around the city's geological high spots and many other locations throughout Scotland. He uses his extensive knowledge of the local area to inform and entertain those who join him on his regular walks. Edinburgh is richly endowed with heritage sites, both natural and cultural. James Hutton developed his ideas that informed his seminal book *Theory of the Earth* in 1788 by studying the local geology. Although Hutton travelled more widely throughout Northern Europe, it was always to his beloved Edinburgh that he returned for inspiration. Hutton's Section in the Royal Park of Holyrood is regularly used by Angus for his trips, and this section is famous in the annals of geology. It was here, so the story goes, that Hutton saw the evidence for intrusion of dolerite in a molten state into the host rocks of Carboniferous age. Thus in the company of an engaging tour guide telling fascinating historical tales and interpreting the excellent geology, with a backdrop of dazzling views over one of the most beautiful cities in the world; what more could a geotourist want?

Conclusions

As has been amply demonstrated, geological tourism has made enormous advances in Ireland and Britain over the last decade or so. The case studies outlined for England, Ireland and Scotland represent only some of the geotourism-related activities that are currently ongoing. In Ireland, a voluntary organization called ES2k has specific aims of raising public awareness of Earth sciences through public outreach and tourism-related activities. In Great Britain, the Regionally Important Geological and Geomorphological Sites (RIGS) organization has been active for many years now in protecting local geological sites and in producing geological trails, leaflets and interpretive boards for the wider public. The British Geological Survey has published a series of guides for the public, including the *Discovering Geology* and *Holiday Geology Guide* series (e.g. *Holiday Geology Guide – St Paul's*, by Robinson and Litherland, 1997) while some private companies, such as Earthwords, now specialize in producing geological literature for the tourist. Finally, in the last few years the two main national broadcasters, BBC (for Britain) and RTÉ (for Ireland), have both commissioned and broadcast major television series on each country's respective geological heritage.

The years ahead will continue to see many challenges for the geological community in Ireland and Britain in terms of making science relevant to the public's everyday life, whether as tourists or otherwise. However, there has been a good start and there are already plenty of opportunities for the visitor to learn more about and enjoy the rich geological diversity of this small group of islands.

References

Bardwell, S., Fairbairn, H. and McCormack, G. (2003). *Walking in Ireland*. Lonely Planet.

Ellis, N. V. (ed.), Bowen, D. Q., Campbell, S. *et al.* (1997) *An Introduction to the Geological Conservation Review*. GCR Series No. 1, Joint Nature Conservation Committee.

English Nature (2004). *Geodiversity and Biodiversity: Making the Links*. Peterborough.

Goodenough, K. and Bradwell, T. (2004). *Rum and the Small Isles*. Scottish Natural Heritage.

GSNI (2000). *Causeway Coast, Northern Ireland Sheet 7. Solid Geology, 1:50000*. Geological Survey of Northern Ireland.

GSNI (2002). *Ballycastle, Northern Ireland Sheet 8. Solid Geology, 1:50000*, 2nd edn. Geological Survey of Northern Ireland.

Larwood, J. G. and King, A. H. (2001). Conserving palaeontological sites: applying the principles of sustainable development. In: M. G. Bassett, A. H. King, J. G. Larwood *et al.* (eds), *A Future for Fossils*, pp. 119–126. National Museum of Wales, Geological Series No 19.

Maher, P. (1998). *An East Clare Landscape Adventure*. Geological Survey of Ireland.

McArdle, P. (1997). *The Wicklow Way – An Exploration of its Rocks and Landscapes*. Geological Survey of Ireland.

McKeever, P. J. (1997a). *Cuilcagh Scenic Drive*. Geological Survey of Northern Ireland and Geological Survey of Ireland.

McKeever, P. J. (1997b). *Upper Erne Scenic Drive*. Geological Survey of Northern Ireland and Geological Survey of Ireland.

McKeever, P. J. (1997c). *Cuilcagh Mountain Walks*. Geological Survey of Northern Ireland and Geological Survey of Ireland.

McKeever, P. J. (1999). *A Story Through Time*. Geological Survey of Northern Ireland and Geological Survey of Ireland.

McKeever, P. J. (2000). *Walk The Sperrins*. Geological Survey of Northern Ireland and Geological Survey of Ireland.

McKeever, P. J. (2001). *Explore South Antrim*. Geological Survey of Northern Ireland and Geological Survey of Ireland.

McKeever, P. J., Kearns-Mills, N. and Gallagher, E. (1998). *Landscapes From Stone*. Geological Survey of Northern Ireland and Geological Survey of Ireland.

McKirdy, A. P., Threadgould, R. and Finlay, J. (2001). Geotourism: an emerging rural development opportunity. In: J. E. Gordon and K. F. Leys (eds), *Earth Sciences and the Natural Heritage – Interactions and Integrated Management*. The Stationery Office, pp. 255–261.

Monro, S. K. and Davidson, D. (2001). Development of integrated educational resources: the dynamic earth experience. In: J. E. Gordon and K. F. Leys (eds), *Earth Sciences and the Natural Heritage – Interactions and Integrated Management*. The Stationery Office, pp. 2442–2449.

Morris, J. H. (1999). *The Copper Coast*. Geological Survey of Ireland.

Parkes, M. A. (ed.) (2004). *Natural and Cultural Landscapes – The Geological Foundation*. Royal Irish Academy, Conference Proceedings.

Robinson, E. and Litherland, M. (1997). *Holiday Geology Guide – St Paul's*. British Geological Survey.

Tietzsch-Tyler, D. (1995). *The Building Stones of St Canice's Cathedral – An Introduction to the Geology of the Kilkenny Area*. Geological Survey of Ireland.

Tietzsch-Tyler, D. (1996a). *The Geology and Landscape in Yeat's Country – Ancient Earth's Crust and Tropical Seas*. Geological Survey of Ireland.

Tietzsch-Tyler, D. (1996b). *The Geology of Allihies Mines – Desert Rivers, Slate Mountains and Copper Ore*. Geological Survey of Ireland.

11

Geotourism in Spain: resources and environmental management

José M. Calaforra and Ángel Fernández-Cortés

Introduction

The European Strategic Plan for the Environment promotes policies of sustainable development through the encouragement of rural tourism, based on the utilization and management of natural and cultural resources. As a member of the European Union, Spain has the opportunity to develop a geotourism market based on its diverse geology, especially in areas declared as Protected Natural Spaces. With this vision there are numerous geological features that spark a tourist interest in Spanish territory, especially in the karstic, volcanic and mining areas.

Systemizing the knowledge about Spain's geological heritage is the function of the Spanish Geosites Project. This Project, initiated by the International Union of Geological Sciences (IUGS) – Geosites

Working Group and also supported by UNESCO, aims to produce a global inventory of the Earth's geological heritage (Wimbledon, 1996, 1998). The second step of this methodology was the selection of the most valuable and representative sites of these geological frameworks (geosites). Spain's geological diversity provides a great number of frameworks of global significance, due to the high quality of outcrops, and it has allowed the selection of illustrative geosites (García-Cortés *et al.*, 2001). In particular, the choice of geosites in Spain has tried to take account of criteria related to the potential use of georesources (Cendrero, 1996), especially from the point of view of tourism – accessibility, proximity to population centres, or the number of tourist activities that can be developed.

The most advanced strategy of tourist use of georesources in Spain is financed by the LEADER II-C Programme of the European Union. This concerns a Network of European Geoparks, which aims to denominate a series of European territories with notable geological value and to plan projects that involve geotourism as a prime means of sustainable development (Eder, 1999). Spain has two European Geoparks; the Maestrazgo Cultural Park (Teruel) and the Natural Park of Cabo de Gata-Níjar (Almería).

With respect to the conservation of geological heritage, it is lamentable that Spain has no specific strategy for conservation of geodiversity, although the national legislature includes two laws that facilitate the protection of geological heritage: the Law of Historic Heritage (since 1985) and the Law of Conservation of Wild Flora and Fauna (since 1989). Most of the Spanish regions have passed laws that develop the Law of Conservation. These place localities of geological interest, including those of tourist interest (Gallego-Valcarce, 1996), within some sort of legal protection, especially the juridical concept known as Natural Monument. Until 1994, 7 per cent of the Protected Natural Spaces in Spain had been declared as such solely because of their geological worth, and 17 per cent where the geological features are predominant over the biotic ones (Gallego-Valcarce and García-Cortés, 1996).

Management of these protected geological features is the responsibility of the environmental authorities. In contrast, in some regions the protection of palaeontological heritage is covered by the Law of Historic Heritage, and so its management falls to the competent authorities for culture. This legal overlap in the management of geological heritage can reinforce its conservation, though on occasions the diversification of responsibility can lead to a failure in coordination of conservation strategies.

Principal geotourism enclaves in Spain

Most of the geological sites on the list drawn up by the Spanish Geological Survey (IGME) are highly important from a scientific standpoint as typical geological elements of the regional environment. At the same time, these settings include sites of significant geological interest from the points of view of recreation, education and tourism. The following sections describe some of Spain's principal geological localities, where flourishing tourist activity and infrastructure have developed that are specifically linked to the geology (Figure 11.1). Geotourism associated with Spain's karstic terrains is the focus of specific analysis in this chapter.

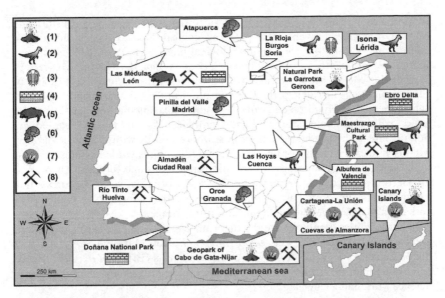

Figure 11.1 Main geotourism enclaves in Spain and their principal interest:
(1) volcanic landscape; (2) dinosaurs' footprints; (3) palaeontological/fossils;
(4) stratigraphical/sedimentological; (5) archaeological-general; (6) archaeological-
hominids; (7) mineralogical/petrological; (8) mining heritage.

Geotourism linked to palaeontological heritage

The fossils and ichnofossils of the continental Cretaceous of the Iberian Peninsula
comprise one of the most significative elements of Spain's geodiversity, particularly the beds of ichnites and dinosaurs in Aragón and La Rioja-Burgos-Soria
(Muñiz and Mayoral, 2001). In the latter region more than 8000 trace fossils and
footprints have been inventoried, which has led to an understanding of the ecological and ethnological aspects of many dinosaur groups (Moratalla *et al.*, 1988;
Casanovas-Cladellas *et al.*, 1991; Platt and Meyer, 1991). This type of georesource
has not gone unnoticed by the tourist industry, and the area has become a cultural
lure, which has boosted the economy of these hinterland areas of Spain. Of note
are the Palaeontology Centre at Villar del Río (Soria), the Enciso Palaeontology
Centre (La Rioja), the dinosaur beds and life-size schematic reconstructions
and, especially, the construction of a Palaeontology Theme Park (named
Dinópolis) in Teruel. The latter arose as an initiative of the Fundación Conjunto
Palaeontológico de Teruel, and aims to use the palaeontological heritage as a
tourist resource, ensuring its correct and proper use by means of scientific evaluation (Royo-Torres *et al.*, 2001).

The region of Aragón (in the northeast of Spain) is where geotourism projects
are strongest. For example, the Maestrazgo Cultural Park (Teruel, Aragón) forms
part of the Network of European Geoparks (UNESCO). The Park contains
extensive natural spaces and a large number of features of cultural interest (protected by special Spanish environmental law) consisting of ten historic centres,
twenty-one monuments, one archaeological zone, two important cave art complexes (comprising a number of caves, and covered by the Declaration of the

World Heritage Site by UNESCO) and more than 600 archaeological sites. The officially recognized inventory of palaeontological deposits has 70 outcrops of interest, in addition to 48 points of geological interest (PGIs). El Maestrazgo is spread over six centres: the Geological Park in Aliaga, the History Museum in Mas de las Matas, the Cultural Park of Molinos, the Centre for Science of Environment in Villarluengo, the Palaeontological Park in Galve and finally the Sculpture Park in Hinojosa de Jarque. The geological and natural heritage of the region will be promoted in the Aliaga Geological Park by means of an educational route with eleven stopping points, where boards with drawings and text will provide explanations for interested amateurs, pupils, students and scientists.

In the Galve Palaeontological Park, dinosaur fossils and footprints, as well as life-sized replicas, can be appreciated. This series of initiatives constitutes a fine example of the integrated use of cultural georesources, geodiversity, biodiversity, and archaeological and ethnographic cultural heritage.

Other localities of interest are the dinosaur egg beds in Lérida (Vianey-Liaud and López-Martínez, 1997; López-Martínez et al., 2000; Martinell et al., 2001) and the avian trace fossils in the Hoyas–Cuenca deposits (Briggs et al., 1997; Evans and Barbadillo, 1997, 1999), of which numerous examples are exhibited in the Science Museum in Cuenca.

Geotourism linked to coastal dynamics

One of the geological complexes with the greatest interest for tourism is the low-lying coastlands of the Iberian Peninsula, specifically the eastern seaboard of the Mediterranean and the Gulf of Cadiz on the Atlantic coast. These localities plainly show the sculpturing effects of coastal geodynamics, which contribute valuable palaeogeographic and palaeoclimatic information. Many of these sites are of outstanding natural beauty and biological diversity, and today have some kind of protection status conferred by Spanish environmental legislation. At the same time they are foci of economic wealth due to tourism and agriculture. Good examples are the littoral zones of the Ebro Delta, the Albufera de Valencia and Doñana. The latter is a complex and varied dune system that closes off the marshes of the Guadalquivir River (Borja et al., 1999); it is declared as a National Park, and is included in UNESCO's 1994 List of World Heritage Sites.

Geotourism linked to anthropological heritage

Spain boasts some deposits that bear witness to the earliest human presence in Europe; the Plio-Pleistocene vertebrate associations exhibit an exceptionally rich taxonomy (García-Cortés et al., 2001). If details of the different deposits and terrestrial ecosystems represented in these beds are combined, the Spanish anthropological records are remarkable for their continuity over the last two million years, during which period deposits of great scientific interest have been laid down. Without doubt, the one that has attracted the most interest in the scientific world is the karstic archaeological series at Atapuerca, which is associated with the characterization of *Homo antecessor* (Carbonell et al., 1995; de Castro et al., 1997) and hominids of the middle Pleistocene (Arsuaga et al., 1993, 1999). This series of deposits has given rise to varied recreational activities based on archaeological explanations of the locality. Thus at Atapuerca the tourist resources consist of guided tours of the deposits themselves, an archaeological park, and the Emiliano Aguirre Museum-Theatre. The irrefutable significance of the scientific discoveries meant that the Atapuerca archaeological outcrop was added to the UNESCO List of World Heritage Sites for the year 2000.

Other important palaeoanthropological deposits are in Orce (Granada) and Pinilla del Valle (Madrid). Significant discoveries about human evolution were made at both these sites (Leurquin, 1995; Gibert, 1998, 2002), which have awakened a tourist interest, and each possesses an archaeological museum.

Geotourism linked to volcanic/hydrothermal regions

The volcanic areas of Spain are also of marked geotouristic interest. The volcanic region of the southeast of Spain boasts a concentration of calcoalkaline and basaltic rocks, as well as some highly interesting ultrapotassic rocks. From a metalogenetic standpoint there are important filonian mineralizations of quartz, gold, alunite and sulphur compounds in Cabo de Gata (Cunningham et al., 1990; Arribas et al., 1995; Fernández-Soler, 1996), and mineralizations of lead, zinc, iron, manganese, copper, tin and silver in the Cartagena–La Unión and Cuevas de Almanzora areas (Martínez-Frías and García-Guinea, 1993; Martínez-Frías, 1999). The unique geology and landscape of the Cabo de Gata-Níjar Natural Park (Almería) are arguments for its inclusion in the Network of European Geoparks (UNESCO).

The volcanic archipelago of the Canary Islands forms a natural laboratory of incalculable worth for the study of the volcanic processes and history of the oceanic islands. Its peculiar geological and geomorphological characteristics (large craters, landslides and lava tunnels) make it a tourist attraction, which is amply protected by the Spanish environmental legislation (Natural Parks of Teide, Caldera de Taburiente, Timanfaya and Garajonay, the last of which was declared a World Heritage Site by UNESCO in 1986).

Of the volcanic peninsular localities, the one that really stands out is the Natural Park of the Garrotxa Volcanic Zone (Gerona); it is one of the most unusual and representative volcanic outcrops of continental Europe as a result of its excellent state of conservation. The area covers $120\,km^2$ and boasts some 40 strombolian and phreatomagmatic volcanic cones, in addition to more than 20 basalt lava flows of highly unusual morphology (Cebriá et al., 2000). The volcanic activity that took place here 11 000 years ago has produced many interesting geomorphological features. For example, the lava emissions obstructed drainage in some valleys and caused lakes to form. These ancient dammed lakes gradually filled with sediment, and today are fertile agricultural plains. The volcanic complex of la Garrotxa has been declared as a Natural Park and is equipped with all the infrastructure needed for tourism, including the Volcanoes Museum ('Museo de los Volcanes') at Olot, Gerona, together with routes through a number of dormant volcanoes (Santa Margarida and Montscopa). Worthy of note is the close link between man and georesources in the volcanic region of la Garrotxa, which is home to about 40 000 people (in 11 municipalities) and where 98 per cent of the land is in private ownership (Ceballos-Lascuráin, 1994).

Geotourism linked to mining heritage

In the southwest of the Iberian Peninsula are some of the largest concentrations of metal and sulphur deposits known in Europe (the Iberian Pyrite Belt), which have been exploited for over 2000 years (Morral, 1990). The deposits of the Río Tinto (Huelva) are particularly noteworthy because of their singular mineralization and exceptional resources (Mitjavila *et al.*, 1997; Leistel *et al.*, 1998; Solomon *et al.*, 2002). The general mining crisis in Spain was felt in the Iberian Pyrite Belt in Huelva province, where the economic-mining crisis began to take effect in 1987. Due to this crisis, all the social agencies of the region signed an agreement to set up the Río Tinto Foundation, aimed at tapping the significant historic capital in mining to spark new tourist initiatives. The study and investigation of the history of mining and metallurgy in Río Tinto, together with their technical, cultural, social and economic aspects, and the conservation and restoration of the environment, has borne fruit in the shape of the Mining-Tourism Park, which includes archaeological zones and features of ethnographic interest.

Another example of conversion of mining activity into tourist resources is the mineralization of mercury in the region of Almadén (Ciudad Real). This mining region is exceptional because of the enormous concentration of the metal, constituting more than 35 per cent of the exploited and existing resources of the planet (Martínez-Frías *et al.*, 1998; Hernández *et al.*, 1999), with mercury resources exceeding all the other large mercury deposits in the world (Idria in Slovenia, and Monte Amiata in Italy). Moreover, the mercury deposits in Almadén occur within a geological context with unique internal characteristics, very different from other mercury deposits, so that its own model of metalogenesis was defined to describe it (Saupe, 1990; Jebrak and Hernández, 1995). The mercury mineralizations in the Almadén area can be grouped morphologically into two types: the first corresponds to stratiform deposits and the second to hydrothermal deposits occurring within volcanic and sedimentary rocks. The market recession of the 1970s and 1980s, together with environmental problems associated with poorly planned mercury extraction (Ferrara *et al.*, 1998; Higueras *et al.*, 2003; Nevado *et al.*, 2003; Rytuba, 2003), brought an end to the mining. Since 1981 the State has made significant efforts to diversify the economy of the region, to the point that mercury extraction only accounts for one-fifth of the total turnover. As part of this initiative, the non-profit-making Foundation of the Mines of Almadén and Arrayanes was created to rehabilitate the Almadén's historic and geological heritage and to promote historic and scientific understanding. Currently, geotourism in the area focuses on the mining installations, document banks and a mining museum.

Vestiges of Roman mines in Las Médulas (León) create another of the places of geotouristic interest in Spain today. The area of the mines of Las Médulas has been declared as a Cultural Landscape – the result of Roman intervention over 200 years in the area, and of other changes experienced in the area up to the present day (Sánchez-Palencia *et al.*, 1998). However, its importance goes beyond the gold-mining remains dating from the Roman period, as it provides an irrefutable demonstration of the profound historic effects and changes in the landscape caused by gold mining in the northeastern Iberian Peninsula. The zone is spectacular because of its mining connotations – the excavation of 600 million cubic metres, the originality of the Roman hydraulic techniques employed in the mines, and the geological context of the mines themselves (occurring in Miocene and Quaternary deposits associated with a Cantabrian mountain system; Pérez-García *et al.*, 2000). This mining area has been recognized worldwide, and this is reflected in its inclusion in 1997 on the UNESCO List of World Heritage Sites as a Cultural Landscape, which combines natural and cultural features. For its part, the Spanish administration declared the area as a Feature of Cultural Interest

(BIC) in 1996 due to its archaeological value, and as a Natural Monument in 2002 due to its geological interest. Today, the management of Las Médulas is the responsibility of a cultural, non-profit-making enterprise whose principal object-ives are the protection, promotion and diffusion of information about Las Médulas and the coordination of events that both public and private organiza-tions undertake in the area. Part of the geotouristic infrastructure in this locality is an archaeological centre and various routes that traverse various stages of the mining exploitation.

Other geotourism initiatives

Many other initiatives and infrastructures exist in Spain, and it is impossible to name them all. Amongst those not mentioned above are the Chera Geological Park (Valencia), the Information Centre of the Middle Cambrian Deposits of the Rambla de Valdemiedes (Zaragoza), the Cultural–Geological Park of Río San Martín (Teruel), plans for Geomining Parks in Sierra Morena and in Linares (both in Jaén province) and the recent discovery of the Giant Geode in Pulpí, which forms the subject of the case study in this chapter.

Karst and geotourism
The karst landscape and its environmental significance

The importance of protecting karstic landscapes as part of a strategy for the con-servation of global geodiversity also covers a wide variety of economic, cultural and scientific values (interests) that are usually present in these same karstic areas. Each of these values has its own significance, and this in turn means that some interests conflict with others. The isolated existence of one of these values highlights the importance of protecting karstic systems. The World Commission on Protected Areas (WCPA-IUCN) summarizes the reasons for the protection of karstic systems (Watson *et al.*, 1997) as being because they:

- are the habitats for species of flora and fauna in danger of extinction
- have deposits of uncommon mineral resources
- are important contexts for scientific studies (geology, geomorphology, palae-ontology, etc.)
- have cultural, historic and prehistoric contexts
- provide 'Windows' for the understanding of regional hydrogeology
- are sources of economic resources (water, oil, industrial rocks, etc.)
- are areas for tourism and recreation, the most notable example being that of show caves.

Karstic terrains play an important role in the earth's geodiversity. Approximately 17 per cent of the earth's land surface is made up of carbonate rocks, with a greater presence in regions of Europe, North America and Eastern and Southeastern Asia. On a global level, only 7 per cent of carbonate outcrops have a typical karstic morphology although, despite this modest representation, it is estimated that up to 25 per cent of the world's population is supplied with water from karstic areas (Ford and Williams, 1989).

The subterranean karstic environment has been stirring geotouristic interest for some years. Habe (1981) estimated that around 650 show caves with artificial access and lighting systems exist around the world. This number does not include the numerous cavities dedicated to caving adventure activities, which have not been modified to accommodate 'mass tourism'. More recent data cite the tourist facilities in caves to total around 750 cavities, of which 180 are situated in North America and receive approximately 16 million visitors every year (Huppert *et al.*, 1993). Examples of show caves that accommodate an extremely high public influx include Mammoth Cave (Kentucky, USA), which receives around 2 million visitors a year, and Cango Cave (South Africa), Nerja Cave (Spain), Frasasi (Italy) and Postojna (Slovenia), with 300 000–500 000 visits per year. Finally, the health-giving properties of certain cave microclimates, especially hydrothermal karstic cavities, for certain respiratory diseases should be mentioned. This type of tourist attraction to caves boasts some very well-known examples in Banff (Canada) and Budapest (Hungary).

Geotourism related to the karst landscapes

Spain possesses numerous karstic systems which are of enormous national significance because of their extraordinary diversity. Twenty per cent of Spanish territory is comprised of karstified strata, be they carbonate or evaporite rocks, with ages ranging from Palaeozoic to Cenozoic (Ayala *et al.*, 1986; García-Cortés *et al.*, 2000). Outstanding from a geomorphological point of view are the karstic landscapes carved out of the Palaeozoic limestones in the Picos de Europa, the Pyrenees, and the internal zones of the Betic Cordillera. The Mesozoic carbonate formations of the Iberian Cordillera, the Cantabrian Coast and the Betic Cordillera exhibit a wide range of exokarstic landforms, such as the remarkable polje-type depressions (Zafarraya, Granada), the karren (lapiés) fields (Tramontana, Mallorca) and the 'rock cities' (El Torcal, near Antequera, and the Enchanted City in Cuenca). The endokarst landforms are also widely represented, with more than 10 000 caves known in Spain, of which a great many extend over appreciable lengths or vertical development. There are nine sinkholes exceeding 1000 m in depth, such as the Sistema de la Trave, which is 1441 m deep and is the sixth deepest cave in the world (Puch, 1998). Another example is the Ojo Guareña Complex (Burgos), with its 100 km of galleries, which makes it the eleventh longest cave on the planet (Martín-Merino and Ortega-Martínez, 2001).

Many of the protected spaces in Spain are karstic areas, and are deemed exceptional because of their geological features. These spaces include the national parks ('Spanish first level natural space protection') of Picos de Europa, Ordesa, Tablas de Daimiel and the Isla de Cabrera. There are several natural parks ('second level of protection') with representative karst areas (e.g. Sierras de Cazorla and Segura, Subbetic Sierras), several so-called natural spaces (Torcal de Antequera) and natural monuments (e.g. Cueva de Castañar, which has formed in the Precambrian limestones of Cáceres; Cueva de las Ventanas in Granada and the

Cueva de los Murciélagos in Córdoba). Lastly, the karstic gypsum formations of the Mesozoic (mainly Triassic) and the Cenozoic (Palaeogene and Neogene) represent karstic systems of global significance. The most important example is the Sorbas Gypsum Karst (Almería), whose density and variety of endokarstic and exokarstic landforms make this protected enclave an exceptional site on a world scale (Calaforra, 1998, 2003; Calaforra and Pulido-Bosch, 2003).

The above facts show how important karst is in Spain's geological heritage. Its intrinsic worth, together with the social demands upon it, make it worthy of special consideration in the context of land-use planning and management, in order that its conservation is assured. Accordingly, given the variety in the karstic terrain, it is essential not only to protect and conserve it but also to develop its use for tourism, education and the advancement of scientific knowledge.

The opening of show caves is not a recent phenomenon in Spain. The first caves were opened during the first half of the nineteenth century. They were associated with thermal spas, and were operated as a complementary activity for visitors to these centres. Nowadays there are more than 10 000 karstic cavities, of which about 70 are show caves (Figure 11.2, Table 11.1). Examples of these are the Drach Cave (Mallorca) and the Nerja Cave (Malaga), each of which is visited by 500 000 people annually, and the Gruta de las Maravillas (Huelva), which sees 160 000 visitors per year (Pulido-Bosch et al., 1997).

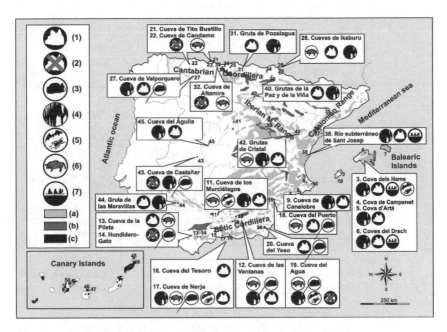

Figure 11.2 Principal karstic outcrops in Spain: (a) limestone; (b) gypsum; (c) lava tubes (not karstic), indicating the most important show caves equipped for public access and/or dedicated to speleotourism (see also Table 11.1) and their characteristics: (1) full tourist access; (2) restricted tourist access; (3) speleotourism-type visit; (4) well-preserved speleothems; (5) biospeleological interest; (6) rock paintings; (7) river/lakes boat route.

Table 11.1 Selected top-50 show caves in Spain (see Figure 11.2 for iconographic description of these caves)

1	Cova Forada dn d'En Xeroni	St Ferrán and St Frencesc (Formentera)	Betic Cordillera (Balearic Islands)
2	Cova d'En Marçà	Sant Joan (Ibiza)	Betic Cordillera (Balearic Islands)
3	Coves dels Hams	Manacor (Mallorca)	Betic Cordillera (Balearic Islands)
4	Cova de Campanet	Campanet (Mallorca)	Betic Cordillera (Balearic Islands)
5	Coves d'Artá	Canyamel-Capdepera (Mallorca)	Betic Cordillera (Balearic Islands)
6	Coves del Drach	Manacor (Mallorca)	Betic Cordillera (Balearic Islands)
7	Cova d'En Xoroi	Alaior (Menorca)	Betic Cordillera (Balearic Islands)
8	Cova de L'Atzubia	L'Atzubia	Betic Cordillera
9	Coves del Calenobre	Bussot (Alicante)	Betic Cordillera
10	Cueva de las Calaveras	Benidoleig (Alicante)	Betic Cordillera
11	Cueva de los Murciélagos	Zuheros (Córdoba)	Betic Cordillera
12	Cueva de las Ventanas	Piñar (Granada)	Betic Cordillera
13	Cueva de la Pileta	Benaoján (Málaga)	Betic Cordillera
14	Sistema Hundidero Gato	Benaoján (Málaga)	Betic Cordillera
15	Cueva de Doña Trinidad	Ardales (Málaga)	Betic Cordillera
16	Cueva del Tesoro	Rincón de la Victoria (Málaga)	Betic Cordillera
17	Cueva de Nerja	Nerja (Málaga)	Betic Cordillera
18	Cueva del Puerto	Calasparra (Murcia)	Betic Cordillera
19	Cueva del Agua	Iznalloz (Granada)	Betic Cordillera
20	Cueva del Yeso	Sorbas (Almería)	Betic Cordillera (gypsum)
21	Cueva de Tito Bustillo	Ribadesella (Asturias)	Cantabrian Cordillera
22	Cueva de Candamo o de la Peña	San Román de Cancamo (Asturias)	Cantabrian Cordillera
23	La Cuevona de Ardines	Ribadesella (Asturias)	Cantabrian Cordillera
24	Cuevas de Puente Viesgo	Puente Viesgo (Cantabria)	Cantabrian Cordillera
25	Cueva del Pendo	Camargo (Cantabria)	Cantabrian Cordillera

Table 11.1 (*Continued*)

26	Cuevas de Arredondo	Arredondo (Cantabria)	Cantabrian Cordillera
27	Cueva de Valporquero	Vegacervera (Léon)	Cantabrian Cordillera
28	Cuevas de Ikaburu	Urdazubi-Urdax (Navarra)	Cantabrian Cordillera
29	Cuevas de Zugarramurdi	Zugarramurdi (Navarra)	Cantabrian Cordillera
30	Cuevas de Mentrokillo	Astitz (Navarra)	Cantabrian Cordillera
31	Gruta de Pozalagua	Carranaza (Vizcaya)	Cantabrian Cordillera
32	Altamira	Santillana del Mar (Cantabria)	Cantabrian Cordillera
33	Cueva del Soplao	Rionansa (Cantabria)	Cantabrian Mountain Range
34	Cueva de Oñati – Arrikrutz	Oñati (Guipúzcoa)	Cantabrian Mountain Range
35	Cova de la Font Major	L'Espluga de Francoli (Tarragona)	Catalonian Coastal Range
36	Cueva Meravelles	Benifallet (Tarragona)	Catalonian Coastal Range
37	Abrigos rupestres-Ulldecona	Ulldecona (Tarragona)	Catalonian Coastal Range
38	Río subterráneo de San José	Vall d'Uixó (Castellón)	Iberian Mountain Range
39	Cueva de los Casares	Riba de Saelices (Guadalajara)	Iberian Mountain Range
40	Gruta de la Paz y de la Viña	Ortigosa de Cameros (La Rioja)	Iberian Mountain Range
41	Cueva de Los Enebralejos	Prádena (Segovia)	Iberian Mountain Range
42	Grutas de Cristal	Molinos (Teruel)	Iberian Mountain Range
43	Cueva de Castañar	Castañar de Íbor (Cáceres)	Iberian Mountain Range
44	Gruta de las Maravillas	Aracena (Huelva)	Iberian Mountain Range
45	Cueva del Aguila	Arenas de San Pedro (Ávila)	Tajo River Basin
46	Cueva de Anzo and Pintada	Galdar (G. Canaria)	Volcanic Canary Islands
47	Cenobio de Valerón	Sta María de Guía (G. Canaria)	Volcanic Canary Islands
48	Cueva de los Verdes	Haía (Lanzarote)	Volcanic Canary Islands
49	Jameos del Agua	Haía (Lanzarote)	Volcanic Canary Islands
50	Cueva del Viento	Icod de los Vinos (Tenerife)	Volcanic Canary Islands

The subterranean formations of the volcanic archipelago of the Canary Islands, which have been developed for the tourist market, deserve a special mention, as do the mining remains – also a strong tourist draw – such as the Mina de la Jayona (Badajoz). In Andalusia, even in the middle of the nineteenth century, there were some caves which were fitted out, to some degree, to make for more comfortable visits (Cueva de Ardales, Gruta de las Maravillas in Aracena). However, it was the opening of the Nerja Cave in 1959 that really marked the beginning of the development of cave tourism in Spain, which was consolidated during the second half of the twentieth century.

Caves equipped for tourism in Spain receive more than two-and-a-half million visitors a year, and yield a significant economic return for the municipalities in which they are located – calculated to be in excess of 15 million euros (Rivas et al., 2002). Many of these municipalities accommodate populations of fewer than 5000 inhabitants, and this fact underlines the importance of the show caves to the local economies. The majority of the tourist caves are in public ownership, as is their management. In the main, it is the local administration that is responsible for their operation. This is the case, for example, for Gruta de las Maravillas (Aracena, Huelva), Caverna de la Peña de Candamo (Candamo, Asturias), Cuevas de Arredondo (Arredondo, Asturias), Cuevas del Castillo and de las Monedas (Puente Viesgo, Cantabria), Cueva de los Enebralejos (Prádena, Segovia), Cueva Meravelles (Benifallet, Tarragona) and Cueva de las Ventanas (Píñar, Granada), among others. There are also examples of caves operated by councils, autonomous (i.e. regional) governments and even agencies of the National Administration, such as the Altamira Caves (National Museum and Altamira Research Centre, run by the Ministry of Education and Science), the Cueva de Castañar de Íbor and la Mina de la Jayona (run by the (Regional) Ministry of the Environment of Extremadura), and the Cueva de Valporquero (León Council) and the Cueva del Pendo ((Regional) Ministry of Culture of Cantabria). The Cueva del Agua of Iznalloz (Granada) is the only subterranean research laboratory of Spain that is allowing an exhaustive environmental control before the aperture to tourist visits of the cave (Calaforra and Sánchez-Martos, 1996; Sánchez-Martos et al., 2002; Calaforra et al., 2003).

At the present time, the only organization that binds this new tourist sector together at a national level is the Association of Spanish Show Caves (ACTE), which is linked to the International Show Cave Association (ISCA). Nevertheless, ACTE unites only 23 of the show caves in peninsular Spain, the Balearic and Canary Islands. The objectives of this association include the promotion of subterranean tourism, and the encouragement of the conservation and sustainable use of the tourist caves. Of all the caves belonging to the ACTE, fifteen are presently open to the public, whilst the remainder are being modified to receive tourists (Cueva del Agua in Granada, Cueva de la Lastrilla in Cantabria, Cueva de Belda in Malaga; Cueva del Viento in Tenerife, Cueva de Anzo in Gran Canaria and Cuevas de Mentrokillo in Navarra). This association does not encompass the remaining show caves that are already being exploited, including caves as important as the Nerja Cave (which belongs to the International Show Cave Association – ISCA), the Cueva de la Pileta (Malaga) or the majority of the show caves on the Balearic Islands.

Many of the caves hosting tourist activity have been conferred with some form of protection status, either before they were opened to the public or since they have been equipped for tourist visits. The protection statutes conferred have been:

- Feature of Cultural Interest (BIC, 'Bien de Interés Cultural') – Cueva de la Lastrilla, Cueva de Santián and Cueva del Pendo in Cantabria, and Cenobio de Valerón in Gran Canaria
- Natural Monument – Cueva de los Murciélagos in Córdoba, Cueva de las Ventanas in Granada, Cueva del Soplao in Cantabria, and Cueva de Castañar in Cáceres
- National Monument – Cueva de los Casares in Guadalajara, and Cueva de Nerja in Málaga.

In turn, the United Nations Education Science and Culture Organization (UNESCO) lists as part of the Heritage of Humanity such gems occurring within Spanish karstic terrains or caves as the Altamira Cave (1985), the Enchanted City of Cuenca (1996), the Atapuerca archaeological excavations (2000) and various incidences of 'Rock Art of the Mediterranean Arc' (1998), the last-mentioned including tourist attractions such as the Ulldecona Cave Art Shelters (Tarragona).

The geographical distribution of the Spanish show caves (Figure 11.2) coincides with the largest outcrops of karstifiable rocks – Cantabrian and Betic Cordilleras (Table 11.1). The lava cavities are an exception to the above; their formation was contemporaneous with the rocks that contain them and most correspond to the lava tunnels on the Canary Islands archipelago. Whilst they have nothing in common with the karstic cavities in terms of genesis, lithology, structure or geological age, their socio-economic repercussions in a local context are very similar to those of the caves hollowed out of carbonate strata. Thus, the vast majority of the underground volcanic features are open to tourism (Cueva de Anzo, Cueva de los Verdes, Jameos del Agua, Cueva Pintada and Cueva del Viento).

The distribution of show caves according to administrative regions coincides with those regions boasting larger numbers of caves in general. Nevertheless, in the regions that attract more tourism, such as Andalusia, Cantabria and the Balearic Islands, the proportion of show caves is higher. Archaeological attributes predominate in the show caves in the northern regions (Cantabria and the Basque Country), as a result of the large number of caves in the north of Spain that accommodate internationally renowned prehistoric deposits and cave art (Cueva de Altamira, Tito Bustillo, Sierra de Atapuerca deposits). In cases where the cave paintings are regarded as important on an international scale, the caves have been closed to tourism in order to protect them. Instead, replicas have been constructed that reproduce the cave's morphology and its paintings, and these are open to tourists (Cueva de Altamira and Cueva de Ekain in Guipúzcoa).

Recently, the show caves have been incorporating a new facility linked to the sudden surge in interest in so-called 'speleo-type' visits or 'speleo-adventure tourism'. In some karstic areas where cavities are already equipped with a certain infrastructure, speleotourism excursions are being developed with the aim of exploiting part of the karstic heritage within a context of conservation and sustainability. This type of activity is being developed in many areas, some outstanding examples being in the Sorbas Gypsum Karst (Almería), the Cueva del Gato (Benaoján, Malaga) and the Cueva de los Chorros (Riopar, Albacete).

Case study 11.1 describes the Pulpí Geode – a unique geological phenomenon.

Case study 11.1: The giant gypsum Pulpí Geode (Spain)

The Pulpí Geode, in southeast Spain, is a geological phenomenon unique in the world due to its size, and the perfect shape and transparency of the gypsum crystals it contains (Calaforra and García-Guinea, 2000). Its discovery in 1999 by mineral collectors was widely publicized in the worldwide media and in famous scientific journals like *Science* (Vol. 286, 2000, p. 2120). It was found inside an old iron and lead mine, 3 km from the coast and 50 m deep, in rocks of Triassic dolomite that form part of the Betic Cordillera. The volume of the void of the Pulpí Geode is $10.7 \, m^3$ (≈ 8 m long, 1.8 m wide and 1.7 m high) and the average size of the gypsum crystals is $0.5 \times 0.4 \times 0.3$ m, with some crystals of 2 m in length (see Figure 11.3).

The geological uniqueness of the Pulpí Geode means that its protection as part of the geological and mining heritage of the planet is essential. However, there are two problems that mean that this heritage could disappear: the scarce or complete lack of Spanish legislation dealing with this type of phenomenon; and pressure from mineral collectors and Natural Museums to dismantle it (García-Guinea and Calaforra, 2001). Moreover, the mineral matrix of the Geode is part of a once flourishing mining activity that became established in the southeast of the Iberian Peninsula during the eighteenth and nineteenth centuries. For this reason, opening of the mine and access to the Geode by tourists has to be seen as part of a joint scheme of conservation and equipping the mine for tourism (Calaforra *et al.*, 2001). Regrettably, two large crystals were also removed from its interior before the discovery of the Geode was communicated to the authorities.

The following sections detail the problems of prospective tourist visits to the Geode, and the environmental techniques used to study them.

Figure 11.3 Detail of the interior of the Giant Geode of Pulpí (Almería, Spain).

Genesis of the Geode

The large crystal sizes, their perfect shape, high transparency and minor solid inclusions, which have given rise to such clean crystals, must have been produced in a unique geological environment. Mineralogenesis of the geode can be summarized in four stages (García-Guinea *et al.*, 2002):

1. Karstification of Triassic dolomites under conditions of pronounced acidification, in the presence of hydrothermal fluids rich in hydrogen sulphide
2. Deposition of fine needles of celestite in the walls of the void generated ($SrSO_4$)
3. The influence of the fresh water–saltwater mixing zone in the carbonate aquifer and mixing with hydrothermal fluids (H_2S)
4. Gradual cooling with slow growth of gypsum crystals sealing in the fine celestite needles.

The small entrance hole into the Pulpí Geode was totally closed, and was opened accidentally by collectors looking for gypsum crystals as they picked at one of the fractures in the mine.

Microclimatic study of the Geode

After the discovery of the Geode, one of the first steps towards its conservation was to initiate an investigation to describe its microclimate under natural conditions and its response to occasional visits by small groups of visitors – in short, to define to what extent visits to the Geode could impact on its natural environment. Using the results of the monitored visits, different situations were simulated with respect to the number and frequency of visitors, modelling what could happen if the Geode were opened to tourists.

The monitored visits were typified by a restricted number of people, a limited time within the Geode, and direct contact between the air within the Geode and the visitor. Dataloggers, especially designed for the narrow range of measurements expected, were installed to measure the physical characteristics of air temperature, temperature at the crystal surface, relative and absolute humidity, dew point, carbon dioxide content, atmospheric pressure and air speed. Thirty experimental visits were undertaken, with groups of between one and three people remaining in the interior of the Geode for between 5 and 30 minutes.

Continuous monitoring of variables that are relatively simple to measure, such as temperature, carbon dioxide concentration, and in particular the calculation of recovery time following monitored visits, forms a very useful tool for determining the 'visitability' of an enclosed space like the Geode. For example, a look at the temperature evolution shows that as the number of visitors or the time spent inside the Geode increases, a gradual caloric accumulation is produced. Following the visit of three people for ten minutes, the humidity inside the Geode took approximately seven hours to recover fully and the air inside the Geode recovered its initial temperature (19.3°C) four to five hours after the visitors had left.

One of the most sensitive variables for detecting the impact of human presence is the measurement of carbon dioxide in the air. This variable was also measured in the Geode, and the recovery curve confirmed that it takes several days before the initial values are recovered.

Another of the risks of continuous presence of people inside the Geode is condensation on the gypsum crystals as a result of an increase in temperature, and water vapour in the air caused by respiration. In the case of show caves, this problem is normally associated with the preservation of rock art (Ek and Gewelt, 1985; Villar *et al.*, 1986; Sarbu and Lascu, 1997; Bourges *et al.*, 2001). In the particular case of the Giant Geode, condensation of water on the crystals caused by human presence could lead to fatal corrosion of the crystals. Condensation of water vapour on a surface occurs when the dew point temperature of the air is higher than the temperature of the rock surface. Some examples of how to measure and interpret these parameters in cave environments are provided in Dragovich and Grosse (1990), Dublyansky and Dublyansky (1998, 2000) and De Freitas and Schmekal (2003).

A study of condensation is extremely important in the case of the Geode, since condensation on the crystals' surface would literally dissolve them. Both dew point and air temperature are monitored in the interior of the Geode, together with the ratio of condensation ($g_{water\ vapour}/m^2h$), during any controlled visit. The phenomenon of condensation on the gypsum crystals occurs during visits of two or three people for more than ten minutes. After such a visit, the difference between the dew point of the air and the temperature of the rock is positive. This caloric situation lasts for 1 h 40 min, during which time there is an effective condensation of $1.55\ g/m^2$, followed by a negative ratio of condensation, which causes the evaporation of the condensed water in only 3–4 minutes. The total recovery time value of the initial natural conditions was 27 hours (Figure 11.4).

Vulnerability of the Geode to geotouristic visits

All in all, condensation of water vapour on the gypsum crystals of the Geode could be the critical parameter that limits human presence inside it. Continuous visits of two or three people for more than ten minutes would provoke the appearance of condensation/evaporation phenomena, bringing with them the risk of corrosion of the magnificent gypsum crystals. Bearing in mind that the carbon dioxide content is another critical variable, the recovery time of the

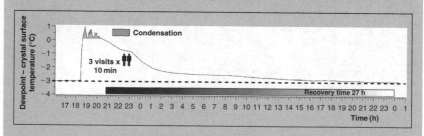

Figure 11.4 Influence of visits to the interior of the Geode on the risk of condensation of water vapour on the gypsum crystals.

Geode environment would exceed one day. The results obtained in the environmental monitoring of the Geode suggest that it is impossible to allow visitors inside it, not only because of the mechanical impact of the visitor on the crystals but also due to the risk of condensation of water vapour, as well as a toxic risk to visitors owing to carbon dioxide accumulation.

For these reasons, the conclusion directed to the competent environmental authorities is to recommend that the mine be equipped for tourism only if there is to be no physical contact between the visitors and the interior of the Geode.

Conclusions

There is no specific law in Spain regarding the conservation of its geological heritage. Its conservation is put into practice by means of Landuse and Management Plans specific to each Natural Park. This situation has the advantage that the regulations relate to the specific needs deriving from the geological singularity of the area, but it also carries the disadvantage of a lack of overall conservation strategy of Spain's geological heritage.

Geotouristic interest in Spain seems to have been focused on three main sectors:

1. Areas of karstic interest (caves and their surroundings)
2. Areas of palaeontological interest, especially outcrops containing dinosaur remains
3. Areas related to present and past volcanic activity.

This chapter has concentrated on cave geotourism, where the majority of problems arising today are related to the management of the environment within the caves. These problems derive essentially from the disproportionate number of visitors and the fact that there has been a lack of understanding of the strong interaction that exists between a show cave and its karstic surroundings.

Nevertheless, there are many other initiatives with a potential for geotourism that are currently starting up and which may provide a salutary socio-economic lesson for particular rural areas in Spain. A typical example is the re-evaluation of the geo-mining heritage, currently undergoing a phase of abandonment and deterioration. It includes tourist initiatives such as the utilization of certain mines and their minero-industrial surroundings. The giant Pulpí Geode is an emblematic example of how the evident tourist interest of the surrounding area must be tempered by environmental restrictions that clearly limit visits by the public. It is evident that the need to develop geotourism in order better to understand our natural surroundings must occur within the ambit of the divulgation of geodiversity, but always within the margins of sustainability that would permit the conservation of our geological heritage.

References

Arribas, A., Cunningham, C. G., Rytuba, J. J. *e al.* (1995). Geology, geochronology, fluid inclusions, and isotope geochemistry of the Rodalquilar gold alunite deposit, Spain. *Economic Geology and the Bulletin of the Society of Economic Geologists*, 90(4), 795–822.

Arsuaga, J. L., Martínez, I., Gracia, A. *et al.* (1993). 3 New Human Skulls from the Sima-De-Los-Huesos Middle-Pleistocene Site in Sierra-De-Atapuerca, Spain. *Nature*, 362(6420), 534–537.

Arsuaga, J. L., Lorenzo, C., Carretero, J. M. *et al.* (1999). A complete human pelvis from the Middle Pleistocene of Spain. *Nature*, 399(6733), 255–258.

Ayala, F., Rodríguez-Ortíz, J. M., del Val, J. *et al.* (1986). *Mapa y memoria del karst de España 1 : 1 000 000.* Madrid: Instituto Geológico y Minero de España.

Borja, F., Zazo, C., Dabrio, C. J. *et al.* (1999). Holocene aeolian phases and human settlements along the Atlantic coast of southern Spain. *Holocene*, 9(3), 333–339.

Bourges, F., Mangin, A. and D'Hulst, D. (2001). Le gaz carbonique dans la dynamique de l'atmosphère des cavités karstiques:l'exemple de l'Aven d'Orgnac (Ardèche). *Comptes rendus de l'Académie des Sciences de Paris, Sciences de la Terre et des Planètes*, 333, 685–692.

Briggs, D. E. G., Wilby, P. R., Pérez-Moreno, B. P. *et al.* (1997). The mineralization of dinosaur soft tissue in the lower Cretaceous of Las Hoyas, Spain. *Journal of the Geological Society*, 154, 587–588.

Calaforra, J. M. (1998). *Karstología de yesos-Gypsum Karstology.* Universidad de Almería-Instituto de Estudios Almerienses.

Calaforra, J. M. (2003) *The Gypsum Karst of Sorbas, A Subterranean Journey through the Interior of Gypsum.* Publicaciones Calle Mayor.

Calaforra, J. M. and García-Guinea, J. (2000). La Geoda gigante de Pulpí. *Boletín de las Sociedad Española de Espeleología y Ciencias del Karst*, 1, 52–53.

Calaforra, J. M. and Pulido-Bosch, A. (2003). Evolution of the gypsum karst of Sorbas (SE Spain). *Geomorphology*, 50(1–3), 173–180.

Calaforra, J. M. and Sánchez-Martos, F. (1996). An example of an environmental monitoring programme of a cave before its possible tourist use: 'Cueva del Agua' (Granada, Spain). In: A. A. Cigna (ed), *Proceedings of the International Symposium Show Caves and Environmental Monitoring.* Stazione Scientifica di Bossea, pp. 251–259.

Calaforra, J. M., Moreno, R., García-Guinea, J. *et al.* (2001). La Geoda gigante de Pulpí: patrimonio geológico y minero. *Medio Ambiente*, 37, 42–43.

Calaforra, J. M., Fernández-Cortés, A., Sanchez-Martos, F. *et al.* (2003). Environmental control for determining human impact and permanent visitor capacity in a potential show cave before tourist use. *Environmental Conservation*, 30(2), 160–167.

Carbonell, E., de Castro, J. M. B., Arsuaga, J. L. *et al.* (1995). Lower Pleistocene Hominids and Artifacts from Atapuerca-Td6 (Spain). *Science*, 269(5225), 826–830.

Casanovas-Cladellas, M. L., Fernández-Ortega, A. *et al.* (1991). Dinosaurios coeluridos gregarios en el yacimiento de Valdevajes (La Rioja, España). *Revista Española de Palaeontología*, 6, 177–189.

Ceballos-Lascuráin, H. (1994). *Estrategia ecoturística para el Parque Natural de la Zona Volcánica de la Garrotxa.* Departament de Medi Ambient-Generalitat de Cataluña.

Cebriá, J. M., López-Ruiz, J., Doblas, M. *et al.* (2000). Geochemistry of the Quaternary alkali basalts of Garrotxa (NE Volcanic Province, Spain): a case of double enrichment of the mantle lithosphere. *Journal of Volcanology and Geothermal Research*, 102(3–4), 217–235.

Cendrero, A. (1996). Propuesta sobre criterios para la clasificación y catalogación del Patrimonio Geológico. In: Dirección General de Información y Evaluación Ambiental – Ministerio de Obras Públicas, Transportes y Medio Ambiente, *El Patrimonio Geológico. Bases para su valoración, protección, conservación y Utilización*. Ministerio de Obras Públicas, Transportes y Medio Ambiente, pp. 17–28.

Cunningham, C. G., Rytuba, J. J. and Arribas, A. (1990). Mineralized and unmineralized calderas in Spain. 1. Evolution of the Los Frailes Caldera. *Mineralium Deposita*, 25, S21–S28.

De Castro, J. M. B., Arsuaga, J. L., Carbonell, E. *et al.* (1997). A hominid from the lower Pleistocene of Atapuerca, Spain: possible ancestor to Neanderthals and modern humans. *Science*, 276(5317), 1392–1395.

De Freitas, C. R. and Schmekal, A. (2003). Condensation as a microclimate process: measurement, numerical simulation and prediction in the Glowworm Cave, New Zealand. *International Journal of Climatology*, 23(5), 557–575.

Dragovich, D. and Grose, J. (1990). Impact of tourist on carbon dioxide levels at Jenolan Caves, Australia: an examination of microclimatic constraints on tourist cave management. *Geoforum*, 21(1), 111–120.

Dublyansky, V. N. and Dublyansky, Y. V. (1998). The problem of condensation in karst studies. *Journal of Caves and Karst Studies*, 60(1), 3–17.

Dublyansky, V. N. and Dublyansky, Y. V. (2000). The role of condensation in karst hydrogeology and speleogenesis. In: A. B. Klimchouck, D. C. Ford, A. N. Palmer and W. Dreybrodt (eds), *Speleogenesis, Evolution of Karst Aquifers*. National Speleological Society, pp. 100–112.

Eder, W. (1999). UNESCO GEOPARKS – a new initiative for protection and sustainable development of the Earth's heritage. *Neues Jahrbuch fur Geologie und Palaontologie-Abhandlungen*, 214(1–2), 353–358.

Ek, C. and Gewelt, M. (1985). Carbon dioxide in cave atmospheres. New results in Belgium and comparision with some other countries. *Earth Surface Processes and Landforms*, 10, 173–187.

Evans, S. E. and Barbadillo, J. (1997). Early Cretaceous lizards from Las Hoyas, Spain. *Zoological Journal of the Linnean Society*, 119(1), 23–49.

Evans, S. E. and Barbadillo, L. J. (1999). A short-limbed lizard from the Lower Cretaceous of Spain. *Cretaceous Fossil Vertebrates*, 60, 73–85.

Fernández-Soler, J. M. (1996). El volcanismo calco-alcalino en el Parque Natural de Cabo de Gata-Níjar (Almería). PhD thesis, Monografias del Medio Natural 2, Sociedad Almeriense de Historia Natural – Consejería de Medio Ambiente (ed.).

Ferrara, R., Maserti, B. E., Andersson, M. *et al.* (1998). Atmospheric mercury concentrations and fluxes in the Almaden District (Spain). *Atmospheric Environment*, 32(22), 3897–3904.

Ford, D. C. and Williams, P. W. (1989). *Karst Geomorphology and Hydrology*. Chapman & Hall.

Gallego-Valcarce, E. (1996). Patrimonio Geológico: aspectos legales, protección y conservación. In: Dirección General de Información y Evaluación Ambiental – Ministerio de Obras Públicas, Transporte y Medio Ambiente, *El Patrimonio*

Geológico. Bases para su valoración, protección, conservación y Utilización. Ministerio de Obras Públicas, Transportes y Medio Ambiente, pp. 79–86.

Gallego-Valcarce, E. and García-Cortés, A. (1996). Patrimonio Geológico y Espacios Naturales Protegidos. *Geogaceta*, 19, 202–206.

García-Cortés, A., Rábano, I., Locutura, J. *et al.* (2000). Contextos geológicos españoles de relevancia internacional: establecimiento, descripción y justificación según la metodología del proyecto Global Geosites de la IUGS. *Boletín Geológico y Minero*, 111(6), 5–38.

García-Cortés, A., Rábano, I., Locutura, J. *et al.* (2001). First Spanish contribution to the Geosites Project: list of the geological frameworks established by consensus. *Episodes*, 24(2), 79–92.

García-Guinea, J. and Calaforra, J. M. (2001). Mineral collectors and the geological heritage. *European Geologist Magazine*, 1, 14–17.

García-Guinea, J., Morales, S., Delgado, A. *et al.* (2002). Formation of gigantic gypsum crystals. *Journal of the Geological Society, London*, 159, 347–350.

Gibert, J., Campillo, D., Arques, J. M. *et al.* (1998). Hominid status of the Orce cranial fragment reasserted. *Journal of Human Evolution*, 34(2), 203–217.

Gibert, J., Sánchez, F., Ribot, F. *et al.* (2002). Human remains in the Lower Pleistocene sediments from the Orce and Cueva Victoria areas (South Eastern Spain). *Anthropologie*, 106(5), 669–683.

Habe, F. (1981). Bericht der kommission fur karstschutz und schauholen der UIS. In: *Proceedings of the 8th International Congress of the Speleological Society, Kentucky* UIS, pp. 442–443.

Hernández, A., Jebrak, M., Higueras, P. *et al.* (1999). The Almaden mercury mining district, Spain. *Mineralium Deposita*, 34(5–6), 539–548.

Higueras, P., Oyarzun, R., Biester, H. *et al.* (2003). A first insight into mercury distribution and speciation in soils from the Almaden mining district, Spain. *Journal of Geochemical Exploration*, 80(1), 95–104.

Huppert, G., Burri, E., Forti, P. and Cigna, A. (1993). Effects of tourist development on caves and karst. In: P. W. Williams (ed.), *Karst Terrains: Environmental Changes and Human Impact*. Reprinted in *Catena Supplement*, 251–268.

Jebrak, M. and Hernández, A. (1995). Tectonic deposition of mercury in the Almaden District, Las-Cuevas Deposit, Spain. *Mineralium Deposita*, 30(6), 413–423.

Leistel, J., Marcoux, E., Thiéblemont, D. *et al.* (1998). The volcanic-hosted massive sulphide deposits of the Iberian Pyrite Belt. *Mineralium Deposita*, 33, 2–30.

Leurquin, J. L. (1995). Orce-Cueva Victoria Project (1988–1992) – human presence in the Lower Pleistocene of Granada and Murcia. *Anthropologie*, 99(1), 170–171.

López-Martínez, N., Moratalla, J. J. and Sanz, J. L. (2000). Dinosaurs nesting on tidal flats. *Palaeogeography Palaeoclimatology Palaeoecology*, 160(1–2), 153–163.

Martinell, J., De Gibert, J. M., Domenech, R. *et al.* (2001). Cretaceous ray traces? An alternative interpretation for the alleged dinosaur tracks of La Posa, Isona, NE Spain. *Palaios*, 16(4), 409–416.

Martínez-Frías, J. (1999). Mining vs geological heritage: the Cuevas del Almanzora natural area (SE Spain). *Ambio*, 28(2), 204–206.

Martínez-Frías, J. and García-Guinea, J. (1993). Yacimientos de plata y chimeneas submarinas asociadas del área de Cuevas del Almanzora. In: L.García-Rossell and J. Martínez-Frías (eds), *Recursos Naturales y Medio Ambiente de Cuevas del Almanzora*. Instituto de Estudios Almerienses, pp. 237–262.

Martínez-Frías, J., Navarro, A., Lunar, R. and García-Guinea, J. (1998). Mercury pollution in a large marine basin: a natural venting system in the south-west Mediterranean margin. *Nature & Resources*, 34(3), 9–15.

Martín-Merino, M. A. and Ortega-Martínez, A. I. (2001). El complejo kárstico de Ojo Guareña (Merindad de Sotoscueva, Burgos). *Boletín de las Sociedad Española de Espeleología y Ciencias del Karst*, 2, 36–42.

Mitjavila, J., Martí, J. and Soriano, C. (1997). Magmatic evolution and tectonic setting of the Iberian Pyrite Belt volcanism. *Journal of Petrology*, 38(6), 727–755.

Moratalla, J. J., Sanz-García, I., Melero-Domínguez, I. and Jiménez-García, S. (1988). *Yacimientos palaeoicnosgicos de La Rioja (huellas de dinosaurios)*. Gobierno de la Rioja/Iberduero.

Morral, F. R. (1990). A mini-history of the Rio-Tinto (Spain) region. *Cim Bulletin*, 83(935), 150–154.

Muñiz, F. and Mayoral, E. (2001). Macanopsis plataniformis Nov Ichnosp from the Lower Cretaceous and Upper Miocene of the Iberian Peninsula. *Geobios*, 34(1), 91–98.

Nevado, J. J. B., Bermejo, L. F. G. and Martín-Dolmeadios, R. C. R. (2003). Distribution of mercury in the aquatic environment at Almaden, Spain. *Environmental Pollution*, 122(2), 261–271.

Pérez-García, L. C., Sánchez-Palencia, F. J. and Torres-Ruiz, J. (2000). Tertiary and quaternary alluvial gold deposits of northwest Spain and Roman mining (NW of Duero and Bierzo Basins). *Journal of Geochemical Exploration*, 71(2), 225–240.

Platt, N. H. and Meyer, C. A. (1991). Dinosaur footprints from the Lower Cretaceous of Northern Spain – their sedimentological and palaeoecological context. *Palaeogeography Palaeoclimatology Palaeoecology*, 85(3–4), 321–333.

Puch, C. (1998). *Grandes Cuevas y Simas*. Espeleo Club Gracia.

Pulido-Bosch, A., Martín-Rosales, W., López-Chicano, M. *et al.* (1997). Human impact in a tourist karstic cave (Aracena, Spain). *Environmental Geology*, 31(3–4), 142–149.

Rivas, A., Durán, J. J. and López-Martínez, J. (2002). Spanish show caves as elements of the geological heritage. In: N. Zupan-Hajna (ed.), *Use of Modern Technologies in the Development of Caves for Tourism, 4th International ISCA Congress, Postojna, 21–27 October*. International Show Caves Association, 155–158.

Royo-Torres, R., Cobos, A. and Andres, J. A. (2001). La Fundación Conjunto Palaeontológico de Teruel: un modelo de promoción palaeontológica. In: G. Meléndez, Z. Herrera, G. Delvene and B. Azanza (eds), *Actas de las XVII Jornadas de la Sociedad Española de Palaeontología (Albarracín-Teruel, 18 a 20 octubre 2001)*. Publicaciones del Seminario de Palaeontología de Zaragoza, pp. 627–633.

Rytuba, J. J. (2003). Mercury from mineral deposits and potential environmental impact. *Environmental Geology*, 43(3), 326–338.

Sánchez-Palencia, F. J., Fernández-Posse, M. D., Fernández-Manzano, J. *et al.* (1998). Las Médulas (León), la formación de un paisaje cultural minero. El Oro en España. *Boletín Geológico y Minero*, 109(5–6), 157–168.

Sánchez-Martos, F., Calaforra, J. M., Fernández-Cortés, A. and González-Ríos, M. J. (2002). Experiencia de visitas masivas a cavidades en condiciones naturales, la Cueva del Agua de Iznalloz (Granada). *Geogaceta*, 31, 31–34.

Sarbu, S. M. and Lascu, C. (1997). Condensation corrosion in Movile Cave. *Journal of Cave and Karst Studies*, 59, 99–102.

Saupe, F. (1990). Geology of the Almaden mercury deposit, Province of Ciudad-Real, Spain. *Economic Geology and the Bulletin of the Society of Economic Geologists*, 85(3), 482–510.

Solomon, M., Tornos, F. and Gaspar, O. C. (2002). Explanation for many of the unusual features of the massive sulfide deposits of the Iberian pyrite belt. *Geology*, 30(1), 87–90.

Vianey-Liaud, M. and López-Martínez, N. (1997). Late Cretaceous dinosaur eggshells from the Tremp basin, Southern Pyrenees, Lleida, Spain. *Journal of Palaeontology*, 71(6), 1157–1171.

Villar, E., Fernández, P. L., Gutiérrez, I. *et al.* (1986). Influence of visitors on carbon concentrations in Altamira Cave. *Cave Science, Transactions of the British Cave Research Association*, 13(1), 21–23.

Watson, J., Hamilton-Smith, E., Gillieson, D. and Kiernan, K. (eds) (1997). *Guidelines for Cave and Karst Protection*. International Union for Conservation of Nature and Nature Resources.

Wimbledon, W. A. P. (1996). Geosites – a new conservation initiative. *Episodes*, 19(3), 87–88.

Wimbledon, W. A. P. (1998). A European geosite inventory: GEOSITE – an International Union of Geological Sciences initiative to conserve our geological heritage. In: D. Barettino, J. J. Durán and J. López (eds), *Comunicaciones de la IV Reunión Internacional de Patrimomio Geológico*. Sociedad Geológica de España, pp. 15–18.

12

Geotourism and interpretation

Thomas A. Hose

Introduction

Despite limited references by a few authors to tourism and geology (e.g. Komoo, 1997; Martini, 1994), until the early 1990s 'geotourism' was neither a published nor a defined term. The first widely available, and Australian, account of geology and tourism (Jenkins, 1992) employed 'fossicking'. 'Tourism geology' has been employed in Malaysia for a branch of applied geology that could support ecotourism's growth and promote geoconservation, much like bioconservation (Komoo, 1997) does for the biological heritage. Seemingly the first widely published definition appeared in a commissioned article for a British professional interpretation magazine (Hose, 1995: 17):

> The provision of interpretive and service facilities to enable tourists to acquire knowledge and understanding of the geology and geomorphology of a site (including its contribution to the development of the Earth sciences) beyond the level of mere aesthetic appreciation.

This came from a working definition for research (Hose, 1994a: 2) informally undertaken for *English Nature* on 'site-specific geological interpretation' at Sites of Special Scientific Interest (SSSIs) and subsequently developed (Hose, 1996) and refined (Hose, 2000a: 136) to:

> The provision of interpretative facilities and services to promote the value and societal benefit of geological and geomorphological sites and their materials, and to ensure their conservation, for the use of students, tourists and other recreationalists.

These various definitions encompass an examination and understanding of the physical basis of geosites along with geoscientists' biographies, research, publications, notes and artwork, correspondence, diaries, collections, workplaces, residences and graves – that is, the 'geoheritage'. The definitions also include an examination of the associated interpretative and promotional media. At the participant level, geotourism is 'recreational geology' – an essentially participatory field observational activity. Its potential for informal adult study is appropriate to modern environmental educational approaches in which there is no substitute for the experience of the authentic. Geotourism could extend the tourism season in suitable locations, especially rural coastal and upland areas.

Geotourism gained late-1990s UK recognition with the first dedicated national conference in Belfast (Hose, 1998a). Geoconservation, defined by the author (Hose, 2003) as 'The dynamic preservation and maintenance of geosites, together with geological and geomorphological collections, materials and documentation', is somewhat interchangeable with 'Earth heritage conservation' (Wilson, 1994), 'Earth science conservation' (Jacobs and Geys, 1993), 'geological conservation' (Black, 1988) and 'geological site conservation' (Wimbledon, 1988). It is a dynamic approach rather than preservation in some notional fixed state, concerned with preventing damage and loss whilst maintaining access. Much of the value of geological geosites lies in the availability of and access to *in situ* rocks and specimens, benefiting from limited disturbance, restricted collecting and removal of rock/soil debris. Geomorphological geosites require the retention of features within a dynamic real-world system.

In developing geotourism research (Hose, 2003), the author recognized:

> Primary Geosites that have geological and/or geomorphological features, either naturally or artificially and generally permanently exposed, within a delimited outdoor area that are at least locally significant for their scientific, educational or interpretative value.

These vary in their elements and size, for several small geosites can be subsumed within a larger one, such as trails incorporating several SSSIs. The English Nature-sponsored Regionally Important Geological and Geomorphological Sites (RIGS) initiatives development (Harley and Robinson, 1991) launched in the 1990s, a similar approach to the 1970s National Scheme for Geological Site Documentation (Stanley, 1993), has lent further value to this definition. Other terms have been used as part of conservation strategies to signify individual sites, principally 'geosite' (Wimbledon, 1996) and 'geotope' (Sturm, 1994). Whilst the former is an abridgement of geological sites, the latter is a response to the use of biotope for biologically important sites (Krieg, 1996). Other geotourism sites are museum and library collections, heritage/visitor centres, geologists' residences, memorials and commemorative plaques/monuments, and are encompassed by:

> Secondary Geosites that have some feature(s) and/or item(s), within or on a structure or delimited area, of at least local significance to the history, development, presentation or interpretation of geology or geomorphology.

Geoconservation measures coupled with tourism promotion are key geotourism elements.

Geotourism research (Hose, 2003) is a multidisciplinary activity encompassing visitor behaviour, typological analysis and interpretative media analysis, together with geosite analysis, conservation and management studies; study analysis is a major approach. It was established by the author following his recognition of the accelerating loss of geosites consequent upon their unrecognized scientific, cultural and potential economic significance. It outlines and explores the geoheritage's intellectual and physical resource base insofar as it impacts upon geosite presentation and promotion and the desired consequence of geoconservation and case. It examines, through surveys ranging from questionnaires to observation and tracking studies, geosite visitors (Hose, 1994b, 1997a, 1998b) and their interaction with interpretative media. It is subsequently apparent (Hose, 1998a, 1999a, 1999b, 2000b) that there is limited recognition of the failure of much on-site interpretative provision to impact upon its target audiences because of a schism between the educators and the public:

> There are three problems which beset all of us in our presentation of geological facts, by whatever means and to whatever audience. They are:
>
> 1. What degree of detail is required in various types of geologic exposition?
> 2. What is the capability of our audience to absorb what we say?
> 3. What rules should we follow in order to communicate in the most effective way?
>
> (Whitmore, 1959: 25)

This underlines the necessity to promote best practice through the development (on the basis of applied research) and dissemination of guidelines on effective interpretation. Geotourism research is intended to improve the value-added component of the geosite visitor experience; a well-designed and implemented interpretative programme can match visitors to resources, manage conservation issues and reduce user conflicts. A fundamental constraint on interpretative provision is that people usually visit the outdoors to socialize and relax rather than to learn. Aestheticism and escapism are their major visit motivational factors, and this has been unrecognized by many geoconservationists. Attempts to promote the geoheritage to general audiences must address this constraint. Geotourism is essentially a geology-focused and visitor-centred sustainable development of 'environmental interpretation', which is described by Badman (1994: 429) as:

> a range of activities carried out by managers of countryside and heritage
> sites. It can be defined as: 'the art of explaining the meaning and
> significance of sites visited by the public'.

Equally it is also a form of 'niche tourism' (Novelli, 2005) or 'special interest
tourism' that (Hall and Weiler, 1992: 5) occurs:

> when the traveller's motivation and decision-making are primarily
> determined by a particular special interest. Therefore the term ... implies
> 'active' or 'experiential' travel.

Modern environmental interpretation evolved from US developments in promoting sport-based wildlife recreation, and can be simply defined (Ham, 1992: 3) as:

> translating the technical language of a natural science or a related field in
> terms and ideas that people who aren't scientists can readily understand.
> And it involves doing it in a way that's entertaining and interesting to
> these people.

In the UK it dates from the mid-1960s, following the establishment of the first
temporary (during 'National Nature Week' in 1964) and permanent (in 1966 at
the Forestry Commission's Grizedale Forest) nature trails and interpretation
should not be confused with education/short-term knowledge acquisition. Whilst
both involve information exchange, the former is based upon revelation (Tilden,
1977: 18). Overall, interpretation has three main functions:

1. Assisting visitors to appreciate site significance
2. Aiding in site management
3. Promoting understanding of the site agency's policies.

The significance assigned to these varies with the priorities of a site's managing
and sponsoring agencies. Heritage tourism's development since the mid-1980s
has been a positive agent in UK interpretative development, aimed at making
its sites meaningful to visitors (Light, 1995: 132):

> through stimulating and arousing their imagination and curiosity ... as a
> means of enhancing the quality of a heritage site, and contributing to the
> satisfaction and enjoyment of visitors.

The development of interpretation

The UK witnessed some of the earliest innovations in popularization of geology.
The first attempt to create a geological theme park was at Crystal Palace, south
London, in 1854. It had educational aims, through the construction and mounting,
upon accurately rendered geological sections, of three-dimensional reconstructions of fossil animals and plants. The first urban geology trail was established by

1881 at a Rochdale (Lancashire) churchyard. The first preservation of fossil finds *in situ* was in 1873, when the remains of fossil trees, a so-called 'fossil forest', were protected by two small sheds at the South Yorkshire County Lunatic Asylum at Sheffield. The second such preserved forest, discovered in 1887 at Fossil Grove in Glasgow, was the first interpreted fossil site with a dedicated visitor centre, and is the UK's longest continuously open geological attraction. However, this early lead in geological interpretative provision was then squandered until the 1960s.

The 1956 designation of Wren's Nest at Dudley as the UK's first purely geological National Nature Reserve created some concern about over-collecting of geological materials. Consequently, an interpretative trail was developed from the early 1960s, eventually supplemented by a mid-1990s on-site display, as a management tool to emphasize observation over literally hammering the finite resource. The Mortimer Forest Geology Trail, the first purposely established educational geology trail, opened in 1973. Such trails have become increasingly common since the early-1990s. Some RIGS groups, most notably the Hereford & Worcestershire Earth Heritage Trust in England, North-East Wales (NEWRIGS) in Wales and the Lothian and Borders in Scotland, have had programmes to produce series for their areas. For example, the innovative 'Steaming Through the Past' (Burek and France, 1997; NEWRIGS, 1997) was based on the route of a preserved steam railway at Llangollen.

The late 1980s witnessed the opening of geology-based visitor centres, such as the National Stone Centre at Wirksworth in Derbyshire and the Charmouth Heritage Coast Centre in Dorset. Both provide exhibitions, talks, identification services and guided walks. Collecting facilities for recreational geologists were also developed. For example, at Writhlington in Somerset during 1984, land reclamation work was carried out following considerable local pressure to remove the past coal-mining 'blight' of pit-head gear and huge spoil heaps (Figure 12.1). The resultant land reclamation unearthed a previously unrecognized Upper Carboniferous land arthropod fauna (and the UK's richest fossil insect fauna). The Writhlington National Nature Reserve was established with a 'rock store' to enable collecting after reclamation work ceased (Jarzembowski, 1989).

Craigleith Quarry, Edinburgh, a waste tip from the 1950s, was one of the longest working (1615–1941) Scottish quarries. In the early nineteenth century, large fossil tree trunks were found and illustrated in Lyell's *Elements of Geology*; it recently also yielded twelve new fossil fish species. Unfortunately by 1993 it had been developed into a supermarket site, with a small quarry section retained, and a free leaflet on its history was issued. It is pertinent to ponder what has been lost from geosites similar to these already obliterated elsewhere.

A major boost to on-site interpretative provision is the numerous interpretative panels placed from the early 1990s at geosites popular with tourists. These include examples developed by English Nature at Scarborough, Yorkshire and Hunstanton, Norfolk (in 1993); Cleeve Common near Cheltenham (in 1998) and Moorfield and Wellfield Quarries near Huddersfield (in 2001) by RIGS groups; and at Brown End Quarry in Staffordshire (originally in 1991 and replaced in mid-2004) by Wildlife Trusts. Another aspect of interpretative, but mainly informational, provision is commemorative monuments and plaques on buildings and geosites. Examples include the 1891 monument to William Smith at Churchill, Oxfordshire, and the plaque at an Edinburgh geosite concerned with Aggisiz's recognition of Scottish glaciation.

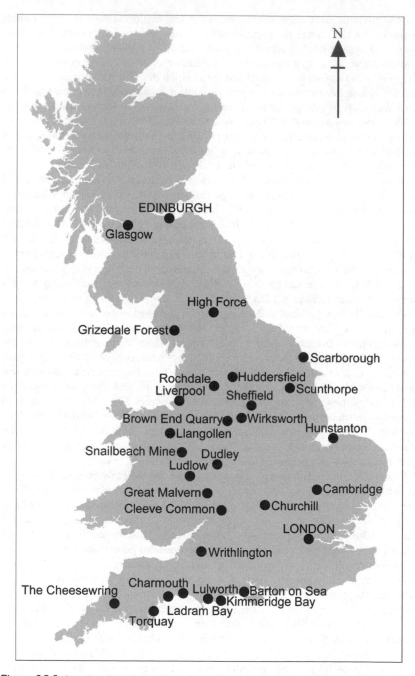

Figure 12.1 Geosites in Britain. The selected geosites evidence a bias towards southern Britain, rather emphasizing the general distribution of such sites in the areas favoured by casual recreationalists from the major urban areas.

Off-site interpretative provision is mainly centred on museums. The Sedgwick Museum, Cambridge University, houses the UK's oldest intact geology collection, the Woodwardian Museum, dating from 1728. It incorporates sixteenth century material, including some of the earliest figured geological specimens. The UK's first dedicated public geology museum was the Geological Survey's *Museum of Practical Geology* opened in London in 1841. It displayed useful minerals and stones, together with their manufactured items. After various closures and removals it reopened in 1935 in purpose-built South Kensington premises, where the displays, mainly three-dimensional representations of the Survey's regional geology guides, were virtually unaltered until the 1970s. The 1973 *The Story of the Earth* was a groundbreaking multimedia exhibition (involving traditional museum displays with projected film, video and audio facilities). It was the first to cover plate tectonics, and was followed by a number of equally innovative, and increasingly computer-controlled, exhibitions. An ongoing exhibition renewal programme, following its incorporation within The Natural History Museum, saw the 1996 opening of two new galleries, 'The Power Within' (geology-based) and 'Restless Earth' (geomorphologically-based). Similar exhibition approaches were sometimes adopted at major provincial museums – for example at Liverpool Museum, where *Earth Before Man* opened in 1973. In the mid-1990s, multimedia exhibitions were opened at the National Museum of Wales and the National Galleries of Scotland. The 'Our Dynamic Earth' centre, Edinburgh, opened in 1999, and is almost entirely computerized multimedia based, lacking the authenticity of actual specimens. New multimedia approaches have become nationally significant in the promotion of geosites, especially on the Internet for the distribution of virtual fieldtrips.

Threatened geoheritage in the absence of interpretation

UK geosites are more threatened today than ever before, especially since public and planners alike usually view the abandoned remains of extractive industrial and civil engineering projects as worthless eyesores ripe for reclamation, landfill and amenity landscaping. The situation can be equated with the UK's industrial sites before the rise of the industrial archaeology and heritage preservation lobbies. Many of the threats facing geosites emanate from the perception of associated dereliction once industrial history sites have been designated and prepared for the tourist and new incoming business ventures. Amenity landscaping, often with the professed aim of safeguarding the environment, for the benefit of the somewhat romantic eye of the urban countrygoer is undertaken at the expense of this extractive industry legacy. Consequently, there are numerous examples of well-preserved mine buildings standing in greenfield isolation from their former adjacent, and now removed or remodelled, spoil heaps (e.g. Snailbeach Mine, Shropshire).

Modern mine and quarry aftercare usually leads to landscaping for leisure, nature (usually wildlife and especially wetland) conservation and agriculture, when retaining quarry faces is an unsatisfactory end-result. However, ample opportunity exists to retain such features when after-use is primarily forestry. The UK waste burial obsession is a major factor in the loss of scientifically important quarry sites. At Scunthorpe, North Lincolnshire, when the UK's last remaining

Jurassic ironstone opencast mines closed they were land-filled despite their suitability, as a rich source of fossils, for geological trails and a visitor centre. Another major threat is civil engineering works for coastal defence, flood prevention and slope stability. For example, at Barton Cliffs SSSI in Hampshire the scientific value of the Eocene stratotype, with some 200 years' worth of published research, was virtually obliterated by mid-1990s coastal defence works.

Whilst general visitor pressure can negatively impact on sensitive geosites, the most visible damage has been from researchers' unwillingness to accept professional codes of practice, especially for rock coring, which sometimes results in the despoliation of the most accessible and photogenic of field-guide exposures. For example, superb sections of dune-bedded Triassic sandstones in the cliffs at Ladram Bay near Sidmouth in Devon and the faces of several of the quarries showing complex Precambrian igneous rocks near Great Malvern in Worcestershire have both been despoiled by rock coring.

Arguably another potential major threat is the commercial collection of fossils and minerals. In the 1980s and 1990s there were several cases of foreign commercial collectors raiding classic UK sites. The legal commercial extraction and sale of specimens has a long history. Most major geology collections contain material bought from commercial collectors and dealers. During the nineteenth century, the sale of fossils supplemented miners' and quarry workers' incomes. Such fossils were a tourist attraction then, and continue to be today, in areas of readily available material such as Dorset and east Yorkshire. A proposed innovative venture in North Wales in the 1990s was the commercial extraction and retail selling of Ordovician fossils from a disused quarry. A threat to the specimens in museum geology collections is that far too many non-geological managers erroneously believe they are robust when in fact they have more conservation-associated problems than those of other museum-based disciplines. This is despite the publication of collections' care and conservation manuals over the past twenty years.

Finally, there is the developing threat of restricted physical access. For example, on the Isle of Arran the landowner (whose land accounts for four-fifths of its field-guide localities) proposed to charge geology field parties in order to generate estate income. Individual landowners, local authorities and charitable trusts have proposed something similar in Dorset and the Isle of Wight. Charging tourists a modest fee to visit waterfalls (e.g. High Force, near Bowlees in County Durham) and show caves (e.g. Kent's Cavern in Torquay, Devon) is a long-established practice. Other ploys are when vehicular access is via a private toll road (e.g. Kimmeridge Bay, Dorset) and where vehicular parking is on private land (e.g. Lulworth Cove, Dorset). Such examples indicate that, albeit unwittingly, tourists have long been prepared to pay for access to geosites of aesthetic value.

The role of interpretation in conserving the geoheritage

UK-based concern for geosites is not new, as witnessed by the Geologists' Association's late-nineteenth century excursion reports. There are early examples of geoconservation arising from public concern centred, much as today, on the potential loss to quarrying of some long-cherished landmark (e.g. the Cheesewring, Cornwall – a granite tor protected in the 1860s). Unlike architectural, archaeological and wildlife conservation, geological conservation is like game conservation – a matter of 'husbandry' (Besterman, 1988). UK geosite conservation and research is based upon tolerance, goodwill and cooperation between geologists, tenants and landowners. UK formal geoconservation education was somewhat neglected until a training pack was co-published by the Open University and the Geological Society in 1994 (Wilson, 1994).

The Nature Conservancy Council and its successors, such as English Nature, categorize geosites within a framework established under the National Parks & Access to the Countryside Act (1949) and the Wildlife and Countryside Act (1981). These are either National Nature Reserves (with six selected for their national geological significance) or Sites of Special Scientific Interest (with 1450 selected for their national or regional geological significance). Their ownership is vested in a variety of private and public agencies and individuals with agreed management strategies, but without statutory right of access. Local authorities are empowered to establish Local Nature Reserves selected for their value to local communities. As part of a major geoconservation scheme (Harley, 1996), an additional category, lacking any statutory protection, is that of Regionally Important Geological/Geomorphological Sites (RIGS). Such sites are selected on the basis of their aesthetic appeal, educational value, historic association, and scientific/research interest and interpretative potential. Additionally, wildlife trusts can designate locally managed nature reserves, but only a tiny minority have any developed geological interest. Some of the country parks, established following the Countryside Act (1968), are areas reclaimed from extractive industry sites – for example, Park Hill Country Park, Staffordshire.

In exceptional cases geosites can be placed on the World Heritage List. In the UK, only the Giant's Causeway (1996) and the Dorset and East Devon Coast (2002) have achieved this status. Recently, geoparks, that have no discrete statutory protection but some UNESCO support have gained UK acceptance. Marble Arch and Cuilcagh, Co. Fermanagh, were the first in late 2001, and Abberley and Malvern Hills became the newest in late 2003. At such geoparks the provision of interpretative facilities, both to promote them to tourists and to encourage geoconservation and in so doing to ensure their economic and environmental sustainability, is important and required management activity in order to maintain their registration and recognition within the European Geopark Network. An overview of Ludlow's geotourism provision (Case study 12.1) exemplifies many of the issues so far raised in this chapter.

Case study 12.1: Ludlow, a case study in geotourism and interpretative provision

The market town of Ludlow is some 210 km northwest of London and 55 km west of Birmingham, in the mainly agricultural Welsh Borderland countryside that has limited access to the UK's arterial rail and road network. Its surrounding countryside is popular with cyclists and walkers, for whom there is some provision within the Forestry Commission's extensive managed woodlands, including a major picnic site and several way-marked walks. Ludlow, because of its castle and many attractive historic buildings, is a popular destination for coach excursions and day visits by car from the Birmingham conurbation, and as a touring centre; it is also promoted for short-break holidays and rural tourism.

Ludlow is built upon Silurian rocks, first recognized in the Welsh Borderland in the 1820s and 1830s by the eminent gentleman geologist Roderick Impey Murchison, but Devonian rocks outcrop nearby. The rocks, produced under subtropical and mostly marine environments around 400 million years ago, are all sedimentary. The 'Ludlow Series', an Earth history time period, is named after the town. These rocks are well exposed at Ludford Corner (Figure 12.2), a few hundred metres south of Ludlow over the River Teme, and at several geosites in the adjacent Mortimer Forest.

Murchison recognized the junction between his Silurian system (mainly limestones and shales) and the overlying Devonian system (mainly sandstones and mudstones) within Ludford Corner's low cliff at the commencement of the cross-bedded sandstones immediately above the Ludlow Bone Bed. Rocks above the Bed were referred to the Lower Old Red Sandstone, based on their appearance, and included fish fossils. The Bed is mainly composed of organic material, especially fish scales, brachiopods, 'worms' and plants. The thin overlying siltstones and mudstones are also known for their fragments of ostracoderms (primitive jawless fish), eurypterids (lobster-like sea scorpions) and primitive land plants. However, the top of the Silurian and base of the Devonian is now placed many metres higher, within the sandstone and mudstone sequence. Ludford Corner has given its name to a subdivision of the Ludlow Series – the Ludfordian Stage. The top Silurian rocks are indicative of the gradual shallowing and infilling of a subtropical shelf-sea. The bottom Devonian rocks represent a change from subtropical shoreline to semi-desert terrestrial conditions, with

Figure 12.2 Ludford Corner. The cliff exposes, from the bottom up: flaggy calcareous siltstones of the Upper Whitcliffe Formation; the Ludlow Bone Bed (marked by – and indicated with a map cover – the deep notch in deep shadow on the bottom right caused by excessive collecting); and 'cross-bedded' Downton Castle Sandstone. Note the commemorative plaque to the right of the seat. On the right is the minor road along and off which are the stops for the Mortimer Forest Geology Trail.

rivers and lakes. The rarest fossil, found in 1990, is that of a pinhead-sized terrestrial predatory mite. Less spectacular but equally significant are the early terrestrial plant fossils, with the oldest known example of plant stomata having been collected near Ludlow.

Ludlow's geosites helped shape the course of early and middle nineteenth century geological investigation, and they have achieved international recognition as world reference points. They are still yielding a lot of scientific interest; much of this is presented in the exhibition and some in the geology trail publications. Fossils such as the world's oldest terrestrial creature and plants are potentially of great public interest because of their uniqueness, local provenance, great age and unusual appearance. The historical importance of the area's rocks in the development of scientific geology is worth noting, as well as the undoubted human-interest element of the lives, personalities and ephemera of nineteenth century geologists. Consequently, its geosites need protection from indiscriminate hammering and collecting. Present interpretative provision consists of a museum exhibition, a commemorative plaque, two self-guided geology trails, and several publications. However, Ludlow's geotourism interpretative media copywriters have a broader range of topics and themes to exploit.

Ludlow Museum – a lesson from its history

Ludlow Museum's history (see Rowlands, 1990) is representative of many similar UK institutions. The original museum was founded in 1833, as a component of the Ludlow Natural History Society. It occupied several premises before moving in 1840 to one of the UK's first purpose-built museums, where it flourished for almost a century before it needed a sponsor to cover its running costs. In 1941 the Society was wound up and its collections were transferred to Shropshire County Council. From 1946 important geological specimens, such as those collected by Murchison, were transferred to the British Museum (Natural History). Because the original purpose-built premises were considered unsuitable, a new local history museum at Buttercross was opened in 1955 but closed in 1993. This resulted in the dispersal by transfer and sale of most of the natural history collections. The new geology displays were integrated within the archaeological, local and social history gallery scheme.

The important local geological material was by then either in London or mainly 'lost' to local schools, individuals and the saleroom. Nobody locally seemed aware of or interested in the importance of the material collected by Murchison and his local collaborators. The historically important collections, which could have underpinned a substantial future geotourism project, were irrevocably lost. The present geological holdings are due to the Museum's first salaried curator, appointed in 1959, who did much to develop awareness, especially through inexpensive local fossil guides, of the local geology's importance. The Museum re-opened in 1995 in the town centre's Assembly Rooms, which also house the Tourist Information Centre. Its geology exhibition covers the geological history of the area as an introduction to the adjacent exhibitions examining Ludlow's archaeology, history and social history. A museum store and workshop, in old school premises acquired in 1973, houses some 50 000 geological specimens. Whilst several notable twentieth century local collections are included, the only remnant of the original collections is of Miocene and Pliocene fossil mammal material, donated in the 1840s by two local army officers, from the Siwalik Hills of India. Today, despite the best efforts of the staff, the museum does not promote public access. Some hint of the richness of the collections is given by the geology exhibition at the town centre site; however, information technology-based approaches, such as CD-Rom and web-located illustrated catalogues, could overcome this situation.

The *Reading the Rocks* exhibition

The *Reading the Rocks* exhibition, open during the spring to late autumn holiday period, was originally accessed for a modest admission charge, through the Tourist Information Centre, but entry is now free. In a roughly 100-m² square room, it encompasses the area's geology, together with an appreciation of its historic importance to the development of scientific geology. It also gives consideration to some of the major nineteenth century personalities involved. It is supposedly purposefully focused on the needs of general visitors, such as tourists, rather than education parties and academic geologists. The latter groups benefit from numerous named specimens of fossils, which have made the area classic for generations of geologists, in under-display drawers. Entrance to the exhibition is via a corridor lined with paintings of palaeo-environmental views of the Ludlow area – an excellent visual introduction for general visitors. Two major exhibition components, popular with younger visitors, are a diorama of early bony fishes and a video-microscope (Figure 12.3).

Beneath the former, in a plinth disguised as a rock outcrop, are glazed drawers of local fossils. To the left of this display is a text panel focused on the Ludlow Bone Bed, evidence from which informed the preparation of a fish display. The latter is a

Figure 12.3 Reading the Rocks, Ludlow Museum. The admixture of traditional and innovative display elements in the gallery is highlighted by the inclusion of: a video-microscope (middle left) and fossil display cases (left); a reconstructed fossil fish case (far right); palaeo-environmental murals and 'information bats' (back wall); and a Murchison biography cartoon panel (centre of left wall to left of entrance).

high-tech, hands-on feature, with both a small desk monitor for the operator and a larger wall-mounted one for general spectators. Several specimens of local fossils are mounted on a manually rotated stage that passes under the variable zoom lens. The video-microscope is part of an island arrangement of three cabinet-top fossil display cases. On the wall backing onto the reception area is a single traditional wooden case packed with Murchison memorabilia, including an open copy of his 1839 *The Silurian System*. Another important and restored Murchison exhibit, mounted on the wall above, consists of two cross-sections of the area's rocks he hand drew for a 1850s lecture to the Ludlow Natural History Society.

Beneath them are innovative cartoon panels on Murchison's life and work, potentially an inspired approach to communicating with general visitors. All incorporate contemporary and modern graphic elements. Some of the latter are quite humorous, with images, for example, of Murchison fox-hunting, exchanging catapult shots with Adam Sedgwick over the Cambrian–Silurian boundary dispute, and holding onto the lines of several sailing ships as he oversees overseas expeditions. However, they are almost overwhelmed by the associated text and other graphical elements. The other main tabletop display, on the opposite wall, examines and promotes the importance of obscure finds such as the earliest terrestrial arachnid and plant fossils from near Ludford Corner. It employs models, backlit illustrations and reproductions of newspaper cuttings (an excellent interpretative ploy) to popularize rather difficult subject matter. Above this display is an account of the structure of the local rocks.

Overall, the compact nature of the various displays and their layout imposes an S-shaped visitor circulation pattern. The gallery's focus is actually upon specimens, with graphics and introductory texts not being strong features. Much of the background information about specimens is discretely placed upon somewhat low-tech, hands-on features – 'information paddles' in green with white outline fossil illustrations on the back. Beneath all the glass-topped display cases are glazed metal drawers with local fossils. All the fossils are taxonomically named, but with no attempt at populist names or descriptions.

The exhibit texts contain numerous references to Ludlow's significance in establishing the Silurian system. For example, a wall panel adjacent to the doors into the other galleries entitled 'Ludlow International' has much dry, factual content that is unmemorable for most visitors. Likewise, the panel adjacent to the fish case, entitled 'The Ludlow Bone Bed', carries texts mixed in style. The first covers a variety of related topics and its storyline stressing that the Bed's geohistorical importance is potentially interesting. The second text is an admirable, if somewhat flawed by complex sentence construction, attempt to explain the process of reconstructing the appearance of fossils from limited evidence. Another panel adjacent to the doors to the other galleries, entitled 'The Rev. T. T. Lewis of Amestrey', focuses on Murchison's slighted and neglected co-worker. Murchison, as was common in his day, failed adequately to recognize the contributions of others to his researches and subsequent writings. Hence, some consideration of the controversy surrounding Murchison and his work is signalled within the exhibition – a good (with the human interest element) interpretative ploy.

Recent research employed observation studies and self-completed questionnaires to assess the exhibition's visitors' characteristics and perceptions (Hose,

1997b). The 64 valid questionnaires returned reflected relatively low visitor numbers. Whilst a self-selected sample inevitably exhibits some bias, it does not necessarily invalidate the findings. The respondents were about equally split between the sexes. Their ages were spread from schoolchildren to pensioners, with a roughly equal split between those aged over and under 44 years. Couples and single persons were major groups correlated with indicated life stage. Compared with other secondary geosites, an unusually high proportion had completed post-compulsory schooling or tertiary education. This reflects the strong resident retiree and income base of professionals originating from the Birmingham conurbation, as well as the limited appeal and initial entry cost barrier. However, only a quarter of respondents were actually retired. Newspaper readership reflected the high educational attainment.

Geological education was relatively high, and a quarter had studied the subject at school/college, with about one-quarter being hobby geologists. Knowledge of the important local geosites and associated publications was restricted to under one-third of respondents. About a quarter of respondents acknowledged the importance of the local fossils, but many expressed neither opinion about nor interest in them. Recognition of the importance of the local rocks centred upon 'importance to science/geology', 'stratotype', 'abundant fossils' and 'ancient life'. Major perceived threats were attributed to road building, development and quarrying, with some concern about over-collecting. Overall, as expected from respondents with a higher than usual interest and training in geology, good awareness and a fair understanding of the uniqueness of, threats to, and need to conserve Ludlow's rocks was evident.

An evaluation of the content and format of the exhibition was also undertaken. This indicated that most panel texts have around 100–150 words with a reading age of 14 or 15 years, with some exceptional ones exceeding 20 years. Panels generally have the space devoted to their principal components as one-quarter text, one-quarter illustrations and one-half white space, making them generally uncluttered. The selected typeface and nature of the illustrations are aesthetically attractive. The volume of the obvious text, compared with other similar exhibitions, is quite low. The use of the 'information paddles' is helpful in this respect.

In summary, the exhibition has a positive impact on knowledge and understanding. General satisfaction levels are quite high, although children benefit from adult support. It is suspected that there is a need to reconsider the specimen labelling and to improve visitor awareness of the hands-on facilities.

The Mortimer Forest Geology Trail

The Mortimer Forest Geology Trail was established in 1973 for education parties and geology students, through the cooperation of the Forestry Commission and the Nature Conservancy Council. It was the first such trail in England, and was developed from 73 sites following 1950s fieldwork to correlate the local Silurian rocks (Holland et al., 1963). When exposures were created by new forest access tracks (Lawson, 1973), some of the more accessible ones were featured in a revised Geologists' Association field-guide (Dean, 1968). This, like the present Trail, included some of the classic sites employed by Murchison in his original description of the Ludlow Series. Amongst these is the last Trail stop at Ludford Corner, where a commemorative plaque, acknowledging the 150th anniversary of Murchison's designation of the Silurian, was unveiled in 1979. However, its short text betrays the copywriter's difficulty (especially common when it was prepared) in addressing the needs of general recreationalists:

> This is the world-famous type locality for the Ludlow Bone Bed in which the fragmented remains of primitive fish are abundant. It marks the beginning of a change in this region about 400 million years ago from open seas to extensive land areas with large rivers. Sir Roderick Murchison in 1830 placed the Fish Bed near the upper limit of the Silurian System.

The limited local value placed on the site can be gauged from the placement of a memorial seat directly in front of the plaque. Given the site's international importance, it merits a more geotourism-focused treatment.

The Trail's route along a busy minor road requires careful use, especially by parties. Its main car park is at the Forestry Commission's High Vinnalls picnic site, the focus of several recreational trails. With only minor gradients for most of its length, underfoot conditions are generally very good in all weathers since either gravel tracks or metalled road are employed, except for a stream section. The geology examined along the route shows the changing rock types and their associated fossil assemblages through geological time. The surrounding countryside is undulating, reflecting the underlying geology, and much of the route affords fine views towards Ludlow. The Trail's Ludford Corner termination lies some 750 m south of Ludlow Museum. Its starting point is a disused roadside quarry near the Forestry Commission's High Vinnalls picnic site, some 5 km west of Ludlow. Its 4.5-km length accommodates thirteen stops marked by numbered wooden posts, at a series of public roadside and Forestry Commission trackside exposures and typically small quarries dug for rough building stone and lime production.

The oldest rocks are seen at the trail's beginning, the youngest at its end. Whilst the approach of beginning with the oldest rocks is a geological convention, it is perhaps not the best approach to leading the casual recreationalist into discovery in the field. There is some benefit in starting with the familiar (and usually youngest) geology and working backwards into deeper time. The trail might better have commenced from Ludford Corner, since it would also have a link between it and *Reading the Rocks*, with users parking their vehicles (thereby reducing traffic) in one of Ludlow's car parks and making it more accessible to those without transport or with limited time. Given the Forestry Commission's support, which originally cleared the sites, the Trail's commencement at a developing visitor facility is understandable. However, site maintenance has not always been timely, and quarry faces and access are often obscured by vegetation, with some of the location posts removed or damaged.

A booklet for the Trail has been available since 1977, and was extensively revised in 1991. The original guide, entitled *Mortimer Forest Geological Trail* (Lawson, 1977), is a 19-page booklet with its glossy white cover having a single trilobite line drawing on it and its pages printed in black on white paper with single-column texts usually devoid of illustrations. Its replacement, the *Mortimer*

Forest Geology Trail (Jenkinson, 1991), is a 24-page booklet with coloured text and illustrations, and was due to be reprinted in 1995. In the 1990s the booklet and the local geological map was produced by the British Geological Survey.

The publication includes a route map showing the underlying geology, which includes a block diagram illustrating the trail's geological setting, topographic features and other information *in situ* – a good approach for the casual user. It fully contextualizes the area's geohistorical importance and incorporates fossil accounts in an introductory section, including a reconstruction of the Ludlovian sea floor, and within the locality descriptions. It also has accounts of biostratigraphy, fossil form, lifestyles, and reconstructions with soft tissues. Overall, the latter publication demonstrates the significant improvement evident in many UK geotourism interpretative publications since the mid-1990s.

The Teme Bank Geology Trail

The Teme Bank Geology Trail was established in 2000 as a 3-km undulating riverside route below, and often paralleling, the preceding trail (Figure 12.4). It is promoted as 'a geological walk through a hundred million years of Ludlow's Silurian history'. Its guide leaflet is supplemented by an on-site interpretative panel. The route, with ten localities, can be completed within an hour, and is easily accessible from Ludlow by two of the town's ancient bridges. It also terminates at Ludford Corner. However, the *in-situ* rocks are not easy to discern, even with the help of the rather small photographs in the leaflet. The introduction opens with:

> The oldest rocks on this walk are the Lower Leintwardine Beds, laid
> down 420 million years ago. At this time, the area around Ludlow was
> a shallow tropical sea along the edge of a large continent. To the west
> was the edge of the continental shelf and the much deeper water of
> a wide ocean. Frequent storms disturbed the sea bed and created
> shell banks.

These concepts might better have been handled by a sketch map or diagram. The description for the first locality is typical of all:

> These are the Whitcliffe Beds, a calcareous sandstone rock, made of sand,
> clay and some lime or calcium carbonate. Look more closely and you
> should be able to see that [the] rock is formed in layers, or bedding
> planes, the most obvious of which is a contorted band about 15 cm thick
> about 2 m above the quarry floor. In front of the rock face you should find
> fallen pieces of rocks. These contain four different types of fossil shell . . .

Other text and diagrams illustrate the common fossils and the formation of the Ludlow anticline. Named rock sequences are employed throughout, which have little meaning to the casual visitor. The generally descriptive locality texts are concise and placed around a route sketch map, with accompanying locality photographs.

Figure 12.4 Teme Bank. The calcareous siltstones of the Upper Whitcliffe beds form the low cliff behind the interpretive panel (on its rather incongruous mounting) that indicates the start of the Teme Bank Trail near the picturesque river crossing of Dunham Bridge. The developing vegetation is already masking much of the geological interest, indicating a major site-clearance need that potentially conflicts with the local biological and aesthetic interests.

The lectern-styled interpretive panel, located at the Trail's start, has a brief introductory text about the river cliff, quarrying for stone for the castle, the local rocks and the Trail itself (Figure 12.4). Its map replicates that on the Trail leaflet, but without any locality information. It also contains the diagrammatic explanation, also replicated from the trail leaflet, of the formation of the Ludlow anticline and the common fossils illustration. Content such as a block diagram demonstrating the relationship between local geology and scenery and/or a palaeo-environmental reconstruction would better have been placed on this panel. Fortunately, the geology text and illustrations of a general countryside interpretative panel on Whitcliffe Common, adjacent to the Trail, compensates for these omissions. In summary, the leaflet is attractive and easily pocketable, but probably tries to cover too much material, resulting in large blocks of small type and illustrations. The panel is a surprisingly poor conclusion to such improved attempts at Ludlow's geotourism provision.

Summary

Ludlow's changing provision from traditional to modern 'hands-on' museum exhibition, from the rather scholarly to more populist trail guides, the placing of a commemorative plaque and an interpretative panel, usually pre-date and sometimes and otherwise mirror developments elsewhere in the UK. Ludlow's modern geotourism provision began much earlier than elsewhere in the UK. Significantly, the positive influence of locally based, geologists determined to promote Ludlow's rich geoheritage is evident in the ongoing development of its geotourism provision.

Conclusions

Whilst geoconservation can be promoted through geotourism for its intrinsic scientific value, it can be argued that there is also a marked personal and societal value component. Geology contextualizes issues of place in the universe and scheme of life, together with some pressing environmental issues, such as climate change and finite mineral and fuel resource management. Geotourism's presentation of geosites can exemplify and contextualize these characteristics. There is little real demonstrable conflict between geoconservation and tourism promotion, and geotourism can thereof be included within sustainable tourism schemes. The UK's major official geosite audit, *The Geological Conservation Review*, noted that (Ellis, 1996: 99):

> Achieving recognition of a site with regard to its importance to conservation is possible through education and site publicity. This is also part of conservation, as is encouraging the 'use' of the site for scientific research or education and training.

An interpretative strategy such as geotourism, interfaced with the formal (school and university) and informal (adult education and interpretative provision) educational environments, can potentially generate the political pressure required for the protection of the geoheritage (Hose, 1997a). The significant contribution that determined individuals can make to geotourism provision, as witnessed by the Ludlow case study, cannot be underestimated. Geotourism's success depends upon identifying and promoting its physical basis, knowing and understanding its user base and, perhaps most difficult but most importantly, developing and widely disseminating communicatively competent interpretative media. The current impetus to such long-neglected studies given by the published geotourism research can only lead to improved interpretative provision and the consequent increased retention and general appreciation of both primary and secondary geosites as significant scientific and cultural societal assets.

References

Badman, T. (1994). Interpreting earth science sites for the public. In: D. O'Halloran, C. Green, M. Harley *et al.* (eds), *Geological and Landscape Conservation*. Geological Society, 429–432.

Besterman, T. P. (1988). The meaning and purpose of palaeontological site conservation. In: P. R. Crowther and W. A. Wimbledon (eds), *Special Papers in Palaeontology No. 40: The Use and Conservation of Palaeontological Sites*. Palaeontological Society, pp. 9–19.

Black, G. P. (1988). Geological conservation: a review of past problems and future promise. In: P. R. Crowther and W. A. Wimbledon (eds), *Special Papers in Palaeontology No. 40: The Use and Conservation of Palaeontological Sites*. Palaeontological Society, pp. 105–111.

Burek, C. and France, D. (1997). Walking and steaming through the past. *Earth Heritage*, 8, 8–9.

Dean, W. T. (1968). *No. 27: Geological Itineraries in South Shropshire*. Geologists' Association.

Ellis, N. V. (ed.) (1996). *An Introduction to the Geological Conservation Review*. Joint Nature Conservation Committee.

Hall, C. M. and Weiler, B. (1992). Introduction: what's special about special interest tourism? In: B. Weiler and C. M. Hall, *Special Interest Tourism*. Belhaven, pp. 1–14.

Ham, S. (1992). *Environmental Interpretation: A Practical Guide for People with Big Ideas and Small Budgets*. North American Press.

Harley, M. J. (1996). Involving a wider public in conserving their geological heritage: a major challenge and recipe for success. In: D. A. V. Stow and G. J. H. McCall (eds), *Geoscience Education and Training in Schools and Universities, for Industry and Public Awareness*. Balkema, pp. 725–730.

Harley, M. J. and Robinson, E. (1991). RIGS – a local Earth-science conservation initiative. *Geology Today*, 7(2), 47–50.

Holland, H. C., Lawson, J. D. and Walmsley, V. G. (1963). The Silurian Rocks of the Ludlow District. *Bulletin of the British Museum (Natural History): Geology*, 8, 93–171.

Hose, T. A. (1994a). *Hunstanton Cliffs Geological SSSI – A Summative Evaluation*. Buckinghamshire College.

Hose, T. A. (1994b). Telling the story of stone – assessing the client base. In: D. O'Halloran, C. Green, M. Harley *et al.* (eds), *Geological and Landscape Conservation*. Geological Society, pp. 451–457.

Hose, T. A. (1995). Selling the story of Britain's stone. *Environmental Interpretation*, 10(2), 16–17.

Hose, T. A. (1996). Geotourism, or can tourists become casual rock hounds? In: M. R. Bennett, P. Doyle, J. G. Larwood and C. D. Prosser (eds), *Geology on your Doorstep*. Geological Society, pp. 207–228.

Hose, T. A. (1997a). Geotourism – selling the earth to Europe. In: P. G. Marinos, G. C. Koukis, G. C. Tsiambaos and G. C. Stournas (eds), *Engineering Geology and the Environment*. Balkema, pp. 2955–2960.

Hose, T. A. (1997b). *Ludlow, Geology and Tourism (Including a Summary of a Visitor Survey of the 'Reading The Rocks' Exhibition)*. Buckinghamshire College.

Hose, T. A. (1998a). Is it any fossicking good? Or behind the signs – a critique of current geotourism interpretative media. Unpublished keynote paper to Irish Geotourism Conference (DoENI/Geological Survey NI/GeoConservation Commission), Ulster Museum, Belfast.

Hose, T. A. (1998b). Selling coastal geology to visitors. In: J. Hooke (ed.), *Coastal Defence and Earth Science Conservation*. Geological Society, pp. 178–195.

Hose, T. A. (1999a). How was it for you? Matching geologic site media to audiences. In: P. G. Oliver (ed.), *Proceedings of the First UK RIGS Conference*. Worcester University College, pp. 117–144.

Hose, T. A. (1999b). Mountains of fire from the present to the past – effectively communicating the wonder of geology to visitors. *Geologica Balcania*, 28(3–4), 77–85.

Hose, T. A. (2000a). European geotourism – geological interpretation and geoconservation promotion for tourists. In: D. Barretino, W. A. P. Wimbledon and E. Gallego (eds), *Geological Heritage: Its Conservation and Management*.

Sociedad Geologica de Espana/Instituto Technologico GeoMinero de Espana/ ProGEO.

Hose, T. A. (2000b). Rocks, rudists and writings: an examination of populist geosite literature. In: A. Addison (ed.), *Proceedings of the Third UKRIGS Annual Conference: Geoconservation in Action*. UKRIGS, pp. 39–62.

Hose, T. A. (2003). Geotourism in England: A Two-Region Case Study Analysis. Unpublished PhD thesis, Department of Ancient History and Archaeology, University of Birmingham.

Jacobs, P. and Geys, J. F. (1993). Theory and practice of Earth science conservation in Belgium. In: L. Erikstad (ed.), *Earth Science Conservation in Europe: Proceedings from the Third Meeting of the European Working Group of Earth Science Conservation*. Norsk Institutt For Naturforskning, pp. 23–31.

Jarzembowski, E. A. (1989). Writhlington Geological Nature Research. *Proceedings of the Geologists' Association*, 100(2), 219–234.

Jenkins, J. M. (1992). Fossickers and rockhounds in Northern New South Wales. In: B. Weiler and C. M. Hall (eds), *Special Interest Tourism*. Belhaven Press, pp. 129–140.

Jenkinson, A. (ed.) (1991). *Mortimer Forest Geology Trail*. Forestry Commission/ Scenesetters.

Komoo, I. (1997). Conservation geology: a case for the ecotourism industry of Malaysia. In: P. G. Marinos, G. C. Koukis, G. C. Tsiambaos and G. C. Stournas (eds), *Engineering Geology and the Environment*. Balkema, pp. 2969–2973.

Krieg, W. (1996). Progess in management for conservation of geotopes in Europe. *Geologica Balcanica*, 26(1), 13–14.

Lawson, J. D. (1973). New exposures on forestry roads near Ludlow. *Geological Journal*, 8(2), 279–284.

Lawson, J. D. (1977). *Mortimer Forest Geological Trail*. Nature Conservancy Council.

Light, D. (1995). Visitors' use of interpretative media at heritage sites. *Leisure Studies*, 14, 132–149.

Martini, G. (1994). The protection of geological heritage and economic development: the saga of the Digne ammonite slab in Japan. In: D. O'Halloran, C. Green, M. Harley *et al.* (eds), *Geological and Landscape Conservation*. Geological Society, pp. 383–386.

NEWRIGS (1997). *Steaming through the Past*. NEWRIGS/Chester College.

Novelli, M. (ed.) (2005). *Niche Tourism; Current Issues, Trends and Cases*. Elsevier Science.

Rowlands, M. (1990). Museum File 20: Ludlow Museum, geology collections. *Geology Today*, 6(5), 166–168.

Stanley, M. F. (1993). The National Scheme for Geological Site Documentation. In: L. Erikstad (ed.), *Earth Science Conservation in Europe: Proceedings from the Third Meeting of the European Working Group of Earth Science Conservation*. Norsk Institutt For Naturforskning, pp. 17–22.

Sturm, B. (1994). The geotope concept: geological nature conservation by town and country planning. In: D. O'Halloran, C. Green, M. Harley *et al.* (eds), *Geological and Landscape Conservation*. Geological Society, pp. 27–31.

Tilden, F. (1977). *Interpreting Our Heritage*, 3rd edn. University of North Carolina Press.

Whitmore, F. C. (1959). Geologic writing for the non-geologist. *Journal of Geological Education*, 7(1), 25–28.

Wilson, W. (ed.) (1994). *Earth Heritage Conservation*. Open University/Geological Society.

Wimbledon, W. A. (1988). Palaeontological site conservation in Britain: facts, form, function and efficacy. In: P. R. Crowther and W. A. Wimbledon (eds), *Special Papers in Palaeontology No. 40: The Use and Conservation of Palaeontological Sites*. Palaeontological Society, pp. 41–55.

Wimbledon, W. A. (1996). GEOSITES – a new conservation initiative. *Episodes*, 19, 87–88.

13

Geotourism's issues and challenges

Ross Dowling and David Newsome

Introduction

Tourism has increased by more than 100 per cent between 1990 and 2000 in the world's 'hotspots' – regions richest in species and facing extreme threats – according to a biodiversity report released by Conservation International (CI) and the United Nations Environment Programme (UNEP). *Tourism and Biodiversity: Mapping Tourism's Global Footprint* is the most comprehensive study of its kind focusing on the impacts of tourism on biological diversity (Christ *et al.*, 2003). Biodiversity hotspots have seen tourism increase by over 100 per cent between 1990 and 2000. In particular, in certain areas the growth has been staggering. Over the past decade, tourism has increased by more than 2000 per cent in both Laos and Cambodia, nearly 500 per cent in South Africa, over 300 per cent in the countries of Brazil, Nicaragua and El Salvador, and 128 per cent in the Dominican Republic.

Tourism generates 11 per cent of global gross domestic product (GDP), employs 200 million people and transports nearly 700 million international travellers per year – a figure that is expected to double by 2020. It is considered one of the largest (if not the largest) industries on the planet. With nature and adventure travel one of the fastest-growing segments within the tourism industry, the Earth's most fragile, high-biodiversity areas are where most of that expansion will likely take place. While tourism has the potential to provide opportunities for conserving nature, tourism development, when conducted improperly, can be a major threat to biodiversity.

With the world's areas of biodiversity under threat, we believe that the time is ready to help capitalize on tourism's natural focus, but to move it away from this emphasis on the biotic environment and towards a more integrated approach with consideration given to the abiotic attributes. Thus ecotourism generally, and wildlife tourism specifically, could benefit from the development of a sustainable geotourism industry. In essence, ecotourism already embraces elements of geotourism, with its emphasis on natural areas, environmental sensitivity and consumer education. On the other hand, wildlife tourism would benefit from an interest in geotourism, as this would provide another option for nature-based tourists wishing to make meaningful journeys to natural environments. This diffusion of tourism would take the 'heat' off the biotic hotspots and instead foster an interest in appropriately planned, developed and managed tourism to some of the world's interesting and diverse landforms (as well as the activities that shape them). However, regardless of whether or not this occurs, the interest in geological tourism has been on the rise for some time.

The rise of geotourism

Interest in geotourism is occurring all over the world. The earth's abiotic environment has always attracted visitors, but it is only in recent years, with the advent of global environmental awareness combined with the era of mass travel, that geological attractions have become better known. A host of examples have been referred to, and in some cases described, in this book. A brief look at some new ones here includes examples of ecotourism in Iceland, England and the USA.

1. *Iceland.* Iceland is one of many countries marketing its geotourism destinations. It states that 'what makes Iceland stand out as a venue is its unique natural beauty and absence of pollution through promotion of its dramatic volcano and glacier scenery'. The Lake Myvatn region of Iceland is an area that lies on the Mid-Atlantic ridge and is geologically one of the more interesting tourist sites on earth. The Ridge is a submarine mountain range that surfaces in Iceland. It is growing by several centimetres a year by pushing apart the tectonic plates that are separating there, with magma flowing on to the Earth's crust from the mantle below. The Mid-Atlantic Ridge crosses Iceland in a diagonal running southwest to northeast. A volcanic eruption can melt a glacier and send huge blocks of ice and water to the lowlands. Pseudo-craters are formed when volcanic material flows into water. Resembling mini-volcanoes, they dot Lake Myvatn. In this smoking stretch of land, there is a myriad of boiling mud pools and fumaroles emitting superheated smoke and gas. Along the southern coast, at Jokulsarlon Lagoon, the area is famous for icebergs that break off into the water. Here there are towering ice cliffs, some carrying a sooty layer of glacial soil, while others have striations of blue and

white colours. In the north of the country lies Mt Krakla, which last erupted in 1984. It lies below the boiling zone, straddling the Ridge, and comprises smoking lava caves, fissures and fragile surfaces. Visitor signs in English and Icelandic warn that 'The ground is extremely hot and therefore dangerous to cross' (McGlinn, 1999). It suggests that visitors should only walk on marked paths, and should never cross the fences around the most dangerous areas.

2. *England.* Even in a predominantly built environment like England, geotourism is on the increase – as evidenced by the examples in the chapters in this book. An example occurs south of the busy, historic cities of Bath and Bristol, where the limestone slopes of the Mendip Hills rise above the flood plains of the Somerset levels. Extending 30 km from Frome in the east, the Mendips come to a dramatic western conclusion in one of England's great natural wonders, Cheddar Gorge. The narrow, steep-walled canyon of the Gorge is the deepest and longest gorge in Britain, and high vertical cliffs line the canyon floor for nearly 3 km. For millions of years, running rivers have cut this dramatic gash through the limestone hills. On both sides, the rugged rock bears the scars of generations of quarrying. A cliff-top Gorge Walk, designated a Site of Special Scientific Interest, leads through the upland estate of the Marquis of Bath. The most popular attraction at Cheddar Gorge is the Cheddar Showcaves. These comprise 100 caves, carved out of soft limestone, which dot the Mendip range. Today more than half a million people a year travel through the gorge, with 300 000 of them visiting the caves (Huntley, 2000). Guides lead visitors down to illuminated caverns through limestone formations carved by underground rivers. Almost 5000 people a year take the cave experience one step further with adventure caving.

3. *The USA.* Haleakala Volcanoes National Park, Hawaii, centres on Mt Haleakala on the island of Maui. The Park preserves the outstanding volcanic landscape of the upper slopes of Haleakala, and was designated an International Biosphere Reserve in 1980. Isolated in the mid-Pacific, the Hawaiian Islands form part of the most remote major island group on Earth. They were formed as the Pacific Plate moved across a volcanic 'hot spot' within the earth's mantle. Lying 4000 km from the nearest continent, they have never had connection to any other land mass. The mountain features the Haleakala Crater, made up of orange- and red-streaked lava walls formed by numerous eruptions over millions of years. The Park has three visitor centres, a range of geological activities, and a number of self-guided trails – including one to the 2682-m summit.

These three examples reflect nations and regions that are unashamedly fostering the development of geotourism. However, such enthusiasm can give rise to a number of development issues.

Development issues

The Stonerose Eocene Fossil Site at Republic in Washington State, USA, is a major regional geotourism attraction. It comprises fossils of the Eocene (Greek for 'dawn of life') Epoch which are 50 million years old. The site is one of the richest sources of fossil specimens in the world. According to Difley and Difley

(2000), these are world-class Eocene fossils that contain the best North American record of upland warm temperate to subtropical habitats. Many of the fossils found are of plants and creatures that no longer exist. Of major significance is the earliest known record of many members of the Rosaceae (rose) family, which gives its name to the site. The Fossil Site includes an interpretive centre, and controlled digging of fossils is one of the major activities encouraged. The fossil beds include almost perfectly formed and preserved leaves, insects and tiny fishes. Visitors are permitted to take up to three fossils per day per person. This is a remarkable situation, and one that may not be sustainable, but at present it constitutes the highlight for visitors who visit this recreational, educational and scientific attraction.

An educational version of digging for fossils at Stonerose occurs at Porcupine Cave, South Park, in Colorado, USA. Each year, the Denver Museum of Natural History and the Western Paleontological Society provides teachers with the opportunity of excavating fossils during a two-week field camp (Babitt, 1998). The cave is located in the Rocky Mountains at an elevation of 2895 m. It is an important geological site due to both the variety and the richness of its fossils.

These examples demonstrate that geotourism cannot simply be regarded as a more 'resistant' option to ecotourism. Indeed, geotourism can give rise to a whole new suite of adverse impacts. However, the key to successful geotourism development lies in appropriate planning, development and management.

Geotourism's potential

Examples abound throughout this book of areas where there is potential for geotourism development. With sound planning, taking into account the sustainable principles of environmental conservation, community well-being and economic benefits, then geotourism offers a potential basis for community and/or regional development for many places around the world. Examples from the literature include possibilities for Saudi Arabia, Chile, India, Canada and Trinidad & Tobago, to name just a few.

The landforms of Saudi Arabia in general, and the Riyadh area in particular, have their own potential for scenic and recreational purposes. In some areas of Riyadh the more resistant higher landforms have been recommended for scenic use. It has been suggested that the more fragile lower lands surrounding the natural lakes, the sand dunes and other features could be developed for other recreational purposes. Overall the country is well endowed with geological and geomorphological features which could provide an excellent base for developing geotourism (Al-Amiri, 1986).

An emerging geotourism area is Temuco in Chile, which is renowned for its volcanoes, national parks, Mapuche settlements and ski resorts (Nicholls, 2003). The town is the gateway to Lake Villarrica and the nearby 2900 m Villarrica Volcano. The volcano is active, and last erupted in 1996. A volcano evacuation plan can be found on the back of each hotel room door in the surrounding area. In the south of the country lies Punta Arenas, the gateway to Patagonia. Here the Torres del Paine National Park is one of the few remaining examples of undeveloped natural beauty in the world, and has been declared a Biosphere Reserve by UNESCO. Tectonic movements 12 million years ago sculpted the mountains, giving them the shape of towers and horns, and this is an imposing site in an area of glaciers, lakes and waterfalls, providing outstanding photographic opportunities. Tourists from all over the world find their way to this remote region, primarily to view the stunning mountain vistas.

One place in Chile with geotourism potential is the Atacama Desert in the northern part of the country. Located four hours by air from the capital city Santiago, Atacama is the driest desert in the world and is home to a variety of spectacular geological formations. Almost completely void of animals and plant life, many areas of the desert have been likened to a lunar landscape – especially at the Valley of the Moon, an area of aeolian carved sculptures sitting amidst wide open spaces. Other areas of the desert offer different experiences, such as the Salar de Atacama, the country's largest salt deposit.

Another potential site identified for geotourism occurs near the village of Lonar, Maharashtra, India (Shivakumar, 2001). The remains of a meteorite are said to be embedded at the bottom of a 2-km diameter crater. The crater is filled by a saline lake, 170 m deep, which dries up at certain times of the year, and the rest of the enclosed area includes freshwater streams and a marsh. The crater is unique, with an almost perfectly circular depression in the basaltic flows of the Deccan Plateau. To date the crater has not been developed for tourism, although the Maharashtra Tourism Development Corporation has announced plans to develop and promote it. Its proximity to the nearby World Heritage-listed Ajanta and Ellora Caves makes it an ideal geotourism attraction. These caves are noteworthy, as three major Indian religions have laid joint claim to the caves peacefully since they were created. These caves have been listed for their remarkable landforms, sculptures and architecture.

In Newfoundland, Canada, there has been a decline in the fishing industry over recent years and thus many communities are now turning to tourism (also see Case study 13.1) as an alternative source of economic activity, revenue and employment (Wilson, 2002). In addition, past tourism has focused on the rocky, cliff shorelines found along the coasts, but now coastal dune areas have been 'discovered'. These dune coastlines have become marketable tourism commodities, based on their sandy beaches and the presence of an endangered piping plover (*Charadrius melodus*). However, this tourism is putting pressure on the coast by causing accelerated erosion and exacerbating the fact that there is only a limited influx of sand currently available for dune replenishment. In the decade from 1989 to 1999, the number of visitors to Newfoundland increased by 33.3 per cent (from 300 000 to 400 000). Beach visiting for pleasure and recreation has also increased, creating significant degradation of the dune system. Trails are now marked by linear blowouts, some almost 2 m deep. All-terrain vehicle (ATV) use is not regulated, and they have caused a proliferation of new tracks and disturbed vegetation, and created considerable litter. Conservation of these areas is required, but a major problem has been the lack of perceived value of the region, especially by local communities. Thus the first step towards sustainable tourism is to inform and educate the residents on the values of the fragile dune systems. A central plank of such an approach will be to overturn the generally held perception that the dunes represent the barrier between the car parks and the coast, and instead to champion the area as having geotourism interest and potential as attractions in themselves. Once this has been carried out then sustainable geotourism development can proceed. According to Wilson (2002), conservation-based management and marketing of the dune-backed coastlines are not incompatible objectives, as Newfoundland's interest in tourism has occurred simultaneously with a growth in environmental

Case study 13.1: Potential geotourism development – the case of Trinidad & Tobago (from Day and Chenoweth, 2004)

The karst landscapes of Trinidad & Tobago illustrate a geological landscape yet to be developed for geotourism, and thus offer the country a great opportunity to plan and develop a sustainable geotourism industry with community and economic benefits.

The islands of this single country lie just off the north coast of South America. They are located on the northern edge of the South American plate, close to the southern boundary of the Caribbean plate. A range of limestone formations outcrop on the surface, presenting a 100-km array of tropical karst landforms. These include karren, caves, springs, valley systems and a range of dolines (sinkholes), including an area of polygonal cockpit karst. The dominant landforms are individual dolines, sometimes clustered in linear groups. There is extensive karren development, including rillenkarren and spitzkarren. Downslope from the doline fields are limestone valley systems and small ephemeral springs. Caves are also common, with the Aripo system extending for over 850 m.

The karstlands have been modified by a number of human activities, including quarrying, logging and agriculture. Tourism has also had an influence on the lands, with regular visitors to the larger caves, especially to see the remarkable oilbird or guacharo (*Steatornis caripenses*). It nests in the caves and is noted for its nocturnal frugivorous foraging.

In the 1970s the government examined the possibility of tourism development to the caves, but so far there have been no commercial developments. However, much of the karst is under increasing human pressure, and on Tobago it is under serious threat from residential and commercial development – ironically, much of it related to tourism. However, only a small part of these areas is protected, although there are some nature and/or game reserves as well as some limited conservation of caves. In order to protect the karst an integrated system of protected areas should be introduced, along with a sustainable tourism development plan.

awareness. However, it is recommended that development should be focused away from the fragile dune areas. If this occurs, then Newfoundland will be able to build a geotourism industry to help replace some of the losses brought about by reduced opportunities in their traditional fishing industry.

Recurring themes for geotourism

Arising from the contributions in the book are several themes that are briefly summarized here:

1. There is no generally accepted definition of geotourism
2. Virtually all countries have some geological resources with the potential for geotourism development

3. The impacts of geotourism are not yet well understood
4. The key to making geotourism accepted by tourists is through proper interpretation
5. Geoparks have the potential to foster geotourism at the community, regional
and national levels.

The term 'geotourism'

There is no universally accepted definition of geotourism. At the macro-level, the word is being championed as a catch-all term referring to the majority of tourists in a 'geographic' sense. Alongside this is the bounded term focusing on 'geological' tourism – the approach we have taken in this book. Even within this definition we see differences in meanings from contributors to this book, from Frey *et al.*'s (Chapter 6) general approach of geotourism being 'the transfer of geoscientific knowledge and ideas to the general public' to the more specific definition given to it by the Geological Society (London) of 'tourism in geological landscapes', as noted by Gates (Chapter 9, p. 157). Indeed, Pforr and Megerle noted that the term has been increasingly debated by the tourism industry, politicians, conserva-tionists, geographers, geologists and academics alike (Chapter 7, p. 119).

Probably the nearest definition to our own given in this book is that of Hose, whose early definition is 'the provision of interpretive and service facilities to enable tourists to acquire knowledge and understanding of the geology and geomorphology of a site (including its contribution to the development of the Earth sciences) beyond the level of mere aesthetic appreciation' (Chapter 12, pp. 221–222). Our view is concurrent with his, and clear, in that geotourism refers to tourism based on geological features and processes in the abiotic landscape.

Thus the definition of 'geotourism' appears to be going down the same route as that earlier trod by 'ecotourism'. It is the age-old story of the purist versus the generalist viewpoint. We are unashamedly sticking to the former, whilst it is obvi-ous that the term is already enjoying a wider populist meaning. However, it is essential that the term be clearly defined and characterized so that a universal meaning can be ascribed to it. This book has exposed a range of meanings; it is now for other fora to debate it further.

Geotourism's potential

Another central finding to emerge from the collection of chapters in this book is that virtually all places have potential for geotourism. People live on land, and the earth's landforms are many and varied. Whilst we can broadly categorize rocks into the three main types of sedimentary, metamorphic and igneous, and landforms into the four main types of mountains, plateaux, hills and plains, in truth each place on earth is different and the rocks and landforms there have their own particular 'story' of formation. This combination of form and process is then further compounded by the contribution of geological time, itself divided into eras, periods and epochs (see Appendix).

Thus any particular place on earth has its own 'sense of place' and 'story of for-mation', apart from any spectacular landscape, landform or geological process occurring today. It is in the discovery of this story that geologists can lay the groundwork for geotourism development, and in the process help communities, regions and nations better to understand their own sense of place. Some of the examples in this book are exemplars for geotourism development, and a large number of potential opportunities are noted. Thus the old adage of not every place having tourism potential (Gunn, 2002) may not apply to geotourism potential, as a central plank of geotourism lies in effective interpretation.

Geotourism's impacts

Examples abound throughout this book of the ways in which geotourism has positively impacted on communities, yet in reality the book also alerts the reader to the many possibilities of adverse impacts being generated by geotourism. In this regard the contributions by Calaforra, as evidenced by the references in Chapter 11, and others are particularly useful. His work on the environmental impacts of tourism, especially in caves, has provided useful guidelines for sustainable tourism development.

If geotourism is to be developed as a sustainable industry, then one of the first tasks to be carried out is to understand the very resource upon which it is proposed to be built. Abiotic features, like their biotic counterparts, also suffer from adverse impacts. The examples given in this chapter for Newfoundland, as well as in some other chapters, indicate that landscapes, landforms, rocks and fossils can all be negatively impacted upon by people. Therefore a key task is to carry out research on the impacts of tourists on the abiotic landscape so that we can move from qualitative to quantitative understandings. While in some geological environments this information is already known, for most it is not. In order to build a solid foundation for a successful geotourism industry, the first thing we must do is understand the geological resource and the possible tourist impact on it.

A sound example of managing the adverse impacts of geotourism is found at Zion National Park, southern Utah, USA. The park is a dramatic landscape of sculptured canyons and dramatic cliffs located at the junction of the Colorado Plateau, Great Basin and Mojave Desert provinces. The Park is promoted as a showcase of geology, and both landforms and their formative processes are highlighted in a world-class interpretive programme. The US National Park website (www.nps.gov.zion/geology.htm) describes the many geological processes in the Park, including sedimentation, lithification, uplift, erosion, landslides and flooding. It is a heavily visited park, and in 1997 visitation was 2.4 million per annum and increasing. As a result of this the Park has introduced a shuttle bus system from the nearby village of Springdale right into the heart of the Park. The buses are all gas powered (Figure 13.1), and as a result both pollution and congestion in the park has decreased. In addition, the Park has focused on a range of educational and interpretive activities, and ranger-led hikes introduce the tourists to the geology of the park (Figure 13.2).

The role of interpretation

Underpinning many of the chapters in the book is the central role of interpretation within geotourism. Scores of books have already been written on interpretation,

Figure 13.1 Shuttle buses at Zion National Park, Utah, USA (photograph courtesy of Ross Dowling).

and others on natural area tourism. A few bridge both topics, but there are virtually no books of geotourism interpretation. A notable exception to this is the contribution of Hose. In the references to Chapter 12 are listed his many contributions to this topic, including his 2003 doctoral dissertation. No doubt an all-embracing book on the topic by this author will be timely and provide essential information on how interpretation can benefit both geological understanding and tourism.

Figure 13.2 Interpretive plaque, Zion National Park (photograph courtesy of Ross Dowling).

Despite the above, a surprising finding from the contributions of this book has been the wide range of interpretive tools currently used in geotourism. At the macro-level, the brief Case study of Our Dynamic Earth (Edinburgh, Scotland) by Mc Keever *et al.* (see Case study 10.5, p. 194) is testimony to a major geotourism attraction (the management of this attraction is explored further in Watson and McCracken, 2003). At the other end of the scale, Case study 9.1 on Harriman State Park, New York, USA (p. 165) is both instructive and innovative, with interpretive resources including a website and series of videos. Somewhere between is the

Figure 13.3 Visitors learning about the geology by ranger-led mule-back tour, Grand Canyon National Park, Arizona, USA (photograph courtesy of Ross Dowling).

unique geological interpretation given of the Grand Canyon by the rangers leading mule-back tours to the Colorado River (Figure 13.3).

There are several similar examples emerging of geotourism's utilization of the Internet for interpretation and promotion. Two examples from the USA are related to the states of Iowa and Arizona. Iowa forms part of the Midwestern states of the USA, which are shaped by a uniform plain with no mountains. However, here lie the extensive Loess Hills of Iowa – one of only two extensive deposits in the world, the other being the huge loess deposits of China. The hills are shaped by silt deposits, called loess, which blew in from the Missouri River floodplain about 30000 years ago. In an interesting development, the Woodbine Loess Hills Computer Club of Iowa decided to showcase the hills through promotion of their local landscape. Primary school club members meet after school two days a week to focus on projects involving science, mathematics and technology (Tevis, 2000). They are currently working on ten projects, and one is the promotion of their own landscape treasure, the Loess Hills. So far the students have generated three posters featuring photos of their scenic landscapes, nature centres and other attractions. This is a good illustration of a small school community sharing its local geological attractions with the rest of the world through Internet technology.

The emergence of geoparks

Whilst the popularization of the conservation movement is a relatively recent phenomena, over the past 130 years humankind has put considerable effort into protection and conservation of the environment through the creation of protected areas. This stemmed from the National Park movement, and today a range of National and Marine Parks and other protected areas span the globe. The outworking of this at the international level has been the establishment of natural and cultural World Heritage Sites, a number of which have been listed for their outstanding geological phenomena. Examples include the Grand Canyon and Yosemite, USA; Sagamartha (Mt Everest), Nepal; and Uluru and the Great Barrier Reef, Australia.

A more recent phenomenon has been the establishment of geoparks by UNESCO to promote places that integrate significant examples of the Earth's geological heritage in a strategy for regional economic development (Chapter 6, p. 102). The move is to establish an International Network of Geoparks, and already a number have been established in Austria, China (Chapter 8), France, Germany (Chapter 7), Greece, Italy, Northern Ireland, Spain and the United Kingdom. We predict that it will be this movement which advances geotourism at a range of levels around the world. Through the international respect and reach of UNESCO, geoparks have already begun to make their mark on communities and regions; with even greater awareness by countries, the geopark movement will become the benchmark for geotourism acceptance by governments, regions, communities and tourists. The danger in this is that such parks simply become the front for governments wanting to commercialize a country's geological assets through the legitimization of tourism, instead of through the perceived less-palatable landuse of mineral exploitation through mining.

Conclusions

Over the last two decades, interest in tourism to natural areas has increased markedly. To date, most of this interest has focused on biotic elements (fauna and flora), with, by comparison, somewhat lesser interest in abiotic features (such as geological landforms and processes). However, in the past decade interest has begun to emerge in the phenomenon of geological tourism, or geotourism. Attractions have developed and tours have been set up. The seeds of this new, emerging industry have been planted, and individuals, communities, regions, nations and international organizations are starting to take notice.

The parallels between ecotourism a decade ago and geotourism today are striking. There is the problem of definition and characterization, impacts and management, education and interpretation, certification and accreditation, and marketing and promotion. In the mid-2000s the ecotourism industry has matured and many of the original issues have been researched and debated, and now appropriate solutions have been discovered. Once a bandwagon for operators who wished to be seen as 'green' in order to cash in on the environmental awareness, the business of ecotourism is now being understood by consumers who are more aware and discerning – and so it will be with geotourism.

Finally, another truth gained from ecotourism also applies to geotourism, in that it is axiomatic that not all geological attributes should be viewed as potential tourism resources. For both the biotic and abiotic, it is imperative to protect some fragile or unusual attributes in order to ensure their continued survival in our increasingly exploitive world. However, where resources are deemed appropriate for geotourism development, then the resource needs to be fully understood – especially in regard to its conservation. Thus it is paramount that geoconservation is fully resourced so that the interface between conservation and tourism in relation to geotourism can be understood, for without this understanding the promise of geotourism will not be reached.

References

Al-Amiri, S. S. A. (1986). Using landforms of Saudi Arabia for scenic and recreational purposes (with special reference to the Riyadh area). *GeoJournal*, 13(2), 143–151.

Babitt, S. (1998). The Porcupine Cave field school. *Science Scope*, 21, 16–18.

Christ, C., Hillel, O., Matus, S. and Sweeting, J. (2003). *Tourism and Biodiversity: Mapping Tourism's Global Footprint*. Conservation International.

Day, M. J. and Chenoweth, M. S. (2004). The karstlands of Trinidad and Tobago, their land use and conservation. *Geographical Journal*, 170(3), 256–266.

Difley, B. and Difley, L. (2000). Digging for roses. *Trailer Life*, 60(11), 45–48.

Gunn, C. A. (2002). *Tourism Planning: Basics, Concepts, Cases*, 4th edn (with T. Var). Routledge.

Huntley, D. (2000). England's Grand Canyon. *British Heritage*, Feb/Mar, 20–25.

McGlinn, M. (1999). Touring the happy side of hell. *New York Times*, 15 August, 10.

Nicholls, M. (2003). A study in contrasts: Chile's natural diversity. *Meetings & Incentive Travel*, 32(3), 35.

Shivakumar, N. (2001). India: cosmic bowl-over. *Businessline, Islamabad*, 19 February.

Tevis, C. (2000). Youth use technology to showcase a unique rural showcase. *Successful Farming*, 98(7), 61.

Watson, S. and McCracken, M. (2003). Attractions and human resource management. In: A. Fyall, B. Garrod and A. Leask (eds), *Managing Visitor Attractions: New Directions*. Butterworth-Heinemann, pp. 171–184.

Wilson, H. W. (2002). Anthropogenic pressures on coastal dune, southwestern Newfoundland. *The Canadian Geographer*, 46(1), 17–32.

Appendix: Geological time

Era	Period	Epoch	Millions of years ago
Cenozoic	Quaternary*	Holocene	0.01
		Pleistocene	0.01–1.8
	Tertiary*	Pliocene	1.8–5.1
		Miocene	5.1–24.6
		Oligocene	24.6–38.0
		Eocene	38.0–54.9
		Palaeocene	54.9–65.0
Mesozoic	Cretaceous	↑	65–144
	Jurassic	Epoch names	144–213
	Triassic	↓	213–248
Palaeozoic	Permian		248–286
	Carboniferous		286–360
	Devonian		360–408
	Silurian		408–438
	Ordovician		438–505
	Cambrian		505–545
Precambrian	Proterozoic		545–2500
	Archaean		2500–3500
	Hadean		3500–4600

*Derived from eighteenth and nineteenth century geological timescale that separated crustal rocks into a four-fold division of Primary, Secondary, Tertiary and Quaternary, based largely on relative degree of lithification and deformation.

Index